"The church in which I work today needs all the encouragement it can get. Fudge's commentary is a strong, theologically-informed exposition of one of the most challenging—and ultimately encouraging—books of the New Testament that will be of especial help to preachers seeking to encourage contemporary believers."

—**WILL WILLIMON,** Bishop, United Methodist Church, Birmingham, Alabama

"Written by a scholar for lay people, this volume presents an interpretation that is clear and transparent. I heartily recommend this commentary as true to Scripture and balanced in explanation of Hebrews."

—**SIMON KISTEMAKER,** Professor of New Testament Emeritus,
Reformed Theological Seminary

"Edward Fudge promises reverent scholarship written for serious Bible students who seek scholarly content in non-technical terms. He holds true to his promise on every page. This is a book written by a kind friend who has moved out into the deep waters of scholarship only to return with encouraging, intelligible, and insightful conversation as he leads us into important textual experiences. The author maintains honest and intelligent dialogue with both Evangelical and Post liberal scholars—a rare and essential conversation and a boon to our understandings. This book should be within arm's reach for every preacher, elder, Bible class teacher and student. This volume can be a critical resource for sermon and class preparation and a tool for small groups and private studies ~ that is, for all who desire to explore with depth and clarity the book of Hebrews. I've just added this book to my short list of essential preparations for preaching Hebrews."

—**DAVID FLEER,** Professor of Bible and Communication,
Director of Annual Conference on Preaching, Lipscomb University

"Despite the great cloud of unknowns swirling about the book of Hebrews, Edward Fudge cuts through the haze and discovers great encouragement for beleaguered believers today. Fudge masterfully distills modern scholarly discussions into readable, elegant prose, putting top-shelf scholarship at eye-level, making it available to all. Some consider Hebrews to be the most difficult and elusive book in the New Testament. Fudge punctuates his commentary in all the right places with boxes of print that lay out the various theological options to Hebrews' most puzzling passages. Saturated in covenant language and adept in biblical and non-biblical sources, Fudge is uniquely qualified to help his readers appreciate the rhetoric, heed the warnings and follow in the steps of the true saints."

—**DAVID B. CAPES,** Professor of New Testament, Interim Dean of Honors College,
Houston Baptist University

"After reading Edward Fudge's commentary, I have it in my head more than ever before that Jesus is our priest who offered to God, not an animal sacrifice, but His own body and blood. The book of Hebrews is such a tribute to Jesus, the man, the Son of God who accomplished 'so great a salvation' for us. If you've never studied Hebrews because you think it's too hard, you will be delighted by this book."

—**Sarah Sumner,** Professor of Theology and Ministry, Graduate School of Theology,
Azusa Pacific University

"Reading the Bible, it turns out, isn't simply a science. It's also an art, and the art requires a kind of connoisseurship. Just as someone could never be a wine connoisseur without having a well-developed taste for wine, an expositor of Scripture needs to have a true love for the text and its author, and Edward Fudge qualifies. His love for Scripture shows on every page of this readable and accessible commentary, as does his skill in the art of interpretation."

—**Brian McLaren,** Author and Networker (brianmclaren.net)

"The Letter to the Hebrews is, theologically, aesthetically and pastorally, one of the richest writings penned by the earliest Christians but one of the most difficult to appreciate. With tremendous clarity and sensitivity, in what is plainly a labour of love, Edward Fudge invites modern believers to rediscover this ancient word of encouragement and its abiding relevance for the church of every age."

—**Chris Marshall,** Professor in Christian Studies, Religious Studies Programme,
Victoria University of Wellington, New Zealand

"Finally, there is a commentary on the often-neglected Book of Hebrews that combines meticulous scholarship with readability and practical understanding. This work is sure to be a favorite of preachers, teachers, and Bible students alike."

—**Jeff Schreve,** Pastor, First Baptist Church, Texarkana, Texas;
From His Heart Ministries

"This commentary takes account of the best in scholarship to serve ordinary thoughtful people, who will find here an important and helpful resource. The commentary is clear not only in language but also in discerning what is central to the book of Hebrews—the human Jesus who is, at the same time, the very Son of God. In the process the author illumines the unique contribution of Hebrews in understanding the way and work of Christ."

—**Ben Wiebe,** Pastor, Mennonite Churches and Churches of Christ in Ontario, Canada;
Adjunct Professor, Union Biblical Seminary, India

"Hebrews in not an easy book; in fact it has often been called a 'puzzle'. Yet, this difficult book contains a depth of teaching and breadth of exhortation and encouragement that can help Christ-followers endure, and stand in faith, in our very difficult world. Thus, we need more teachers and tools that clearly unpack the message of Hebrews, bringing that message to bear in relevant ways to the church today. While many will find points at which to differ with the interpretations offered, Edward Fudge writes clearly and applies the test pointedly in this engaging, accessible little commentary."

—**George H. Guthrie,** Benjamin W. Perry Professor of Bible, School of Christian Studies, Union University; Author of *NIV Application Commentary: Hebrews*

"Scholarly, refreshing, and packed full of encouragement for today's Christian. Eminently read-able, this volume is like having an enlightened friend walk with us through the challenges of life as reflected in this ancient book, all the while pointing us to the faithful friend who will never leave us or forsake us. Coming out of the author's deeply spiritual heart, this book inspires greater spirituality in the heart of the reader. It is a joy to recommend it!"

—**LANDON SAUNDERS,** Founder and President, Heartbeat

"Here is nourishing food for the soul. But behind the apparent simplicity of this commentary lies a meticulous examination of the original text as well as judicious consideration of the conclu-sions of other exegetes."

—**DESMOND FORD,** Good News Unlimited, Queensland, Australia

"Readers at any level will profit from this author's always clear elucidation of the ancient Greek text and its English translations. I have read this commentary as critically and as carefully as any I've ever examined, and I have seen with fresh eyes how Jesus our high priest has gone outside the gate to serve and to heal a hurting world, and how he beckons us anew to follow him. If I had more classes to teach, more sermons to preach, or more translation teams to guide, this book would be high on my recommended list."

—**GERALD KENDRICK,** Translation Officer (Ret.), United Bible Societies

"This new commentary on Hebrews is a delight to read. Edward Fudge deftly handles the weightiest of theological material in a fresh and invigorating way, reminding us that Hebrews is indeed an encouraging word to Christians of any era. This book will be a staple for preachers and teachers of adult Bible classes."

—**MATT SOPER,** Senior Minister, West Houston Church of Christ, Houston, Texas

"Christians have long recognized that the Epistle to the Hebrews provides one of the most original theological perspectives in the New Testament, and one of the least accessible. Edward Fudge goes a very long way toward acknowledging Hebrews' profundity while aiding its accessibil-ity. Through his study of the text, his attention to the long history of interpretation of this writing and his own wise pastoral applications, Fudge has written a guide to Hebrews that I am happy to commend to students and pastors alike."

—**DAVID BARTLETT,** Professor of New Testament, Columbia Theological Seminary, Lantz Professor of Preaching, Emeritus, Yale Divinity School

"Fudge's skill as a biblical scholar, his pastoral love for people, and his career-long special inter-est in the book of Hebrews make this commentary a mandatory asset for both the scholar and the casual reader. My wife and I regularly use it as part of our devotions, something we do with no other commentary."

—**NEAL PUNT,** author and retired pastor, Christian Reformed Church

"In reading through this commentary, I have been impressed anew with a first-century preach-er's ability to bring a positive word from God to Christians under stress. But it is in the nature of things for faith always to be under assault. Therefore I am grateful for this practical and readable study of Hebrews for this generation. Read it, and take heart for your own struggle."

    —**RUBEL SHELLY,** President, Rochester College

"Much imagery in the Epistle to the Hebrews is obscure to moderns. It is a book I try to avoid preaching on! But Edward Fudge clarifies the imagery and Hebrews makes a lot more sense to me now. I won't be so afraid of preaching on it!"

    —**FOSTER EICH,** Associate Priest, St. Bartholomew's Episcopal Church,
                  Florence, Alabama

"This is one of the finest works on Hebrews that I have read. Fudge writes with a clear focus, steers clear of tangents, and captures the spirit of the letter. Demonstrating extensive research and sound scholarship, he writes for both the ordinary and the more accomplished student of Hebrews. Not shying away from controversial passages, he addresses them forthrightly, generally including his view with a careful acknowledgment of differing opinions."

    —**DAVID L. EUBANKS,** President-Emeritus, Johnson Bible College

"This commentary on Hebrews achieves the author's purpose of providing 'Ancient Encouragement for Believers Today.' While the writer demonstrates familiarity with recent scholarship and rich insights, he has written in a style that does not require a terminal degree in theology to understand. The reader may disagree with some of the author's conclusions, as I do, but this commentary is well worth reading."

    —**FLAVIL R. YEAKLEY, JR.,** Professor, College of Bible and Religion, Harding University

"God has gifted Edward Fudge as a teacher to make His word understandable to the student and challenging to the scholar. This commentary is the result of that gifting."

    —**JOHN J. VOSS,** Chaplain, Children of Promise, Inc.

"This work is informed by scholarly research but communicates clearly to the non-specialist. Laity and clergy alike will find it to be an accessible and informative guide through the rich and complex message of Hebrews."

    —**DAVID F. WATSON,** Assistant Professor of New Testament,
                  United Theological Seminary

"Fudge's commentary on the Book of Hebrews is a momentous accomplishment that the Lord has given him the wisdom to write for His glory! It is a scholarly work, yet written in a simple, understandable and refreshing way, for believers today to be encouraged in their walk with Jesus and to fulfill all that He has called and gifted them to be and to do in His Kingdom."

    —**DAN HUBBELL,** leader, international house church movement

"Believing that the biblical book of Hebrews has been pushed back in a corner and largely forgotten, Edward Fudge brushes away the dust and reopens this ancient 'word of encouragement.' Those who stand in the pulpit, those who sit in the pew and the non-Christian seeker all will benefit from his exegetical insights and relevant contemporary applications."

    —**STAN REID,** President, Austin Graduate School of Theology

"Insightful and reflective, this commentary makes the book of Hebrews a touchable, tangible word of encouragement for today. Throughout the journey, Edward Fudge keeps the spotlight shining on Jesus Christ, the author and perfecter of our faith."

—**WYATT E. FENNO,** Preaching Minister, Montgomery Church of Christ, Albuquerque, New Mexico; author *Living Waters*

"We need more commentaries like this one, which is characterized by careful exegesis on the one hand and sound exposition on the other. It will be a significant help to both pastors and teachers."

—**ROY R. MATHESON,** Professor Emeritus of New Testament, Tyndale Seminary, Toronto, Canada

"If your congregation faces an aging membership, declining numbers, a shortage of volunteers, tension over a variety of issues and confusion over your neighbor's apparent apathy toward the church, then Hebrews has a good word for you. Edward Fudge's fresh version and interpretation faithfully witness to Jesus, the Ground Breaker of our faith, who is still working for us. This is the church's hope."

— **DWIGHT ROBARTS,** Senior Minister, Skillman Church of Christ, Dallas, Texas

"Blending accessible scholarship with a remarkable piety, Fudge addresses opposing interpretations of Scripture with fairness and balance. I plan to use this commentary for personal devotions as well as a reference for preaching."

—**FRANK COATS,** Elder, Texas Annual Conference of the United Methodist Church

"Edward Fudge has highlighted the book of Hebrews in such an encouraging and accessible style, that it could be called a devotional commentary. Fudge's passion for preaching Jesus in a manner that is easily understood, shines through on each page."

—**STEVE FARMER,** Pastor, Christian Gospel Temple, Cross Plains, Tennessee

"Fudge has written a concise, informative and thorough commentary. In 'problem' areas of the biblical text, he offers solutions, yet does not try to force his judgments upon the readers, challenging them all the while to think 'outside the box.' I commend this book to all serious students of the word of God."

—**TOM SEALS,** College of Bible and Ministry, Lipscomb University

"Edward Fudge has skillfully bridged the gap between the world of the ancient text and the world of the contemporary believer who seeks to hear the voice of God through the pages of Scripture. He successfully conducts serious exegetical exploration without introducing overly-technical jargon or explicit citations of Greek vocabulary and syntax. Both the non-biblical studies specialist and the preacher-teacher will find his approach refreshing and helpful. Readers also will find valuable his concise, clear, and cogent discussion of thorny theological issues raised by the text of Hebrews."

—**MARK HAHLEN,** Department Chair and Professor of Bible, Dallas Christian College

"If you seek a commentary to strengthen your confidence in God's saving grace by the powerful example of Jesus raised and glorified, Edward Fudge on Hebrews will satisfy. Fudge manages assertiveness without arrogance in his own reading of the text as he points to Jesus who shows the way to the Father. With personal insights that address conditions in today's world, this commentary is thorough without being wordy. Avoiding a less-than-helpful dependence on what others have said, the author's adept use of original sources results in a reading of the text that is both theologically responsible and practically helpful. The one who wrote Hebrews did so to encourage. Edward Fudge has done the same."

—**ROGER McCOWN,** Preaching Minister, Brentwood Oaks Church of Christ, Austin, Texas

"Edward Fudge has written a very insightful, non-technical, devotional commentary on the Book of Hebrews. His recurring 'Why & Wherefore' sections provide excellent summaries of the text and explain the logical connections of sections to context. Today's Christian will find much helpful light in Fudge's commentary in opening up the meaning of a book often thought to be dark and difficult."

—**DONN LEACH,** Professor Emeritus of Bible, Manhattan (Kansas) Christian College

"The author's verse-by-verse commentary is a humble and thoughtful analysis of the original meaning and current applications of Hebrews. Fudge balances personal reflection with orderly analysis, and often proffers the reader with succinct summaries of different positions that commentators have taken on particularly difficult passages. Though the author has worked through the Greek text, he writes in a manner that is consistently accessible to the layman—the result being a pleasant blend that readers of all backgrounds today can welcome and absorb."

—**JONATHAN M. WATT,** Professor of Biblical Studies, Geneva College; Adjunct Professor of Biblical Studies, Reformed Presbyterian Theological Seminary

"Edward Fudge dissects the mysterious book of Hebrews with a stirring combination of practicality and scholarship. His goal seems to be the simplicity of depth. I think he hit his target!"

—**TERRY RUSH,** Senior Minister, Memorial Drive Church of Christ, Tulsa, Oklahoma

"I have long looked to Edward Fudge's writings and advice to assist me in the difficult job of presenting relevant biblical messages to our congregation week to week. I am thrilled that he has tackled Hebrews and left his wisdom in such a useful format for all of us to use in the years to come. This commentary is brilliant."

—**MARK MOORE,** Preaching Minister, Springfield (Virginia) Church of Christ and former missionary to Uganda

HEBREWS

Ancient Encouragement for Believers Today

HEBREWS

ANCIENT ENCOURAGEMENT
FOR BELIEVERS TODAY

Edward William Fudge

Foreword by Haddon W. Robinson

A New Commentary
for Use With All Standard Versions

LEAFWOOD
PUBLISHERS
Abilene, Texas

HEBREWS:
Ancient Encouragement For Believers Today

Copyright 2009 by Edward William Fudge

ISBN 978-0-89112-625-6

Library of Congress Cataloging in Publication Data

Fudge, Edward William (1944-)
Hebrews: Ancient Encouragement for Believers Today
    1.   Bible. N.T. Hebrews – Commentaries
    ISBN 978-0-89112-625-6
    Copyright 2009 by Edward William Fudge

Printed in the United States of America

Cover design by Marc Whitaker, MTW Design
Interior text design by Sandy Armstrong

Leafwood Publishers is an imprint of
Abilene Christian University Press.

1648 Campus Court
Abilene, Texas 79601
1-877-816-4455 toll free

For current information about all Leafwood titles, visit our website:
www.leafwoodpublishers.com

Visit the author's multimedia website www.EdwardFudge.com

09 10 11 12 13 14 / 6 5 4 3 2 1

DEDICATION

*This book is
gratefully dedicated to*

W. MARK LANIER

*brother in Christ - faithful encourager
comrade in study and teaching
generous sponsor - genuine friend*

Through [Jesus] then let us continually offer up a sacrifice of praise to God, that is, the fruit of lips that acknowledge his name. Do not neglect to do good and to share what you have, for such sacrifices are pleasing to God.

Hebrews 13:15-16

ACKNOWLEDGEMENTS

The author gratefully acknowledges the following individuals for their valuable contributions to the writing of this book:

CRAIG CHURCHILL, Theological Librarian, Abilene Christian University—for extraordinary hospitality and research support;

JEREMY FUDGE, Dallas, Texas, and **TODD FOSTER**, Houston, Texas—for their assistance in connection with the creation of The Common Version;

DAVID CARR, New South Wales, Australia—for proofreading several drafts of the manuscript;

CHARLES G. MICKEY, MATT SOPER and **BRENT ISBELL**, all of Houston, Texas—for reading the manuscript and for offering important constructive suggestions in both style and content;

PEGGY VINING—who, having recently completed her Ph.D. at Catholic University of America with emphasis on New Testament Greek, found the time to read the manuscript with a special eye on remarks concerning the original language;

SARA FAYE FUDGE, my wife and chief copy reviewer, a former English teacher who is honest in her criticism and lavish in her praise—for her stylistic suggestions and for her patience with an obsessive-compulsive husband;

HADDON W. ROBINSON—for his gracious generosity in contributing the Foreword to this book. Dr. Robinson is the Harold John Ockenga Distinguished Professor of Preaching at Gordon-Conwell Theological Seminary, of which he is also a past President. He is widely regarded as an expert in the area of preaching, and was named one of the twelve most effective preachers in the English-speaking world in a 1996 Baylor University poll. Dr. Robinson has authored six books, including *Biblical Preaching*, which is currently being used as a text for preaching in 120 seminaries and Bible colleges throughout the world.

Contents

Foreword

Haddon W. Robinson

When I was growing up in New York City, all of my friends were Roman Catholic. My mother, however, was part of a group known as The Plymouth Brethren. When it came to discussing religion with the other fellows in my gang, I felt overmatched and undermanned. The Catholics knew how to do religion.

The Catholic families in my neighborhood attended Saint Joseph Church. Frankly, I thought it was what a real church should be. It looked like a church on the outside and when worshippers entered the darkened sanctuary they faced a large white basin filled with holy water. Over to the side of the church closer to the front there blazed scores of candles which I was told represented prayers for the sick and for the dead. The focal point of the church was a large altar and to one side stood a huge statue of Joseph who looked down with a gentle smile on the parishioners who attended mass each week.

The hall in which our church met, on the other hand, was located in another part of the city. It wasn't actually a church, but only a large plain rented room on the second floor above a bank. To get to it, we had to climb a steep flight of stairs. Those stairs presented no problem for me, but some of the older folks climbed them with considerable difficulty. Nothing about that room looked like what I and my friends knew a real church should look like. I told my friends I worshipped in a cathedral that towered several stories above the street. I knew, of course, that I was bearing false witness.

Buildings aside, my friends always won the discussion of comparative religions when they asked, "Who is your priest?" "Well, we don't exactly

17

have a priest," I would explain. "We have a man named Mr. Johnson who makes the announcements at the close of our service." It was all a bit embarrassing having a religion without a priest. If it weren't for my mother, I would have gladly become a member of St. Joseph Catholic Church.

That must have been something like what some of the first readers of the letter to the Hebrews must have felt. They, and possibly their parents, had come to believe that Jesus was the long prophesied Messiah in the First Testament. They had become Christ Followers. No longer did they worship in the temple but instead they met in homes. They gave up the trappings of the religion of the Jews that appealed to the senses. The massive temple dwarfed other buildings in Jerusalem. Worshipers smelled the incense and heard the bells on the garments of the priest and the bleating of the animals being brought to sacrifice. At the temple a worshipper could feel the mystery. The interior of the temple grew increasingly darker with a huge curtain that guarded the sacred center. That curtain had shut God in and the people out.

Christians had traded all of that for small groups gathering in homes. No wonder some of them were tempted to go back to the old familiar forms. The author of the letter to the Hebrews faced a rhetorical challenge. "How do I convince my readers that what they have in Christ is infinitely better than what they have given up?"

For modern Christians unfamiliar with the forms and ceremonies and personnel of the religion of the Hebrews the letter seems a bit much to tackle. They do not realize what they are missing. They need someone to sit beside them to explain what they do not know and to point out what they might easily miss. Edward Fudge does that well. He helps you in your study so that you will be encouraged in your faith as Christians were centuries ago.

Dr. Robinson is the Harold John Ockenga Distinguished Professor of Preaching at Gordon-Conwell Theological Seminary, of which he is also a past President.

About This Commentary

This commentary is written for the serious Bible student who seeks scholarly content in non-technical terms. As such, it bridges a gap that many commentaries simply ignore. While I have considered each word of the Greek text of Hebrews in my own study, no Greek words are included in this work. And, although this commentary represents considerable scholarly research, the results of that research are expressed in the ordinary language of regular people.

For example, highly-technical commentaries regularly refer to Hebrews 1:1-4 as the author's *exordium* (opening section) and the collection of biblical quotations in 1:5-14 as a *florilegium* (bouquet) or a *catena* (collection of passages or comments on passages). Since those specialized terms add nothing to our understanding of the author's message, they do not appear in this discussion of the text.

You will notice that there are no footnotes or endnotes in this book. Quotations from non-biblical authors are few. When they do appear, they are credited by author and page within the text itself. Occasionally other works are cited for additional research. In such cases, books are identified by author, and journal articles by author and title. Complete information is provided in the bibliography which follows the conclusion of the commentary.

NOTE ABOUT THE GREEK OLD TESTAMENT (SEPTUAGINT: LXX)

Here we need to explain the meaning of "LXX" in some Scripture references cited in this book. The Jewish Scriptures, which we call the Old Testament, were originally written in Hebrew (with some small portions in Aramaic). During the century after Malachi, Alexander the Great

(356-323) conquered the Persian Empire, spreading both Greek culture and the Greek language throughout his newly-conquered territories. Beginning about 275 B.C., Egyptian Jews living in Alexandria translated the Old Testament Scriptures from Hebrew into Greek. Tradition says this was begun by 70 (or 72) translators. This Greek Old Testament is commonly called the Septuagint, from the Latin word for "70." That name is abbreviated as "LXX" (the Roman numeral for "70").

The Septuagint was the primary Bible used by Jesus and the early church, and it included some books not contained in the Hebrew Old Testament. These books, called the Apocrypha, are all included in the (Eastern) Orthodox Bible, and some of them are in the Roman Catholic Bible. Protestant Bibles follow the Hebrew Bible which does not include these books. At times the Septuagint differs from the Hebrew text. It adds Psalm 151 to the Book of Psalms, and it combines, divides and/or renumbers other chapters and verses in the Psalms and elsewhere.

Throughout the Book of Hebrews, almost all Old Testament quotations come from the Septuagint. When the Greek citation differs from the Hebrew citation, I have indicated this with a reference that includes "LXX." For example, I identify our author's quotation in Hebrews 1:5b as coming from Psalm 89:27 in our Bible. However, in the Septuagint, that passage is numbered 88:28. This is indicated by a reference to "(LXX 88:28)." The same abbreviation "LXX" also occurs when our author quotes wording from the Greek Old Testament which is different from the Hebrew wording (for example, in Hebrews 2:7).

Reverent scholarship is important, and that has ever been my goal. However, as beneficiaries of the new covenant, our ultimate teacher is God himself (Hebrews 8:10-11). With that reality in mind, let us fix our eyes on Jesus and receive with faith the word that God has spoken by his Son (Hebrews 12:2; 4:2).

Edward William Fudge
March 2009

Introduction to a Book
of Unknowns

What can we know about the person who wrote Hebrews and the people for whom it was first written? When was it written and why? The fact is that we know almost nothing about the origins of the so-called "Epistle to the Hebrews," a title first documented in the writings of Tertullian (approximately 160-220 A.D.)

I say "so-called" because this ancient writing lacks most of the usual elements of an "epistle" or letter (such as the author's name, the addressees and a formal greeting), and because it is possible that the original readers might not have been "Hebrews" at all. Curiously, the author never uses the words "Hebrew," "Jew" or any other form of either word and he (or she) sometimes seems to explain details which one assumes Jewish believers would have known already (Hebrews 7:1-2; Hebrews 9:1-5).

Such uncertainties led one scholar to describe the church's acceptance of Hebrews with the story of a couple who find an orphan boy, "not quite knowing what to do with him, soon discovering his brilliance, embracing him, and spending the rest of their days trying—unsuccessfully—to identify him. Through it all they are dazzled by what they learn from him, never quite sure where to seat him among their other children" (Holladay, 447).

Hebrews does indeed dazzle those who read it with a prayerful heart and a mind focused on Jesus Christ. For even with all the unknowns regarding its origin, this book remains "one of the most beautifully written, powerfully argued, and theologically profound writings in the New Testament" (L. T. Johnson, 1).

Unknown Author

The first known writing identifying Paul as author of Hebrews is Papyrus 46 (or P46) written about A.D. 200 and found in Egypt. However, church leaders a century later still didn't know who wrote Hebrews. Clement of Alexandria surmised that Paul wrote Hebrews in Hebrew and that Luke translated it into Greek. (Of course no one has ever found a Hebrew *Hebrews,* so Clement stands by himself with that idea.) Origen was less sure, confessing that "who really wrote the letter is known to God alone." Elsewhere in Africa, at Carthage, Tertullian nominated Barnabas as the author of Hebrews. Most Christians in the Roman West said they didn't know. Centuries later, in the Reformation, Luther leaned toward Apollos while Calvin favored Luke or a second-century believer named Clement of Rome.

Unknown Recipients

If the identity of Hebrews' first readers were being determined by popular vote, the candidates that have been nominated would stretch all the way from Italy to Egypt. Various scholars have suggested that our unknown author wrote for his friends and fellow-believers living in Rome, Ephesus, Colossae, Laodicea, Corinth, Cyprus, Palestine and Alexandria.

Unknown Date

The date of Hebrews is equally unknown. When the author discusses Jewish priests, sanctuary and sacrifices, he clearly is speaking about people, places and things described in the Old Testament, not the politicized priesthood, commercialized sacrifices and institutionalized Temple of the first century after Christ. We cannot even say for sure whether Hebrews originated before or after the destruction of Jerusalem and its Temple in A.D. 70. Advocates for both views claim internal support from Hebrews itself.

We can state with reasonable confidence that Hebrews was written no earlier than the mid-first century, since its first readers were second-generation believers (Hebrews 2:3-4; Hebrews 13:7). And it was certainly written before A.D. 96, when Clement of Rome quoted from it in his letter to the church at Corinth now called First Clement.

Unknown Circumstances

As we read through Hebrews, we quickly detect that it was written to professing believers who were experiencing a crisis of faith. The text itself suggests several possible causes of this crisis, including persecution, weariness, temptation, boredom and lack of knowledge. In the minds of these believers, the price of discipleship was beginning to outweigh its prize. They had begun to entertain second thoughts about their commitment to Jesus, and they were thinking seriously about returning to their comfortable and familiar past. But what exactly was that past which now seemed so attractive?

Through the centuries, most Christians have assumed that Hebrews was written for Jewish believers who were tempted to abandon Jesus for the religion in which they were raised. There are two main reasons for this assumption. First is the name "Hebrews" itself. Then there is the constant emphasis throughout the book on all the ways Jesus and his priesthood and sacrifice are better and stronger and more enduring than their Old Testament counterparts. Isn't that adequate evidence for the long-held and widespread conclusion that Hebrews was written to Jews who were in danger of forsaking Jesus for Moses?

Some scholars think that it is not (Moffatt, xv-xvii). In fact, the name "Hebrews" is undocumented before about 200 a.d. As a descriptive term, "Hebrews" appears almost exclusively in the Old Testament, where it regularly identifies the people we know as Jews. The word "Hebrew" appears only four times in the New Testament with this sense (Acts 6:1; 2 Corinthians 11:22; Philippians 3:5 twice).

It should not surprise us that the Book of Hebrews frequently quotes, regularly refers to, and always assumes the presence of what we call the Old Testament. After all, those earlier Scriptures were the early church's *Bible.* (For the most part, the early church read the Septuagint, a common Greek translation of the Hebrew Scriptures made between 275-200 b.c.. Nearly all the Old Testament quotations in Hebrews match the Septuagint. Comparisons between Jesus and what came before him are to be expected regardless of the audience: until Jesus came, the Old Testament was God's latest revelation. Hebrews opens with the startling announcement that God who spoke in the past has spoken again in his Son. The full moon always appears bright until the sun rises and dims it by contrast.

The truth is that the original audience really does not matter. Whether the first readers were messianic Jews, Gentile Christians or house-churches containing both Jews and Gentiles (as seems most likely anywhere outside Palestine itself), we know that they faced a crisis of commitment. And regardless of the exact nature of that crisis, they desperately needed strong encouragement to continue trusting in Jesus and to keep hanging on.

But Well Known to Us by Experience

Is that not the situation in which we often find ourselves today? The truth is that the first recipients of Hebrews were very much like us. And, realize it or not, we frequently walk in their shoes. You don't believe me? Consider the following slice of life. Do you recognize anyone in this picture?

We come to Christ with strong commitment and the best of intentions. Our zeal is stoked, our emotions are high. We have seen Jesus in the gospel story and he has claimed our heart. At that moment, we cannot imagine how it could ever be otherwise. But then time passes.

Days turn to weeks, weeks to months and months to years. Earthly pleasures—altogether innocent—attract our attention. Worldly obligations, quite necessary as we live on this earth, distract us and claim our time. Gradually our hearts come "down from the mountain." It almost feels like Jesus has slipped farther away.

We continue serving Christ but, truth be told, we sometimes find it more tiring than triumphant. Sometimes circumstances converge, storm clouds gather and we face a crisis of conscience, a test of faith. Perhaps we pass the test with flying colors, but fellow-workers or associates now seem to look at us in a different way. Somehow we don't quite seem to "fit in."

Time goes on and we sometimes have questions. Why can't we see Jesus? Does God really hear our prayers? In fact, does God really accept us in spite of our faults? We know how we love our children. Can God really love us like that? Eternity sure seems a long way from here. We are so busy. We need a break—a weekend of golf and shopping would probably help.

We love the church—our fellow-believers, fellow-pilgrims, the People of God. But some of those individual people sure get on our nerves. When will they ever grow up? We want to serve Christ, of course, and we used to volunteer for anything that needed helpers.

Sometimes, at the end of the day, we feel almost wiped out. We skip worship meetings for a few Sundays. It will do us good not to see those people quite so often.

Our conscience nags so we return to church. This week's sermon is hard-hitting. We have a duty, a sacred obligation. Yes, we know, and we stumble on. Strange, but this church business is beginning to feel more like Mount Sinai and less like the New Jerusalem. Where are all those celebrating angels? Where did Jesus go? Will we ever recover the thrill and zeal that we enjoyed in the beginning?

Does anything there sound remotely familiar? Perhaps we share more with the unknown original readers of Hebrews than we first thought. The good news is that there was wonderful help for them—and the same wonderful help remains for us! But we should change that word "help" to "Helper" because I am speaking of a person. He is Jesus Christ, the Son of God. Yet he is more than God's Son. He is also *man*—one of us, and he has lived here, faced our problems, encountered the same kinds of people we deal with. He has suffered. (*How* he has suffered!) He has been exhausted and grown discouraged. He has wondered whether the goal was worth the cost. And he has persevered—stuck with it despite everything, even through a horrible death.

In Jesus, God saw everything that he ever wanted from a human being—and God was immensely pleased! A man like Jesus couldn't remain dead—couldn't stay away from God's immediate presence. So God raised the *man Jesus* from the dead, took him up to heaven and gave him the seat next to his own throne. However, Jesus is not just *there*. He is there *for us*, as our representative, just as he earlier had lived and died and risen as our representative on the earth. One day, on a day that God will decide, Jesus will appear again, to give his people the fullness of salvation in new, redeemed heavens and earth.

This is Hebrews' word of encouragement! The problem is that most of us don't know that, because over the years this biblical book has been pushed back into a corner where it was largely forgotten. There for the most part it has languished—gathering spider-webs and collecting dust. Now that is about to change. And are we in for a treat!

Hebrews is Good News!

So far as the origins of Hebrews, we have just reviewed the traditional questions *(by whom? to whom? when? where? why?)* and the traditional answers *(don't know, don't know, don't know, don't know, don't know).* Happily, that uncertainty presents no great cause for concern. In fact, when it comes to Hebrews, we will benefit far more if we agree to forget such questions and to simply listen with prayerful and open hearts to what its ancient anonymous author actually has to say.

FALLEN ON HARD TIMES

Unfortunately, Hebrews has fallen on hard times in the church. Many Christians find it confusing to read and difficult to understand. Even experienced Bible teachers have been known to dismiss Hebrews as a tedious book about the tabernacle and the technical superiority of the New Testament over the Old. In today's fast-paced world, most people find those subjects both boring and irrelevant. With such discouraging opinions filling their heads, more than a few believers often opt to simply turn the pages of their Bibles from Hebrews and to read some other book instead.

That is a terrible tragedy, because Hebrews is bubbling over with *encouragement!* Hebrews is encouraging because it keeps the spotlight shining on *Jesus.* Because it is focused on Jesus, its message is chock full of pure *gospel.* Hebrews also beautifully illustrates how the early church could always be talking and thinking and preaching and studying about Jesus – with no "Bible" except the books we call the Old Testament. It is fair to say that the New Testament is the Old Testament read in light of Jesus. If someone needs convincing of that fact, the book of Hebrews qualifies as Exhibit Number One. In fact, Hebrews is a message of encouragement built around four Psalms—Psalm 8, Psalm 95, Psalm 40 and Psalm 110 (Kistemaker).

THE STORY OF ONE WHO TOOK OUR PLACE

As we move through Hebrews chapter by chapter and verse by verse, we will gradually detect the tones of a wonderful story. It is a story we thought we already knew, one that many of us have heard since earliest childhood. But as we grow more accustomed to the cadence and rhythms of this ancient voice, we will increasingly find ourselves caught up in a beauty and excitement of the story that has often gone missing in the modern telling.

He became a man to live a human life

This is the story of the Son of God who became a human being. That human being was and is the man we know as Jesus of Nazareth. The Son of God became the *man Jesus* to accomplish one specific objective—to put us right with God. He would do that *as a man* by taking our place and doing for us what we could never do for ourselves. These are the thoughts prompted in our author's mind as he reflects on Psalm 8.

He served God faithfully, every new 'today'

As our representative, Jesus lived the life of loving and faithful human obedience that the Father had always wanted from men and women but which he had never received. Jesus did this one day at a time, each new "today." Every morning upon awakening, Jesus listened to the Father's voice. Then he did just what the Father wished—day after day after day.

Jesus followed through, regardless of opposition or distraction or ordinary weariness. Despite temptations of every kind (and he encountered them all), he followed through. When it became obvious that this path of obedience was leading directly to a cross, Jesus still was faithful. Nothing could distract him. Nothing could disturb his resolve. Nothing could detour him around God's path or deter him from doing God's will. When Jesus was beaten, he followed through. His enemies nailed him to a cross, but still he followed through. Our author remembers all this as he thinks about Psalm 95.

He gave God what God had always wanted first

Then, nailed to that cross, Jesus offered that life to the Father as a *present*—a gift wrapped in Jesus' *human body.* Even his act of giving was part of the faithful obedience, and therefore part of the *present.* In offering the obedience lived in his *body,* Jesus also shed his *blood,* a highly significant event in Jewish circles. For centuries the Jews had approached God through a priesthood whose daily work primarily involved the slaughter of physically flawless animals and the presentation to God of their sacrificial blood. These things our author considers as he analyzes Psalm 40.

Those animal sacrifices constantly reminded the Jews of their own failure, and of God's greatest desire—that they love him with all their hearts, then live in faithful fellowship with him by keeping his commandments. In short, God wanted each person to give God his own self as a *living* sacrifice pleasing to God. However, no Israelite (or anyone else) had ever done that. In his mercy, God permitted the sinful Israelite to express repentance and to receive forgiveness by giving him the life of a physically perfect animal.

Because the animal's "life" was represented by its blood (Leviticus 17:11-12), *giving* God that life required that the life first be *taken.* When the animal had been slaughtered, the priest sprinkled, poured and smeared its blood inside the Holy Place and in the courtyard. In this way, the Israelite who sinned gave God the physically perfect "life" of a sacrificial animal as a substitute for the morally spotless life he himself was unable to give. (On the Day of Atonement, the high priest sprinkled blood of the sin offerings inside the Most Holy Place. This unique event prefigured Jesus our high priest, who figuratively "sprinkled" the heavenly sanctuary with his own blood.)

But all of that was entirely *remedial*—a *rescue* effort. It was never what God wanted most. For all those years, all that slaughter and all that blood was only God's *second* choice. If the people had simply loved God, enjoyed his company and done what pleased him, his *second* choice would never have come into the picture. There would have been no slitting of throats, no blood poured on altars or sprinkled on holy furniture. And now that Jesus had given God his *first* choice, the gift of a faithful and loving life in unbroken fellowship with God, there would never be the need again of that *second* choice—that *remedial* business involving slaughtered animals and ceremonial blood.

God saved Jesus out of death and honored him in heaven

God looked at Jesus' obedient life, which he offered in his obedient death, and declared that it was all that he ever had requested or required from the human race. In this way, by his flawless life and death, Jesus rescued his people from their sins and made them intimate friends with Father God. We call this result the "atonement"— the *at-one-ment,* if you please, for God's door is now open wide to anyone represented by Jesus, any time of day or of night.

To show how pleased he was, God raised Jesus out of death. Not as a ghost or bodiless spirit, but with a marvelous human body grander than anyone could possibly imagine. Yet that was only the beginning. God then promoted the *glorified man* Christ Jesus right up into heaven and gave him a throne next to his very own. This passed before our author's mind as he considered Psalm 110.

SUCH GOOD NEWS COMPELS OUR RESPONSE!

Because Jesus represents us as our substitute and proxy, God regards everything that Jesus did for us just as if we had done it for ourselves. And because Jesus represents us, God's response to Jesus makes very clear how God regards every person whom Jesus represents. Such good news calls for our uninhibited response—a life of faith and faithfulness patterned after the faith and faithfulness of Jesus Christ himself.

Because of what Jesus has done for us, because we now have access to the Father, we are called to hold firmly our own confidence in God's promises and faithfulness just as Jesus did, until the very end of our lives. We have a responsibility to encourage each other as we follow Jesus together. Each new "today" we must hear the Father's voice, receive his word to us and digest it with the enzyme of faith.

Slothfulness and indifference are our greatest enemies. Like Jesus, we must learn the Father's wishes and seek daily to fulfill them. Like Jesus, we will encounter temptation, meet opposition, face weariness . . . and some will shed their blood. When these things happen we must—again like Jesus—*follow through.* Jesus has blazed a trail from earth to heaven. He has opened a highway that gives us forgiven sinners access to God. The writer of Hebrews sees the believer's life as a journey—and he exhorts us to keep moving until we reach its end.

One day Jesus will appear again, bringing to perfection all God's plans for his people in the much-anticipated world to come. Until then, Jesus represents us in heaven—Jesus the *glorified man,* who stood in for us to live and die under our name. By his very presence in heaven as *man,* Jesus certifies and guarantees *our* access to the Father. He is one *of* us. He is *us* by proxy. Indeed, in the words of the Scottish Presbyterian preacher John Duncan (1796-1870), "the dust of the earth is on the throne of the universe." That is what it means to speak of Jesus—*our man in heaven* (which was the title of my 1973 commentary on the King James Version of Hebrews).

A New But Familiar Version

Those who regularly use any standard Bible version (most versions produced by a team of scholars, in the tradition of the English Bible) will discover here the familiar and comfortable tones of a long-time friend. To understand why that is so, we need to look briefly at the history of the English Bible.

THE ENGLISH TRADITION BEGINS (1536-1611)

William Tyndale was the first person to translate and print the Bible in English, for which he paid with his life in 1536. (John Wycliffe had produced a hand-written English Bible two centuries earlier.) Tyndale's New Testament in particular laid the foundation for English versions that followed—the Coverdale Bible, the Great Bible, the Geneva Bible, the Bishops Bible and others—culminating in the King James Version (KJV) of 1611.

Critics immediately attacked the newborn KJV, charging it with upstart impertinence because its translators dared to tamper with the older translations. Defenders of the KJV replied that this new version stood squarely within the *tradition* of English-language Bibles that preceded it. They also explained that revisions included in the new Bible were needful for the sake of accuracy and to match the ever-changing English language.

THE TRADITION CONTINUES (1611-2008)

The next 335 years saw the production of the English Revised Version (ERV), American Standard Version (ASV) and Revised Standard Version (RSV). In each case, the translators of these versions proudly said that they were preserving for the next generation the best of the *traditional* language of standard English Bibles from centuries past.

In response to their critics, the publishers of the ERV, the ASV and the RSV patiently explained that it was important for them to change the KJV tradition because the English language itself kept changing. The ASV also reflected differences between "English" as spoken in Great Britain and America. The publishers of these versions also noted the discoveries of older biblical manuscripts and textual fragments, and recent research in the disciplines of history, archaeology and linguistics.

Since the publication of the RSV in 1946, American publishers have produced other standard versions, all claiming to perpetuate the broad English *tradition* of biblical phraseology begun by William Tyndale so long ago. These include The New American Standard Bible (NASB), copyright 1960-1995 by The Lockman Foundation; The New International Version (NIV), copyright 1973-1984 by the International Bible Society; The New King James Version (NKJV), copyright 1982 by Thomas Nelson, Inc.; The New Revised Standard Version (NRSV), copyright 1989-1995 by the Division of Christian Education of the National Council of the Churches of Christ in the United States of America; The English Standard Version (ESV), copyright 2001 by Crossway Bibles, a division of Good News Publishers; and The Holman Christian Standard Bible (HCSB), copyright 2001-2004 by Holman Bible Publishers.

These six versions display a striking similarity to each other. For example, 53% of the wording in Hebrews chapter one is identical in all six versions. Add to that the similarities resulting from sheer coincidences of translation and two of these versions prove to be 88% identical in that same chapter. When it comes to the English words used to translate the Bible, there is a living *tradition* that began centuries ago and which still continues today. "Tradition" has to do with sameness. It naturally results in similarity.

THE COMMON VERSION

In addition to a Greek copy of Hebrews, our tools for this task included nine standard versions of the Holy Bible, with emphasis on six of them which were produced within the past 50 years. Those versions were the KJV, ASV, RSV, NASB, NIV, NKJV, NRSV, ESV and HCSB. By analyzing the wording of these traditional translations, we were able to construct (or, better, to *discover)* the common text of Hebrews—both as it had been handed down from earlier centuries and as it is still being shaped today. First we set out to identify identical wording in two or more of the six most recent standard versions. We looked for *common* language, not unique wording.

When a single word, phrase or clause did not immediately reveal traditional text, we probed the texts more deeply for common structural and grammatical elements. Is the verb active or passive? Which comes first, the verb or its subject? Is a noun or pronoun rendered more frequently in singular or plural form? Is it traditional to use a definite article ("the") or an indefinite article ("a," "an") in a specific phrase? If the Greek text leaves some word unstated, but implied or understood, is it more traditional to supply a word (if so, which one?) or to leave the sentence ambiguous as in the Greek? When words or forms appeared with equal frequency in the sample versions, we usually resorted to one or more of the three older standard versions to break a tie, while also considering the clarity and power of the English alternatives.

The result of this process is *The Common Version,* which appears in 48 portions of Scripture text throughout this book. It was created specifically for this commentary, to make it useful for the greatest number of people. Whatever your regular reading Bible and regardless of the version you prefer for study, this text was constructed for you. Consider it an adjunct to your own favorite version—and be blessed!

"The incarnation
was a historical and unrepeatable event
with permanent consequences.
Reigning at God's right hand today
is the man Christ Jesus,
still human as well as divine,
though now his humanity
has been glorified.
Having assumed our human nature,
he has never discarded it,
and he never will."

John Stott, *Understanding the Bible*
(revised edition, London: Scripture Union, copyright 1984, p. 74).

COMMENTARY

HEBREWS 1:1-4

The Son's Great Person and Achievements

[1] Long ago, at many times and in various ways, God spoke to our fathers by the prophets, [2] but in these last days he has spoken to us by his Son, whom he appointed heir of all things, through whom he made the worlds. [3] He is the radiance of God's Glory and the exact imprint of his nature. He is upholding all things by the word of his power. When he had made purification for sins, he sat down at the right hand of the Majesty on high, [4] having become as much superior to angels as the name he has inherited is more excellent than theirs.

WHY & WHEREFORE

The chief character of the Bible is God. And a chief characteristic of God throughout the Bible is that he is a God who *speaks.* Until Jesus Christ appeared, God's "last word"—his greatest word—his highest and noblest word to humankind of which we have any knowledge, was the word given piecemeal across past centuries through the prophets. That word is reported, described and often contained in the Jewish Scriptures, which Christians call the Old Testament. The author of Hebrews acknowledges this foundational fact in his opening sentence. Then he concludes that sentence with a blockbuster announcement of his own:

"God has spoken again . . . through a Son!"

Using our imagination, we visualize what happens next. Like a trumpet fanfare, this announcement reverberates across the earth and through the heavens. All activity suddenly stops; every action freezes. The curtain opens. The whole creation watches with bated breath as the spotlights turn to focus on the Son at God's right hand. This Son was God's agent in creating the universe, which he now sustains and will someday inherit. He is God's mirror-image and revealer, heaven's purifier, our exalted king and savior. As to dignity, rank and honor, even angels cannot hold a candle to him.

UNPACKING THE TEXT

God Who Spoke

1:1 Hebrews opens with a striking announcement expressed in five simple words: "God [who] spoke has spoken." Like a pair of faithful sentries, God's word stands at the beginning of Hebrews and at its close. This word brought the universe into being (Hebrews 11:3), and the same divine word will bring it to its end (Hebrews 12:26-27).

The phrase "at many times" stands for a single Greek adverb which literally means "in many portions." God revealed his word in segments, over a period of centuries. Genuine and faithful prophets spoke exactly what God said to them, and that word was always partial and incomplete. "In many" or "in various" ways translates a second Greek adverb quite literally.

The focus here is on variety. For centuries before Jesus was born, God spoke to the Jewish fathers by the prophets on many occasions in an assortment of ways. In the opening pages of Genesis we find God speaking directly to Adam, Cain and Noah, to Abraham, Isaac and Jacob. God spoke through a rainbow (to Noah), an angel (to Hagar), dreams (to Joseph), a burning bush (to Moses), Urim and Thummim (to high priests), a small voice (to Elijah) and a vision in the temple (to Isaiah). During the final centuries of Old Testament history, God spoke through oracles (Amos), life experiences (Hosea, Jonah, Ezekiel), symbols and symbolic acts (Ezekiel), sermons (Haggai), mystical signs (Zechariah) and by questions and answers (Malachi).

God also spoke in a variety of venues. He addressed Adam in unspoiled Eden and Noah in a fallen world. God spoke to Abram in Ur, Isaac in Palestine and Jacob in Haran. His word came to Joseph in Egypt, to Moses in Midian and to Daniel in Babylon. God's communications covered the spectrum. He addressed his people by parables and promises, in encouragement and in exhortations. God spoke through the prophets to the fathers in all these ways. By the time Jesus was born, God's people assumed that revelation was complete. However, God was yet to speak again. This time he would speak more completely and more clearly than he ever had spoken before.

"Long ago" is literally "of old." The expression refers to past centuries before Jesus was born. "The fathers" were the Jewish ancestors through whom eventually God would redeem the world. As such, they were the spiritual predecessors of all who ever believe in Jesus. If Hebrews was first written for a group of Jewish believers, "the fathers" were their fleshly forefathers.

"The prophets" mentioned here were men and women through whom God delivered special messages from time to time. First-century believers in Jesus, whose faith was deeply rooted in the Old Testament Scriptures, would naturally think of writing prophets like Moses and David, Isaiah and Amos, whose work Scripture preserves, as well as non-writing prophets such as Miriam, Deborah, Nathan, Elijah and Huldah, whose work Scripture describes, but which it does not contain.

At times God spoke through non-Jewish prophets living among the nations (Numbers 22-24). However, unless their stories intersect the salvation-story that is Scripture's theme, the Old Testament is silent concerning their existence. Some Jews and Christians alike have wondered whether God might ever have spoken through such persons as Siddhartha Gautama (the Buddha) in India, Lao-Tzu and Confucius in China or Socrates in Greece. Certainly they all taught some things consistent with biblical revelation. Perhaps we will never know. However, Hebrews tells us something that we can know for sure. If God ever did speak through these wise men (a premise we cannot merely assume), their messages were only a small part of the whole. We can also be sure of this—however wise those men might have been, they all have been superseded now by the Son.

These 'Last Days'

1:2 In using the phrase "these last days," the author is not calculating calendar-time, as if he sees the future approaching and observes that the End is near. He is speaking of salvation-time in God's agenda. This period described as the "last days" is the time of the Messiah—the agent through whom God rescues his people from sin and all its effects.

This concept of a final period of divine intervention was announced by the Hebrew prophets, and it was widespread by the time of Jesus. The pious community at Qumran that produced the Dead Sea Scrolls believed that it was living in the time of the End. The Present Age of anticipation would soon give way to the Coming Age of the Messiah (or perhaps two Messiahs, one royal and one priestly). The people who wrote the books in our New Testament also expected the Messiah to come at the end of the Present Age. What no one seemed to expect was the very thing that actually transpired. To everyone's surprise, Jesus appeared while the Present Age was still in progress. With Jesus' appearance, the Coming Age also arrived on the scene—and with it the time of messianic fulfillment. Salvation-history entered a new and long-awaited era (N.T. Wright, *Suprised by Hope*, chapters 12–15).

Yet earth-clocks continued to tick. To all appearances, the familiar visible events of world history continued as before. How can we say, then, that the Coming Age and the "last days" have begun? We can say that because events that belong to the End Time have started to occur.

(God's people generally understand end-time prophecies best in retrospect; prophetic meanings almost always become clearer after the fact.) Consider the following:

- Messiah has appeared;
- the resurrection has begun (God called "Number One!" and Jesus was raised. God then put the resurrection on "Pause," to be resumed at a time known only by him);
- the Spirit has been poured out;
- God has forgiven sins and is giving his people a new nature to serve him; and
- one *man* is already glorified with God in heaven!

Yet the End Time includes an interim. Although the End has begun, its finalization remains in the future and the old order continues to exist (2 Peter 3:3-10). When Jesus appears again, God will complete the End that he began at Jesus' first appearing. The Present Age and the Coming Age are now like two overlapping circles. We live in *both* Ages—the time of "already" and "not yet." The prophet David in particular foretold the Messiah's double-phased work with an unknown interim separating the two phases (Psalm 110:1 – note the word "until"). Peter refers to these two stages of the last days, separated by an interim also indicated by the word "until" (Acts 3:19-21).

Like the sudden merger of two swiftly-descending mountain streams flowing down from opposite points, the overlapping of the Present Age and the Coming Age creates undercurrents pulling in opposing directions. For the believer, the result is pressure or tension. The New Testament refers to this as "tribulation" or "affliction." If the Coming Age did not pull Jesus' people upward and forward, they would feel no pressure. However, the Present Age would then pull them backward and downward into the whirlpool with all that is passing away.

God has Spoken Again

God who spoke in the past has spoken again. This time he has spoken to us, that is, to those who will live and who do live with this tension between Present and Coming. The phrase "by his Son" is literally "in a son" or "in one who is a son." This is no mere prophet. It is the very Son of God—a son who shares the nature of the Father.

Today we understand that this Son became the man Jesus Christ. However, at this point in Hebrews our author has not yet disclosed that information. Viewing the matter from our perspective two millennia later, we think it completely natural that God who spoke through earlier prophets also spoke through Jesus (and even in a superior manner with a superior message). It is important for us to remember that when Jesus was born, the mainstream Jews generally had a different point of view.

They believed that prophecy had ended with Malachi. This belief was so strong that anyone who wanted to claim a new message from God had to attribute that message to some person who had lived long before. Based on that conviction, a small library of writings claiming ancient authority appeared both before and shortly after Jesus. These writings are called the Pseudepigrapha (literally "false writings") because they claimed as authors such earlier figures as Jeremiah's scribe Baruch, Isaiah, Solomon, Moses, the Twelve Patriarchs, Enoch and even Adam and Eve.

Introducing the Son

In Hebrews 1:2-3, our author shines four colored spotlights, as it were, on the Son through whom God has spoken in these last days. In these lights we see him progressively as (1) God's Son/heir, (2) the divine agent in creation, (3) who shares God's eternal nature, (4) and who is now enthroned at God's right hand.

The Son is the heir to whom God gave the nations for an inheritance (Psalm 2:8). He did not receive his inheritance as pre-incarnate Son but as glorified man, about which our author will say more in chapter 2. The imagery of Son/heir reappears in Psalm 110, a text to which our author will return throughout the book. He is particularly interested in verse four of this Psalm, which speaks of the priestly service that Jesus performs at God's right hand in heaven during the interim (the "until" mentioned in verse one) between his first and his final appearing.

Through this pre-incarnate Son, the "Word" of John's Gospel prologue (John 1:1-18), God made the worlds. "The worlds" encompass the totality of the created universe (Hebrews 11:3), although the Greek word here literally refers to the aeons or special eras of time in which God works out his saving purpose.

1:3 As God's word in creation first spoke light into being, so the Son who is God's Word (John 1:1) is also his emanation and brightness. The Son is the effulgence of God's shining glory—radiating out from the Father and reflecting back in return. As beams to the sun, or rays to a light, or flames to fire, so is the Son to the Father. Without the Son and apart from him, humankind is in the dark concerning both God and salvation. The word "glory" also reminds us of God's shining presence among his people from the time he rescued them from Egyptian slavery and thereafter.

The Son is the exact imprint, representation or image of the Father's nature, being or person. The word translated "imprint" here was used of a personal stamp or seal, and also of the impression it made in clay or wax. We might say that the Son is the Father's signature. Our author uses a figure of speech that anyone can understand. But human curiosity is seldom satisfied with simplicity, as later theological history would make very clear.

A few centuries removed from Jesus' birth, the bishops of the established church engaged in great philosophical debates concerning the precise nature of God as Trinity, and of Jesus Christ as Son of God. Their efforts were made more difficult because Scripture does not talk about God in abstract or theoretical terms. Instead, it speaks in language that is personal and practical.

For example, our author next notes that what the Son created, he now continues to uphold and to sustain. "The word of his power" is specifically a "spoken word" and the phrase can be translated also as "by his powerful word." The word that upholds the universe is potent and effective.

Purification for Sins

We fallen human beings have many problems, but the greatest and most serious of them all is our problem with sin. The Son (who we already know became man as Jesus, a detail our author does not reveal until chapter 2) also "made purification for sins." This is one of many ways that Hebrews describes how Jesus dealt with our sin problem. Elsewhere we read that Jesus:

- made propitiation for sins (Hebrews 2:17);
- dealt with sin so that God is merciful to iniquities (Hebrews 8:12)
- dealt with sins so that God does not remember them (Hebrews 8:12; 10:17);
- brought redemption from transgressions under the first covenant (Hebrews 9:15);
- put away sin (Hebrews 9:26);
- bore sin (Hebrews 9:28);
- offered one sacrifice for sins forever (Hebrews 10:12); and
- brought about forgiveness of sin (Hebrews 10:18).

With all these concepts at hand, what is the meaning of "purification" in this verse? Commentators have offered at least nine explanations (MacLeod, "The Cleansing of the True Tabernacle"). The following three appear most likely.

1. Perhaps this "purification" is simply a synonym for atonement or reconciliation. Purification is certainly one effect of an atonement (Leviticus 16:30). In that case, it refers to the overall saving effect of Jesus' sacrifice on the cross. However, the Greek word here translated

"purification" appears only once in the New Testament as a broad term for Jesus' saving accomplishment (2 Peter 1:9). If that is what our author intended here, he could have said it far more clearly.

2. This "purification" might refer to the cleansing of the conscience. Our author later speaks of Jesus' blood that cleanses—literally "purifies" (the verb form of the noun "purification" here)—our consciences (Hebrews 9:14). Might this "purification for sins" refer to the result of that cleansing? That seems unlikely because the cleansing in chapter 9 is from "dead works" and not from sin or guilt. Our author relates hearts sprinkled clean from an evil conscience with bodies washed with pure water—a clear reference to the process of conversion and perhaps to baptism in particular (Hebrews 10:22). Yet that cleansing is a subjective purification that occurs individual by individual. Hebrews 1:3 refers to an objective purification that Jesus accomplished one time for all who are finally saved.

3. On a more cosmic scale, this "purification" in Hebrews 1:3 might well refer to the cleansing of the heavenly sanctuary by Jesus' blood following his ascension and before his installation as king/priest at God's right hand. Our author later refers to this event, stating that it was necessary for "the heavenly things" themselves to be *purified* with better sacrifices than those used to purify the earthly tabernacle and its sacred paraphernalia (Hebrews 9:23). Just as the earthly sanctuary was purified with blood from its contamination by human sin (most grandly on the Day of Atonement), so Jesus Christ cleansed the Most Holy Place of the heavenly sanctuary by his own blood. But what is the connection between sin and the sanctuary—whether on earth or in heaven?

The answer is found in the Old Testament's understanding of sin's effects and God's provision for their remedy (Clifford & Anatolios, 52-56). When an Israelite committed a sin, two evils resulted. Sin made the sinner guilty. Even worse, sin defiled the sanctuary, the Most Holy Place, which was God's dwelling. The Hebrew expression for the "sin offering" might also be translated as "purification offering." Viewed this way, an Israelite offered this sacrifice for two reasons. He did so to obtain personal forgiveness, but also to purify the sanctuary.

Understood in this light, the purification of Hebrews 1:3 refers to Jesus' purification of the heavenly sanctuary by sprinkling his blood (this all is metaphor, corresponding to literal service performed by Levitical priests) as the first order of business upon his arrival in heaven (see Hebrews 9:12; 12:24). Our author does not explain how the heavenly sanctuary was fouled. Perhaps the contamination resulted from all the sins committed (or perhaps from those forgiven) from Adam onward. Yet of this we may be sure—every trace of defilement in the heavenly sanctuary has been removed by the blood of Jesus Christ. Jesus' one-time sacrifice of himself has removed sin's guilt and its defilement, objectively and subjectively, internally and externally, on earth and in heaven.

The tense of the participle translated "made purification" and its relationship to the main verb tell us that Jesus made this "purification" *before* he sat down at God's right hand. Jesus made only one sacrifice for sin forever. That sacrifice involved his entire life, death and exaltation.

- Jesus *prepared* the sacrifice by living his faithful, sinless human life in a human body.
- Jesus *performed* that sacrifice by offering his body, his life, his shed blood on the cross. The Father declared that the sacrifice was perfect, then he raised Jesus from the dead and took him up to heaven.
- Jesus *presented* that sacrifice by sprinkling his blood in heaven. Then, his sacrifice completed, Jesus took his seat at God's right hand in the heavenly sanctuary, inside the curtain, in the Most Holy Place of heaven itself. In that exalted position, Jesus, the Son-of-God-made-man through whom God spoke as prophet, now also reigns as king (Psalm 110:1) and intercedes as priest (Psalm 110:4) during these "last days" that separate his first and his final appearing.

In contrast to the Levitical priests, who stood every day performing their sacred rites that never cleansed the conscience, Jesus accomplished complete atonement involving both heaven and earth. Then he took his seat until the time arrives for him to come again bringing salvation (Hebrews 9:25-28). To sit at God's "right hand" signifies honor and authority. Out of respect for the divine name, our author uses the word "Majesty" to refer to God.

Seated at God's right hand

1:4 Although the Son became lower than angels when he became a *man,* he has now become far superior to angels. This verse has two tiny Greek words that indicate a comparison. The author is about to show just how much better, how far superior, how much more excellent is the Son's "name," rank and position than that held by any of the angels.

Our author first welcomed us with a view of the Son seated in glory at God's right hand. He is there because he has accomplished redemption by his single offering of himself. Although he was always God's very substance and express image, although he was active in creation, he is now honored even more and exalted far higher than ever before.

"And why?" we ask. Because the Son became and forever will remain a *man,* and that as *a* man—*the* man—*our* man— he has accomplished a perfect work of complete redemption. He has been raised up to heaven by God the Father. He has taken his inherited seat as universal heir and Lord at God's right hand in heaven. Now it is time to rejoice! And that is what our author does next, in a bouquet of scripture verses that celebrate the exalted position of the Son at God's right hand.

HEBREWS 1:5–14

No Angel Can Begin to Compare

5 For to which of the angels did God ever say,

"You are my Son,
today I have begotten you?"

Or again,

"I will be to him a father,
and he shall be to me a son"?

6 And again, when he brings the firstborn into the world, he says,

"Let all God's angels worship him."

7 Of the angels he says,

"He makes his angels winds
and his ministers a flame of fire."

8 But of the Son he says,

"Your throne, O God, is forever and ever;
the righteous scepter is the scepter of your kingdom.
9 You have loved righteousness and hated wickedness;
therefore God, your God, has anointed you
with the oil of gladness beyond your companions."

10 And,

"Lord, in the beginning you laid the foundation of the earth,
and the heavens are the work of your hands.
[11] They will perish, but you remain;
they will all wear out like a garment.
[12] Like a cloak you will roll them up;
like a garment they will be changed.
But you are the same and your years will never end."

[13] To which of the angels has he ever said,

"Sit at my right hand until I make
your enemies a footstool for your feet"?

[14] Are they not all ministering spirits sent out to serve for the sake of those
who will inherit salvation?

WHY & WHEREFORE

The Son at God's right hand in heaven ranks far higher than any angel
in honor. That is very clear. But why does our author feel the need to develop this point? He wants us first to appreciate and celebrate the Son's
exalted position. Then, as we read further in this ancient sermon, its
author will discuss *how* and *why* the Son came to occupy this place. Our
author first dazzles us with an opening scene featuring the Son. Then he
shows us flashbacks that explain that scene. Next he walks us through the
process that finally led to that point.

Have we caught it yet? The opening scene—of the Son at God's
right hand—once did not exist. As great as he was before becoming a
man, the Son now enjoys a position of recognition that was not always
his. How did that occur? God named him heir of all things and this is
part of his inheritance. But why is he heir? Because he has made purification for sins, which first required him to become a *man.* However,
we are getting ahead of ourselves. The important thing now is that the
Son is glorified at God's right hand in heaven. It is time to celebrate
that fact!

With that, the author of Hebrews takes us by the hand for a stroll
through the gardens of the Scriptures, heading directly to the many-col-
ored Psalms. He inspects the radiant hues, picking one blossom here,

another there, until he has assembled a dazzling bouquet of seven texts. The Bible verses in this bouquet, he explains, all illustrate ways the Son's rank surpasses the position of every angel in the universe.

UNPACKING THE TEXT

Our host gently spreads out his Scripture bouquet to reveal seven spectacular flowers in four stunning hues—each color matching a spotlight from the previous verses. Again we see the Son from four perspectives, in the same order as before. The Exalted One before us is God's Son/heir (vs. 5-9), the divine agent in creation (v. 10) who shares God's eternal nature (vs. 11-12) and who is now enthroned at God's right hand (v. 13).

These themes possibly reflect an early Christian hymn. More likely, the seven Bible verses that illustrate them represent a collection of messianic scriptures (all from what we call the Old Testament, of course) which was already familiar among first-century believers. Some commentators have questioned any relationship between Hebrews 1:5-14 and the rest of the book. In fact, these verses compose "a fitting introduction to a sermon whose main teaching point is the definitive atonement provided through Christ" (Schenck, "A Celebration of the Enthroned Son ... ," p. 471).

God's Son/heir

1:5a The Scriptures referred to angels in general as "sons" of God. However, they never report God saying to any specific angel: "You are my Son, today I have begotten you" (or "become your father"). This unique pronouncement was reserved for God's Son (Psalm 2:7). The early church interpreted this whole psalm in light of Jesus Christ. When they read Psalm 2, the first believers envisioned humanity's rejection of God and his servant Jesus (Psalm 2:1-3; Acts 4:25-28), followed by God's triumph through his Christ (Psalm 2:4-9; Revelation 19:15), and ending in a future messianic judgment with two contrasting outcomes (Psalm 2:10-12; John 3:16). The early church also saw this psalm in the background of major events throughout the story of Jesus, including his baptism, his transfiguration, his resurrection and his divine induction as high priest in heaven.

The word-order in this quotation emphasizes "Son" and "I," putting the stress on the Son's position and on his divine appointment to that position. The New Testament presents Jesus as God's "Son" with a variety of meanings. He is God's Son:

in essence—   by eternal nature
in the flesh—   by miraculous conception
in glory—   by resurrection and by God's decree.

1:5b The second quotation in our bouquet has God saying: "I will be to him a father, and he shall be to me a son." This statement comes from Nathan's prophetic oracle regarding David's royal son (2 Samuel 7:14/1 Chronicles 17:13) and it is paraphrased in Psalm 89:27 (LXX 88:28).

This promise of God originally referred to Solomon (1 Chronicles 28:5-7), but it found its greatest fulfillment in Jesus Christ. The pronouns "I" and "he" are both emphatic in position and stress the personal relationship described. These first two quotations in our author's bouquet also appear together in some of the Dead Sea Scrolls discovered at Qumran.

1:6 This "again" can be read either with the main verb ("when he *again brings* the firstborn into the world") or it can be read as a connector between the previous quotation and the quotation that comes next. God's command for all angels to worship the Son would fit equally well at Jesus' incarnation, his resurrection or his Second Advent. Angels are involved in all three events.

The word translated "world" literally means "inhabited earth" which suggests Jesus' entrance into the present world at his birth or at his resurrection. However the same word appears in the next chapter where it clearly refers to the world yet to come (Heb. 2:5). The truth we must see is that all God's angels, of every rank and order, are commanded to worship the Son. Our author almost certainly is quoting a Greek version of Psalm 97:7—the third flower in his bouquet.

1:7 This verse and the next contain a pair of Greek words which used together mean "on the one hand" and "on the other hand." The author explicitly contrasts angels, who are ministers or servants, and the Son who is addressed as "God." The fourth bouquet flower is Psalm 104:4 (LXX 103:4).

1:8-9 Psalm 45:6-7, the fifth flower, was originally written to celebrate the marriage of a king. Our author boldly includes it here although (no doubt, *because*) it identifies the Son with the eternal God. His throne stands for his reign, which is marked by righteousness or justice, and which for that reason will always endure (Isaiah 9:7; 11:4-5). During his earthly life, Jesus loved righteousness (justice) and hated wickedness (lawlessness). Because of Jesus' righteous life of faithful obedience, God anointed *("christ-ed")* him and positioned him at his right hand above every created being (see Philippians 2:8-11). The oil of gladness or of joy represents both festivity and coronation. With our author, we celebrate the Son who is also heir!

Creation Agent/Divine Nature

1:10-12 Our author's sixth selection, Psalm 102:25-27, returns to the second and third views of the Son above—as the divine agent in creation who also shares God's eternal nature. This psalm is the cry of a person in trouble, who appeals to God who is eternal. Our author quotes three verses from Psalm 102 and unashamedly applies the language to the Son at God's right hand.

The passage begins by addressing the "Lord" who "in the beginning" made the heavens and the earth. Our author does not hesitate to put the Son in that picture as the person being addressed. The Son was the agent of creation and was himself uncreated. The Greek Old Testament (Septuagint) regularly replaces the Hebrew name for God with the Greek word for "Lord." In the New Testament, this same Greek word for "Lord" regularly refers to Jesus Christ. It was not difficult, therefore, for Christian believers who used the Septuagint to read passages that spoke of God and to transform them in their minds to speak also of the Son of God.

Creation, which includes the angels, is temporary. It ages, changes and will finally pass away (see Hebrews 12:26-28). By contrast, the Son is eternal. He continues the same (Hebrews 13:8) and he will always remain (Hebrews 7:24-25).

Man at God's Right Hand

1:13 The final flower in this scripture bouquet is Psalm 110:1, which revisits the perspective of the fourth spotlight in the introductory verses. This is the most-referenced Old Testament passage in the New Testament. It is quoted or referred to in Matthew (22:41-45; 26:64), Mark

(12:36; 14:62), Luke (20:41-44; 22:69), Acts (2:34-35; 5:31; 7:55), Romans (8:34), Ephesians (1:20), Colossians (3:1), Hebrews (1:3, 13; 8:1; 10:12; 12:2), 1 Peter (3:22) and Revelation (3:21).

This imagery of the "right hand" appears often in the Psalms. It sometimes refers to a place of blessing and honor (Psalm 16:11; 45:9; 80:17). Most often it describes God's strength or security on behalf of the person he blesses. The metaphor of enemies made one's footstool comes from the ancient custom of the defeated king bending to kiss the conqueror's feet (Psalm 2:12), or the victorious sovereign putting his feet on his captive's neck (Joshua 10:24).

1:14 This biblical passage is already in our author's bouquet and it is Psalm 104:4 (LXX 103:4). Already quoted in verse 7, this verse refers to angels as God's ministers or servants. That is their role, regardless of rank: ministering spirits. Their work includes serving believers, human beings living on the earth, who will one day inherit salvation. And that salvation, as we are about to hear, is no small matter indeed.

HEBREWS 2:1-4

Do Not Neglect this Salvation

[1] Therefore we must pay much closer attention to what we have heard, so that we do not drift away from it. [2] For if the message spoken through angels was binding and every transgression and disobedience received a just penalty, [3] how shall we escape if we neglect so great a salvation? It was first spoken by the Lord, and it was confirmed to us by those who heard him. [4] God also testified by signs and wonders and various miracles, and by gifts of the Holy Spirit, distributed according to his will.

WHY & WHEREFORE

Today the eternal Son sits at God's right hand in heaven, exalted far above angels in a glorified humanity that was not always his. He received this honor from the Father about 2,000 years ago, in recognition of his cosmic victory over the devil and his successful rescue of human earthlings from the guilt and consequences of sin. Our author now warns against neglecting the deliverance that the Son has accomplished. The grandeur of this salvation defies description: the Lord himself revealed it, his hearers reported it, and God reaffirmed it by significant manifestations of special gifts and awesome power. If violating the ancient Mosaic Law delivered by angels carried severe consequences, we can be sure that ignoring the Son's accomplishment now must bring a penalty unimaginably greater.

UNPACKING THE TEXT

Caution is Imperative

2:1 There is an old saying that when you see a "therefore" in the Bible, you should stop and ask what it is "there for." Literally "on account of this," this "therefore" connects the grand vision we have just seen of the Son at God's right hand (and the bouquet of Bible verses that followed it) to the caution that lies just ahead (and the carefully-reasoned analysis of Psalm 8 that follows the caution).

The words "must" and "much closer" (or "more careful") are exceptionally strong in the original language. It is fair to translate the first part of our author's sentence something like this: "Because of these things, it is absolutely necessary for us to be extremely careful to pay attention!" (Fudge, 25.) This is the first of five times that our author temporarily interrupts his teaching to issue a warning or to make an appeal based on what he has just said (Hebrews 2:1-4; 3:12-4:13; 5:11-6:12; 10:19-39; 12:14-29).

The author preaches to himself as well as to us, repeating "we . . . we . . . we." The God who speaks has spoken in the Son. We must now pay attention to the things we have heard. "Pay attention to" and "drift" are seafaring words in the original language, where they sometimes referred to holding a ship fast to port rather than letting it drift off course. Greek writers also used the word for "drift" (or "slip") to talk about an arrow slipping from its quiver, nasty language slipping into a conversation, and food slipping down the windpipe. Our author insists that we keep a firm grip on the message we have heard about the Son of God, whether from his writing or from other reliable sources.

But why is drifting even a temptation? For the first readers of Hebrews, it is appealing because they are tired—"tired of serving the world, tired of worship, tired of Christian education, tired of being peculiar and whispered about in society, tired of the spiritual struggle, tired of trying to keep their prayer life going, tired even of Jesus. The threat . . . is not that they are charging off in the wrong direction; they do not have enough energy to charge off anywhere. . . . Tired of walking the walk, many of them are considering taking a walk, leaving the community and falling away from the faith" (Long, *Hebrews*, 3).

Throughout the New Testament, "faith" means active trust and reliance. For the author of Hebrews, the most obvious way to demonstrate trust in God is by holding fast, pressing on, following through. Such perseverance marked Jesus' own faith and faithfulness. Those who know Jesus and trust in him will also demonstrate perseverance. To do otherwise is to be guilty of sinful neglect and to bring down fearful consequences.

2:2-3a As surely as the Son outranks and outshines any angel, just that certainly God's message delivered through the Son outweighs any message delivered through angels. To the first readers of Hebrews, the message spoken through angels was the Law that God gave to Israel at Sinai. Although the Sinai story in Exodus 19-20 does not mention angels, some other Old Testament passages do (Deuteronomy 33:2; Psalm 68:17). The non-scriptural Book of Jubilees portrayed "the Angel of the Presence" dictating the Law to Moses (Jubilees 1:29), and both Stephen (Acts 7:53) and Paul (Galatians 3:19) gave angels a role at Sinai. Our author also points to the Law of Moses by his choice of words—"binding, "transgression," "disobedience" and "just penalty" are all technical *legal* terms.

"Transgression" and "disobedience" both describe deliberate lawbreaking. The first includes sins of commission (what we have done); the second covers sins of omission (what we have left undone). The word translated "disobedience" literally means refusing to hear. Its use here brings us back to the great announcement that God is speaking through the Son. It also reminds us that we had best listen with both ears.

"Neglect" means making light of, not caring for, or disregarding. The same Greek word is used at Hebrews 8:9 of God's disregard for Israel after they broke his covenant and ignored his gracious works on their behalf.

So Great a Salvation

The word here translated "salvation" appears seven times in Hebrews. Once it refers to rescue from the Flood (Hebrews 11:7) and six times to rescue from sin. In this book, Jesus is the source of salvation (Hebrews 2:10; 5:9), which is sometimes perceived as a present reality (Hebrews 2:3; 6:9) and other times as a future gift (Hebrews 1:14; 9:28). As we begin reading Hebrews, this tension between *already/not yet* alerts us to take seriously the author's confident assurances and also his urgent warnings.

By making one sacrifice for sin, Jesus has sanctified his people and perfected them forever (Hebrews 10:10, 14). And how do we recognize those who are his people? Our author says that Jesus' people are known by their persevering faith (Hebrews 3:6, 14; 4:11; 6:11; 10:23, 36, 38-39). Every day is a new *today*, a fresh opportunity to hear God's voice and not to harden one's heart (Hebrews 3:12-15). God holds us accountable for the decisions we make throughout life. But when we finally reach the end of our race, we will know that God is the one who equipped us, energized us and brought us safely there (Hebrews 13:20-21). We sometimes think of divine sovereignty and human responsibility as alternatives, but our author sees them as two sides of the same reality. (See this illustrated graphically in a brief Powerpoint presentation at http://www.EdwardFudge.com/Romans8_28.ppt .)

The grandeur of the salvation magnifies the evil inherent in its neglect. The question arises spontaneously from the reality: how will any of us possibly escape God's punishment if we commit such a horror? The inquiry is rhetorical—escape would be impossible. The inferior word delivered by angels was sure and violations of it were strictly punished. How much more serious is the fate of anyone who carelessly regards the greater message of salvation spoken by the superior Son? True believers will diligently hold fast to Jesus the Son of God, constantly trusting his sacrifice and the atonement which it has made a reality. Neglect and indifference are tools and tricks of the enemy, whose goal is to spread disbelief and finally to destroy.

2:3b-4 Hebrews opened with the statement that God has spoken in these last days through the Son (Hebrews 1:2), who is later identified as the "Lord" (Hebrews 1:10). Now we learn that the content of that communication is "salvation" and that it first was spoken by the Lord—whom we recognize as Jesus Christ. The message had been confirmed (guaranteed or accredited) to our author and his first readers by those who heard Jesus, marking author and original readers as a generation removed from Jesus' life on earth in the body. "Confirmed" is another legal word in the list we began in verse two. Those who confirmed the accuracy of the word might or might not have been apostles, a word our author uses only once and then in reference to Jesus (Hebrews 3:1).

God himself, who has spoken through Jesus, has also testified (another legal word). In this way, he endorsed or corroborated the testimony of those who confirmed what the Lord Jesus had said. God did this by action rather than by words, testifying by signs and wonders, by miracles and by gifts of the Holy Spirit. The phrase "signs and wonders" regularly appears in the Septuagint as a summary of God's mighty deeds in delivering Israel from Egyptian slavery (Deuteronomy 4:34; Psalm 135:9; Jeremiah 32:20-21). "Signs" *signify* God's involvement in the powerful deeds and "wonders" point to their awe-inspiring effect on observers.

The New Testament continues this Old Testament phrase, to which it adds "miracles," literally "powerful deeds" (Acts 2:22; 2 Corinthians 12:12). God also endorsed the testimony of those who confirmed Jesus' message by gifts (literally "distributions") of the Holy Spirit as it pleased him. Rather than restricting the period of spiritual gifts, this verse leaves the time open, subject only to God's will.

HEBREWS 2:5-8

Humankind's Position as God Intended It

⁵ Now he has not subjected to angels the world to come, about which we are speaking. ⁶ But one has testified somewhere,

"What is man that you are mindful of him,
or the son of man that you care for him?
⁷ You made him for a little while lower than the angels;
you have crowned him with glory and honor.
⁸ You have put all things in subjection under his feet."

For in subjecting everything to him, he left nothing that is not subject to him. But now we do not yet see everything in subjection to him.

WHY & WHEREFORE

Earlier we described Hebrews as a sermon about Jesus built around four particular Psalms. Our author now reflects on words from Psalm 8, the first of the four. As we listen, our thoughts drift back to a Judean night very long ago. In the silence, a shepherd boy named David views the starry heavens and contemplates his own place in the cosmos. Compared to the panoply of stars overhead, he is so tiny as to go unmentioned. Yet, as unthinkable as it is, the Creator notices human beings and acts on their behalf. More than that, our author remembers, God placed men and women over the whole creation. Or has he? As we look around us, that is certainly not what we see now.

UNPACKING THE TEXT

2:5 God did not subject this world to angels, either now or in its future renewal. He put it in subjection to human beings. From the beginning, God intended for men and women to shine with dignity in their role as caretakers of the rest of creation. In expectation of such responsible stewardship, and with no hint of exploitation or greedy consumption, God in creation subjected the world and all creatures on it to human beings made in his own image.

2:6 Our author quotes David's words from Psalm 8:5-6 to establish this point. The psalmist views the stars and feels insignificant by contrast. (His reaction was in response only to what he saw with the naked eye. The shepherd boy could never have imagined creation as described by scientists today—containing "a hundred billion galaxies, each with a hundred billion stars" (Polkinghorne, 22). Can God be interested in and mindful of his human creatures to remember them? "Indeed he is!" comes the answer. He is genuinely concerned about humankind, and he is therefore faithful to care for them.

This part of Psalm 8 uses a poetic structure called "parallelism," which means that the phrase "son of man" is synonymous with "man" and stands as a representative of humankind as a whole. As noted above, God intended for humans to exercise benevolent sovereignty over their fellow-creatures. This intention reappears in the prophetic vision of Daniel 7, where a figure "like a son of man" (="like man") travels in clouds to heaven and is ushered into the throne-room of the Ancient of Days. There he receives a kingdom from God (Daniel 7:13-14). By the end of this vision we understand that the one "like a son of man" represents God's people in general, who eventually participate in his rule (Daniel 7:18, 22, 27).

Jesus' favorite title for himself in the Gospels is "Son of Man" (or "son of man"). The term is full of messianic implications, based on its use in Daniel 7 and in the non-scriptural Enoch (see comments under Hebrews 1:2 above). Our author uses the phrase to mean a human being in general, the same sense it has in Psalm 8. However, as he reflects on the psalm more deeply, he gradually comes to understand that the only human being who now fits the psalm's exalted description of "son of man" is the man Jesus–the "son of man" who experienced his entire life and underwent his death as the ultimate representative for his people.

2:7 God made humankind for a little while lower (or, "but a little lower") than the angels (LXX Psalm 8:6; the Hebrew text says lower "than God"). God crowned human beings with glory and honor. Some English versions add: "And have appointed him over the works of your hands." Most recent translations omit the clause, which does not appear in two important early Greek manuscripts.

2:8 In short, says the psalmist, God subjected everything under humankind's control. And that, our author observes, is an all-inclusive statement permitting no exception. If God truly subjected everything to humankind, nothing remains wild and untamed, independent of man's authority and control. Yet as we look around us, that is not what we observe–at least not yet. Does this mean that God's purpose has been overcome? Is there now, anywhere in the universe, a man who exercises glorious sovereignty by God's own appointment?

HEBREWS 2:9–18

Jesus Fulfills Human Destiny

⁹ But we see Jesus, who for a little while was made lower than the angels, crowned with glory and honor because of the suffering of death, so that by the grace of God he might taste death for everyone. ¹⁰ For it was fitting that God, for whom and through whom are all things and through whom all things exist, in bringing many sons to glory, should make perfect the source of their salvation through sufferings. ¹¹ For both he who sanctifies and those who are sanctified all have one Father. For which reason he is not ashamed to call them brothers, ¹² saying,

"I will proclaim your name to my brothers;
in the midst of the congregation I will sing your praise."

¹³ And again,

"I will put my trust in him."

And again,

"Here am I and the children whom God has given me."

¹⁴ Since the children share in flesh and blood, he himself likewise partook of the same, so that through death he might destroy him who had the power of death, that is, the devil, ¹⁵ and free those who through fear of death all their lives were held in slavery. ¹⁶ For surely it is not that he helps angels but that he helps descendants of Abraham. ¹⁷ Therefore he had to be made like his brothers in every respect, so that he might become a merciful and faithful high priest in service to God, to make propitiation for the sins of the people. ¹⁸ For

because he himself was tempted and has suffered, he is able to help those who are being tempted.

WHY & WHEREFORE

Is there now a man, anywhere, in the exalted place for which God created humankind? We do see one such man. He is Jesus, and he is crowned with glory and honor! The eternal Son who was God's agent in creation and who shares God's nature became a *man*. For a little while, he became lower than angels. As man, he lived and died for us and in our stead. In the process, he destroyed the devil and freed humankind from death's binding fear. God raised Jesus from the dead and exalted him far above angels at his own right hand. Now perfected as high priest through suffering, Jesus helps his brothers and sisters who also suffer.

UNPACKING THE TEXT

One Man in Glory!

2:9 If we search the whole world, we cannot find any human being who exercises sovereignty over the rest of God's creation. However, if we look beyond this present earth, we get a different view. There we do see one man—even now—crowned with "glory and honor." For the glorious Son at God's right hand in heaven, the "Lord," is none other than the *man* Jesus, here identified for the first time by his proper name.

Jesus is now crowned with "glory and honor," in fulfillment of human destiny as expressed in Psalm 8. But the expression "glory and honor" suggests more than that. The same Greek phrase also described Aaron's vestments at his inauguration as high priest (LXX Exodus 28:2, 40). Jesus has achieved man's destiny, but he has done so for his brothers and sisters, for whom he now intercedes as high priest.

Before he was exalted to this high position, the Son first became very low. Although by nature he always ranked higher than angels, the Son became the *man* Jesus, in a rank lower than angels, and as a man he also experienced death. Jesus' death demonstrated human cruelty and evil, but even more it was an act of divine grace.

For Whom Did Jesus Die?

Since Saint Augustine in the fourth century, and especially since the Reformation, Christians have understood the statement that Jesus tasted death "for everyone," or "for all," in more than one way.

- Reformed or Calvinist Christians believe that all those for whom Jesus died will finally be with God in eternity. But some humans will not be finally saved. Reformed believers therefore explain that Jesus died (and thereby ensured final salvation) for all the "elect" (those whom God has chosen), who include all sorts of individuals—i.e., representatives from all people groups and nationalities.
- Arminian or Wesleyan Christians believe that Jesus' death made salvation possible for everyone ("all" without exception), but that it guaranteed the final salvation of none.
- Despite the obvious difference, these two groups actually share much ground in common. I have identified some of these areas of agreement in the article, "What Calvinism and Arminianism Have in Common," originally published in *Christianity Today* and now available online at www.EdwardFudge.com/written/article1.html.
- Christian Reformed author Neal Punt seeks to reconcile truths from both sides scripturally in a proposal which he calls "evangelical inclusivism" (www.evangelicalinclusivism.com). According to Punt, Jesus died for (and will eternally save) every human being—except those who throughout life knowingly reject the truth they have from God—whatever that truth might be. According to this understanding, Calvinists correctly say that those who are finally saved must give God all the credit, and Arminians correctly say that those who are finally lost must themselves accept all the blame.

Jesus experienced death, not for himself but *for* all men and women. Not for us in some vague and general way, but specifically with reference to sin. Jesus' death *for* all men is further described in verse 17, where we also learn that Jesus "made propitiation" *for* his people's sins. The Greek verb here translated "made propitiation" for sins, is a form of the same verb with which the Greek Old Testament describes a sin offering.

More specifically, Jesus died as our representative, just as he had lived as our representative. By his perfect *doing* and his perfect *dying*, in his *action* and in his *passion*, Jesus took our place, stood in our stead, experienced life and experienced death—bearing our nature and wearing our names (Hebrews 10:5-10; Exodus.28:9-12, 29-30).

Jesus represented us on earth in order to represent us in heaven. The Son of God, who was always higher than angels, became *man*—Jesus—although he would never abandon his deity. Having taken on our nature, he would never abandon his humanity. When Jesus had done everything that God desired, by his life and by his death, God raised him from the dead and exalted him to his right hand in heaven (Hebrews 12:2). Now, as the exalted and glorified *man* Jesus, the Son is both higher and more than he ever was before. Still the Son, he is now also Jesus. Always divine, he is now also human. Forever perfect in essence and character, he is now perfected through suffering to be high priest for those he came to save.

Perfected Through Suffering

2:10 The demotion and exaltation of the Son who became Jesus had a single purpose—"to bring many sons [and daughters] to glory" and so to fulfill the destiny of humankind. Sin interrupted God's original plan for his children. For Jesus to complete that plan means their salvation. God's people begin to taste that salvation here and now (Hebrews 6:4-5). They will experience it fully in the world to come (Hebrews 2:3, 5).

If Jesus was to accomplish salvation, he had to be perfected or made whole by experiencing suffering. In the Greek Old Testament, a priest's consecration "perfects" the priest (LXX Exodus 29:9; LXX Leviticus 16:32; LXX Numbers 3:3). Having suffered all that his people suffer, except sin itself, Jesus became the origin or source of salvation. The "biblical consolation for those who suffer is not that God suffers right along with us, but that Jesus Christ, our faithful high priest, suffered as one of us" (DeYoung, "Divine Impassibility . . .," 49 [emphasis omitted]).

His Brothers and Sisters

2:11 He who sanctifies is Jesus. Those who are sanctified ("saints") are believers—people he makes holy to serve God through him. God is the father of believers and he is Jesus' father also. Precisely for that reason, Jesus freely calls them his brothers and sisters, without shame or embarrassment. The brother-sister relationship exists when people share a common father. Because Jesus is willing to claim us as his kin, we who claim God as our father must freely recognize all his other children as our brothers and sisters, regardless of denomination, nationality, social standing or financial circumstances. Then, having said it, we must live as if we believe it to be the truth.

2:12 In support of the point he just stated, our author puts words from Psalm 22:22 (LXX 21:23) in the mouth of Jesus. In this Psalm, the speaker says he will proclaim God's name to his "brothers" and sing God's praise in the midst of the congregation. Psalm 22:1 begins with the cry of Jesus on the cross, "My God, my God, why have you forsaken me?" From that dismal start through verse 21, the forsaken one describes his peril and pleads for God to deliver him.

However, when we reach verse 22, everything changes and protest turns to praise. From verse 22 through the end of the psalm, the speaker affirms that God will rescue him, and describes how he will serve and praise God in gratitude for his deliverance. The entire psalm fits Jesus perfectly— from his suffering as one forsaken, through his rescue, and finally in his rejoicing with his brothers and sisters in the assembly of God's people.

2:13 Our author pictures Jesus making two more statements that emphasize his solidarity with his people. The first quotation ("I will put my trust in him") comes from Isaiah 8:17. It shows that Jesus, like all his human brothers and sisters, depended totally on God.

The second quotation ("Here am I and the children whom God has given me") comes from Isaiah 8:18. In it, Jesus identifies fellow-humans as his personal inheritance and reward from the Father for his faithful obedience unto death (see John 17:2; Ephesians 1:18). The prospect of

Hebrews' Diverse Views of the Atonement

An important conversation is underway these days concerning the atonement. Christians in general—whether Roman Catholic, Orthodox, Protestant, Evangelical or Fundamentalist—agree on the basic fact, which the Bible makes perfectly clear. By the life, death and resurrection of Jesus Christ, God has dealt with sin and has rescued sinners from its dreadful consequences. Most participants in the current discussion agree on what to *proclaim*. They differ on how to *explain*. It is really not surprising that such differences exist. For centuries, some of the church's greatest thinkers have struggled to explain just *how* Jesus' death reconciled the world to God, in the process formulating a number of interesting theories. Following are some of the major theories and the people credited with framing them.

- *Ransom theory*. This explanation is attributed to Origen of Alexandria (185-232). In a common version of this theory, Jesus' death was the price that ransomed or bought back the human race from Satan, who had taken ownership of the human race when Adam and Eve sinned in the Garden of Eden. Jesus then tricked Satan by rising from the dead, leaving him with neither ransom nor prey.
- *Recapitulation theory*. Popularized by Athanasius of Alexandria (296-373), this theory focuses on Jesus' incarnation. Since Adam, humans had walked a path of sin, resulting in guilt and condemnation. In Jesus, the Son of God became a man to reverse that pattern and to create a new reality. By becoming a human who pleased God perfectly, Jesus changed human destiny and enabled humans to share his divine nature. This is the theory of Eastern Orthodoxy.
- *Satisfaction theory*. Popularized by Anselm of Canterbury (?-1109), this theory reflected legal principles of the

Middle Ages, which demanded "satisfaction" for offenses against the honor of another person. In this view, sin offends God's infinite honor, which demands infinite satisfaction. By sacrificing his own life of infinite value, Jesus (who is himself divine) satisfied God's honor, enabling God to forgive humankind.

- *Moral influence theory*. This view was proposed by the French philosopher Peter Abelard (1079-1142), in reaction to the *satisfaction theory* and the *ransom theory* which came before. According to Abelard, Jesus' death set an example of self-sacrificing love so overwhelming that it unleashed a spiritual power able to change the hearts and lives of sinners.
- *Victor theory*. In this understanding, favored by Martin Luther (1483-1546), Jesus and Satan engage in cosmic conflict. By his sinless life, death and resurrection, Jesus conquered Satan and, as victor, set sinners free. This theory is also known as the Christus Victor theory, so named after the title of a book by G.E.H. Aulen, who died in 1977. (For a more recent version, see Chandler, *Victorious Substitution*.)
- *Penal substitution theory*. This understanding explains that a just and holy God must punish sin with death. However, God loves sinners and wants to save them. Jesus volunteers to be punished in their place and dies on the cross as their substitute. God's justice satisfied, he forgives sinners who believe on Jesus. One form of this view says that the personal guilt of sinners was transferred to Jesus, and the personal righteousness of Jesus is transferred to sinners who believe. Critics of this explanation attribute it to John Calvin (1509-1564) or to later Calvinists. Its defenders insist that it is the primary biblical view.

If we follow the author of Hebrews, we will not restrict our thinking to any single explanation of the atonement. Instead, we will marvel that in Jesus, God has accomplished a salvation so enormously exhaustive that it encompasses elements from all of the traditional atonement theories—yet it still remains a mystery too deep to explain. That broad range of meaning is evident even within this present section (Hebrews 2:9-18).

As we read through these verses, we are impressed that Jesus died a *substitutionary* death—"for everyone" (v. 9). The Son of God became "lower than angels" in order to "bring many sons to glory" (v. 9-10). By his own life, death and judgment, Jesus re-routed the path ordained for humankind so that it would end in glory rather than in failure. The ancient writers referred to this process as the *recapitulation*. By the same life and death as a man, Christ "destroyed" the destroyer and became our conquering hero or *Christus Victor* (v. 14-15). We were in "bondage" and Jesus set us "free"—a word-picture suggestive either of a ransom or a *victor* (v. 15-16). *Moral influence* is also involved, for Jesus was both "tempted" and "suffered" so that he could "help" those who undergo the same experiences (v. 18).

Jesus "made propitiation for sins" (v. 17). This is a complex phrase, traditionally interpreted in keeping with the penal theory. Today, its meaning is at the center of controversy. Whatever the rest of the New Testament might add to the picture, our examination of Hebrews reveals that Jesus "made propitiation" by giving God the *satisfaction* of faithfully doing God's will throughout life in his human body, and then offering that faithful life to God in his body by shedding his blood on the cross.

eternal companionship with all his brothers and sisters was surely part of "the joy" set before Jesus that motivated his ultimate obedience unto death (Hebrews 12:2).

This second quotation is lifted from a longer sentence spoken by Isaiah regarding his own children and their prophetic names. In their original context, the quoted words are not spoken by Jesus and they mean something entirely different from the point our author is making.

Rabbinical exposition included such use of biblical language—our author is not doing anything improper or surprising in his own time. This example does remind us that Jesus "fulfilled" the ancient Scriptures in more ways than one. This example illustrates one of those ways.

Victory Through Death

2:14 God's children experience human frailty and death, and Jesus accepted the same in his identification with them. Although tempted in every respect, Jesus never broke faith with the Father. Because he never sinned, death had no power over him (Acts 2:24). When Jesus entered the realm of the dead, he did so as death's invader and destroyer—not as its victim or captive (Isaiah 49:24-26; Luke 11:21-22). There he confiscated the keys to death and Hades, and triumphantly made his exit (Revelation 1:17-18).

But the victory climaxed a genuine struggle. Jesus, the *Son of God* made man, truly *died*. And Jesus, the Son of God *made man*, truly *arose*, "still bearing in himself the wounds of the conflict, and the wounds remaining for evermore the marks of the Eternal" (Lewis, "Creator and Creature . . .," 151).

2:15 From the day that Adam first introduced sin into the world (and into the human race), the devil had used it as a club to intimidate humankind. In this way, death became "a henchman in the devil's service" (Lane, *Commentary* I, 61). Jesus' death disarmed the devil, and death no longer holds its former terror. As the representative and head of a new and redeemed humanity, Jesus conquered death, immobilized Satan and liberated every human being from death's present rule.

Jesus' victory over death even transformed the Greek vocabulary. Before Jesus died and rose, the Greeks called their burial-ground the *Necropolis*—"city of the dead." Since Jesus arose from the dead, however, we call it a "cemetery"—from the Greek word meaning a "sleeping place."

2:16 Again our author emphasizes that Jesus became a man to help human beings rather than angels. Humankind needed redemption. The Son of God became a man to provide it.

2:17 In order to save men and women, Jesus was made like us in every respect. As *man*, he truly experienced temptation, sorrow and desire.

Therefore he is able to show mercy to men and women whom he represents as high priest. As man's *representative*, Jesus lived a life of faultless and loving obedience to the Father.

Jesus 'Made Propitiation' for Sins

Jesus remains wholly faithful to the Father while representing his people. He is the ideal high priest according to God's own stated standard (1 Samuel 2:35). It was as high priest designated by God that Jesus made "propitiation" for sins. And, as our author will later explain, it was by becoming a *man*, and then by becoming the *faithful* man, that Jesus was able to make propitiation. For the offering by which he accomplished this priestly function was in fact his own faithful human life.

The Greek word here translated "to make propitiation" appears only one other time in the New Testament. That is in Jesus' parable of Two Men at Prayer, in which the penitent tax-collector pleads for God to "be merciful" (Luke 18:13). Translated literally, the tax-collector begs God to "be *propitious*," in the original sense of that English word. In the Septuagint, the Greek translation of the Old Testament from which our author usually quotes, "propitiation" is interchangeable with "atonement."

This is our author's first explicit mention of Jesus as high priest, although he hinted at that role when he said the Son has made purification for sins (Hebrews 1:3). Jewish literature written after Malachi includes future references to both a priestly and a royal messiah. Yet in all that literature, no one ever suggests a priestly messiah who offers himself as a sacrifice for sin, or who intercedes for his people in heaven (Attridge, *Epistle to the Hebrews*, 97-103). These two great acts, which summarize Jesus' ministry as high priest, exceed the reach of human imagination.

2:18 Because Jesus was genuinely tempted and truly suffered, he is now fully able to help his people who at any moment are suffering or being tempted. Jesus "does not wag his head at human misery and cluck, 'There but for the grace of God go I.' Instead he says, 'There because of the grace of God, I am'" (Long, 42).

Jesus Was Faithful, Unlike Israel

¹ Therefore, holy brothers, partakers of a heavenly calling, consider Jesus, the apostle and high priest of our confession. ² He was faithful to the one who appointed him, just as Moses was in all God's house. ³ For Jesus has been counted worthy of more glory than Moses, just as the builder of a house has more honor than the house itself. ⁴ For every house is built by someone, but the builder of all things is God. ⁵ Moses was faithful in all God's house as a servant, for a testimony to those things that would be spoken later. ⁶ But Christ was faithful as a Son over God's house, and we are his house if we hold fast the confidence and the boast of our hope.

⁷ Therefore, as the Holy Spirit says:
  "Today, if you hear his voice,
   ⁸ do not harden your hearts as in the rebellion,
    on the day of testing in the wilderness,
   ⁹ where your fathers tested me, tried me,
    and saw my works for 40 years.
   ¹⁰ Therefore I was angry with that generation and said,
    'They always go astray in their hearts,
    and they have not known my ways.'
   ¹¹ So I swore in my anger, 'They shall not enter my rest.'"

WHY & WHEREFORE

Our author now comes to Psalm 95, the second of four psalms from which he tells the Story of Jesus. This Psalm speaks of Jesus' life-long faithfulness to the Father. This obedient life qualified Jesus to offer himself as a sacrifice that could take away sin, make his people holy and perfect them forever. The question that remains is whether we will be faithful also. The answer to that question ultimately reveals the validity of our profession. In a mixed multitude of any size, it is almost certain that some who profess faith with their mouths actually lack it in their hearts.

UNPACKING THE TEXT

Consider Jesus

3:1 Jesus has been revealed as God's greatest spokesman. God has installed him as merciful and faithful high priest. On that basis, our author now appeals to his readers as "holy brothers" (and sisters, too; the Greek word usually includes all siblings regardless of gender). In New Testament usage, "holy" describes the state of all people whom God has set apart from the world for his own special purpose. Without holiness no one can see God (Hebrews 12:14).

In the gospel message, these saints received a heavenly invitation to be God's people, participants—sharers and partners—in the way of life. They welcomed the invitation by faith. Now our author urges them to consider Jesus. The word here translated "consider" means to look thoughtfully and with great care. It includes seeing with the mind as well as with the eyes. This activity requires a significant investment of time, but it is time well-spent.

The majority traditional English text says "Jesus," in keeping with the better Greek manuscripts, although some manuscripts and some translations have "Christ Jesus" or "Jesus Christ." The distinction between these terms is not absolute. As a general rule, when our author refers to "Christ Jesus," he usually points to the risen and glorified Jesus of Nazareth at God's right hand. When the word order is "Jesus Christ," the author usually focuses on the person or experience or achievement of Jesus as a man and as one of us. Here our author combines both views, urging us to contemplate and reflect on the Son who became *man*—one of us— who is now our heavenly Lord. Consider Jesus "in all his offices, his splendor, his rank and his glory" (Fudge, 36).

We have been introduced to Jesus already as God's final and finest spokesman. As one whom God sent with authority, Jesus is also the

Apostle of our profession. As one who made propitiation for our sins and now represents us before God, he is also our "high priest" (2:17).

The confession or profession mentioned here is the acknowledgement to others that one claims Jesus as God's spokesperson and savior whom he sent to earth. Our author is concerned that his readers cling tightly to that confession by believing its content and continuing to express it as an act of faith (Hebrews 4:14; 10:23).

God's House/Household

3:2-4 Our author now compares God's people and purpose to a "house" and its "household," the people who reside in it. The metaphor is a bit fluid and involves both figures. Moses served God faithfully in the role he was assigned in God's house/household, and our author praises Moses for his faithful service. Jesus also served God faithfully in all his assignments. When we think of the great structure of redemption, God himself is the grand builder, the master architect, the skilled superintendent. We admire a beautiful house, but we honor the builder and not the bricks. The highest honor always goes to God.

3:5-6a Jesus receives greater glory than Moses. Moses was a *servant in* God's house/household (Numbers 12:6-8). Christ is a *Son over* the house/household. This is the first time in Hebrews that Jesus is called by his title "Christ." The statement that Christ is *faithful* as a *Son* over God's house brings to mind three Old Testament contexts in which our author more than once expresses uncommon interest.

- In the days of Eli, God said through Samuel: "I will raise up for myself a *faithful priest* who will do everything in my heart and in my soul, and I will build him a faithful *house*" (LXX 1 Samuel 2:35). We will consider the context of this promise when we come to Hebrews chapter 7.

- A few years later God promised David a royal heir of whom he said: "I will be his father and he will be my son" (2 Samuel 7:14; 1 Chronicles 17:13), words which our author has applied to Jesus before (Hebrews 1:5). Concerning this royal heir, the next verse in the Greek text of Chronicles says: "I will make him *faithful* in *my house*" (1 Chronicles 17:14).

- Within a period probably no greater than 75 years, God gave two oracles promising to provide a *faithful king* and a *faithful priest.* The author of Hebrews applies the double imagery to Jesus who, in fulfillment of Psalm 110, is at once both the *royal heir* seated at God's right hand (Psalm 110:1; Hebrews 1:3, 13; 8:1; 10:12; 12:2) and also the *eternal priest* after the order of Melchizedek (Psalm 110:4; Hebrews 5:6, 10; 6:20; 7:11, 15-17).

3:6b We now learn what is meant by God's house as it relates to Jesus. That house is "the assembly" or church. It does not consist of any denominational or undenominational membership found in record books on earth. It rather includes all the "firstborn [ones] who are enrolled in heaven" (Hebrews 12:23).

Are we ourselves included in that enrollment? Here we must be content to live with a divine *if.* We are his house, *if* we grip firmly the confidence grounded in assurance, the boldness that boasts in Christ who is the basis of our hope. It is not enough to begin this pilgrimage, only to fall along the way. The faith that accompanies salvation will not stop until it reaches its goal. Hope that is anchored in Jesus and his atonement will not finally drift away from that anchor. The original readers of Hebrews needed to hear that reminder in their day. It is equally important for us today.

Although this speaks of our responsibility, it is ultimately a sign of God's own faithfulness and power. God is the one who equips his people and who works in them what pleases him (Hebrews 13:20-21). For this reason our author is not being inconsistent when he alternates warnings with words of assurance. Some Christians read Hebrews and conclude that steadfastness *makes* us God's house. Other Christians (including me) read Hebrews and conclude that steadfastness *confirms* that we are God's house. Either way the outcome is the same: saving faith trusts and obeys until the very end. Reaching the destination infallibly validates the pilgrim's quest and authenticates the pilgrim's profession.

"Confidence" here translates a word that originally meant political "freedom of speech." Later the word came to include the boldness and assurance in general which such freedom produced (Hebrews 3:6; 10:35). In a religious setting this confident assurance shows itself by uninhibited openness as expressed, for example, in prayer (Hebrews 4:16; 10:19).

Faithless in the Wilderness

3:7-8 There was once a notable community that did not hold fast to its confession, our author continues. He points to the generation of Israelites who followed Moses out of Egypt, only to perish in the wilderness. They received God's blessings and heard his good word. Yet most of them fell from divine favor through disbelief. The same thing can happen to those similarly situated today. Quoting from Psalm 95:7-11 (LXX 94:7-11) our author issues the strong exhortation: "Therefore, as the Holy Spirit says: 'Today, if you hear his voice, do not harden your hearts.'"

Psalm 95 is a call to worship God who alone is divine (v. 3). He who created all things and now sustains them (v. 4-6) also chose his people Israel and made covenant with them (v. 7). God did all that, the psalmist says, but it is not enough to look to the past. God desires a living relationship with his people and that happens forever in the *present*. The psalmist therefore considers it urgent in his day that those who hear God's voice "today" not harden their hearts. The Greek verb here translated "harden" is a form of the word that gives our word "sclerosis." We are dealing with a serious spiritual pathology, more deadly and dangerous by far than atherosclerosis (hardening of the arteries).

The original event mentioned here occurred during Israel's wanderings in the wilderness (Exodus 17:1-7). Although God had wondrously provided for them in the past, Israel showed an unbelieving heart by refusing to trust him to provide in the future. Because they distrusted God in their hearts, they were quick to murmur and to complain about his provisions for their needs. Both the psalmist and the author of Hebrews a millennium later exhort their audiences not to distrust God—not to murmur and sin—but to have full confidence in him. In that confident trust they are to hear God's word every *today*, and just as often not to harden their hearts.

The first readers of Hebrews were in danger of leaving Jesus—whether for Moses or for someone or something else does not ultimately matter. Our author's use of Psalm 95 suggests that their threatened apostasy grew out of an essential lack of trust in Jesus as perfect sacrifice, Savior and high priest. They professed with their mouths to believe in Jesus, but the faith in their hearts was shaky.

3:9-11 Our author continues quoting from Psalm 95. For 40 years the wilderness generation put God to the test. Because of such unbelief, God swore in his anger that they would not enter his rest. "The fundamental failure of the desert generation was their refusal to believe that God was actually present among them, directing them through his word. Refusing to acknowledge his presence and voice, they forfeited the possibility of entrance into God's rest" (Lane, *Commentary* I, 90).

HEBREWS 3:12-19

We Are to be Faithful 'Today'

¹² Take care, brothers, lest there be in any of you an evil, unbelieving heart that turns away from the living God. ¹³ But exhort one another daily, as long as it is called "today," so that none of you may be hardened by the deceitfulness of sin. ¹⁴ For we have come to share in Christ, if we hold fast our first confidence firm to the end. ¹⁵ As it is said,

"Today, if you hear his voice,
do not harden your hearts as in the rebellion."

¹⁶ For who were they who heard and rebelled? Was it not all those who came out of Egypt led by Moses? ¹⁷ And with whom was he angry for forty years? Was it not with those who sinned, whose bodies fell in the wilderness? ¹⁸ And to whom did he swear that they would not enter his rest, if not to those who were disobedient? ¹⁹ So we see that they were not able to enter because of unbelief.

WHY & WHEREFORE

Our author urges his readers to take care to avoid an "evil unbelieving heart" that would "turn away from the living God." This is a goal in which they can help each other. It is an important goal, because those who truly share Christ will retain confidence in him until the end. Privilege and blessing from God do not inoculate them from this danger, as shown by the example of the ancient Jews.

UNPACKING THE TEXT

The Importance of 'Today'

3:12 For this reason the readers should exercise great care to avoid an evil heart that refuses to believe God's word. Like the hard heart in the preceding verses, such a heart distrusts God, rejects his message and chooses not to live by faith. The person who "turns away" from God in this way literally commits "apostasy" (that English word comes from the Greek verb translated "turn away"). Despite public professions of faith, there is nothing to stop a distrustful and unfaithful heart from forsaking Jesus completely.

3:13 For the psalmist who wrote about ancient Israel and for our author alike, "today" is the critical time that calls for care and caution. "Today" is the day we hear God's voice. "Today" we must not harden our hearts. To prevent that from ever occurring, believers are encouraged to exhort each other daily—that is, every new "today" that comes. Such admonishing helps maintain a tender heart and prevents it from becoming hardened through sin's deceitfulness. This is a mutual ministry project in which all believers are privileged both to give and to receive, although the leaders of the faith community have a special responsibility (Hebrews 13:17).

3:14 Are we truly Christ's partners who share in and partake of his life and blessings? We validate and confirm that profession by holding fast our confidence of hope until we reach our final goal.

A 'Lost' Generation

3:15 The unfaithful generation in the wilderness had ample opportunity to believe in God instead. Our author repeats for emphasis the exhortation of Psalm 95:7 with which he began: "Today, if you hear his voice, do not harden your hearts as in the rebellion."

3:16 The rebellion within ancient Israel was no small incident involving only a few inconsequential people. With few exceptions, it was the work of an entire Israelite generation. They heard God's voice, and they chose to ignore it.

3:17 With whom was God angry for forty years? His anger was well justified; it was directed at those who sinned. Their judgment was both certain and tangible, as the corpses littering the wilderness bore silent witness (Numbers 14:33).

3:18 The next question reaffirms the justice of God's reaction. To whom did God swear that they would not enter his rest? It was to those who were disobedient.

3:19 These details lead to one certain conclusion: the Israelites could not enter God's rest because of unbelief. Blame for their fate rests on their heads alone. Moses was faithful. God was faithful. Their fall was due to their own unbelief.

HEBREWS 4:1-13

God's Promise Brings Rest, Not Wrath

[1] Therefore, while the promise remains of entering his rest, let us fear lest any of you should seem to have come short of it. [2] For good news was preached to us just as to them, but the message they heard did not benefit them, because it was not united by faith in those who heard. [3] For we who have believed enter that rest, just as God has said,

"As I swore in my anger,
 'They shall not enter my rest,'"

although his works were finished since the foundation of the world. [4] For he has somewhere spoken about the seventh day in this way:

"And God rested on the seventh day from all his works."

[5] And again in this passage,

"They shall not enter my rest."

[6] Since therefore it remains for some to enter it, and those who formerly received good news failed to enter because of disobedience, [7] again he sets a certain day, "Today," saying through David after such a long time, in the words already quoted,

"Today, if you hear his voice,
 do not harden your hearts."

⁸ For if Joshua had given them rest he would not have spoken later about another day. ⁹ There remains, therefore, a Sabbath rest for the people of God. ¹⁰ For those who have entered God's rest have also rested from their works as God did from his. ¹¹ Let us therefore make every effort to enter that rest, so that no one may fall through their example of disobedience.

¹² For the word of God is living and active, sharper than any two-edged sword, piercing as far as the division of soul and spirit, joints and marrow; it judges the thoughts and intentions of the heart. ¹³ And no creature is hidden from his sight, but all things are naked and exposed to the eyes of the one to whom we must give account.

WHY & WHEREFORE

It is not enough to hear the gospel or to attach oneself to the believing community. God's good news benefits only those who internalize it personally by faith and assimilate it into their daily lives. Those who do that will enjoy God's *rest,* which comes in two successive stages. First is the "rest" of a finished salvation, which the believer enters upon trusting in Christ. Second is the eternal "rest" that awaits us at the end. This section closes with a reminder that God's living word penetrates and inspects the most private reflections of our hearts—a message that both warns and comforts.

UNPACKING THE TEXT

Hearing is Not Enough

4:1 Throughout Hebrews, our author warns against unbelief which manifests itself in disobedience, against a hardened heart that causes one to drift away from Jesus, and against outright rejection of Jesus Christ and the sacrifice he offered once for all time for sin.

In issuing these warnings, our author remembers the mixed multitude we know as ancient Israel, which included both believers and unbelievers—a distinction known with certainty only by God. In the same way, the community that professes faith in Jesus also is spiritually-mixed. Some who pilgrimage with this community are true believers. Others are not. With this in mind, our author urges the seriousness of godly fear.

A promise now remains for us, although the Old Testament community has long since died. The content of that promise is entry into God's own rest. God offered this rest to the liberated Jews under Moses, our writer explains, but they forfeited it through unbelief. God is now repeating the offer to believers in Jesus.

The warning now is to "fear" lest anyone should seem to come short of God's rest. The word translated "come short" can also mean "to come too late." The error to be prevented might therefore be mistakenly thinking that God's promised rest is no longer available. Or it might be failing to continue to the end where the reward is received. The whole tenor of Hebrews favors the second view.

Our author's original readers were weighed down with discouragement. They had given up their original world-view and lifestyle (whether that was related to Judaism or to something else) to follow Jesus. They had suffered hardship for their faith. They had endured afflictions specifically for Christ's sake, and they had watched their comrades undergo the same ordeals. To some of them, it surely seemed that all their sacrifices had been in vain. Rather than entering into rest they had entered into distress. Our author explains that God's promised rest was not fulfilled in the past. For that reason, he concludes, it still awaits those who come to God through Jesus Christ.

4:2 Merely hearing good news does not guarantee that one will experience the blessing which that news announces. The first generation of liberated Israelites is evidence enough of that. God announced good news ("gospel") to them concerning a promised land. But ancient Israel did not benefit from the good news Moses had announced. What was their problem? They heard God's good news with their ears, but they did not receive it internally. Our author describes this with a metaphor involving the human body and nutrition. Just as food must be digested and assimilated in order to benefit the body, so God's word must be "united" or "mixed" with faith if it is bless the hearer. Hearing God's word and then ignoring it is as futile as savoring the most exquisite cuisine, but spitting out each bite instead of swallowing it. This truth is as important for us as it was for ancient Israel.

Sharing God's Rest

4:3 Believers in Jesus enter one aspect of God's rest now and will enter another aspect of it in the future. Already, anyone who trusts in Jesus rests from all attempts to merit God's favor and forgiveness. Jesus fully atoned for sin by his single offering of himself—nothing else remains for us to do to make peace with God, to gain access into his presence or to establish the basis for a clear conscience.

Any person who professes to trust in Jesus, but who lives in anxiety and uncertainty regarding God's acceptance, has not yet grasped the reality of this gospel truth. Yet for some reason, many of us find it easier to believe that God accepts other sinners than it is to believe that he actually accepts us personally.

Because God swore in his anger that Israel would not enjoy his rest, we can draw two conclusions. First, God himself enjoys a rest of some sort. Second, God always has intended for humankind to enjoy it with him. God began his rest when he finished creating all that exists—his creative "works" have been "finished since the foundation of the world." Since then God has been on sabbatical, we might say, while constantly observing humankind in search of people who would join him in it.

Even in Genesis, there is some suggestion that God's "rest" following the creation was to be ongoing. Throughout Genesis 1, the account of each day's work concludes with a statement that "there was evening and there was morning, the [number] day." However, the description of the seventh day does not include that standard phrase (Genesis 2:1-3). The natural implication is that, from God's point of view, the seventh day— God's *rest-day*—did not come to an end but continued in perpetuity.

4:4-5 Two separate texts from the Jewish Bible (which our author quotes in its Greek translation) support our two conclusions just mentioned. The first text is Genesis 2:2, which tells us that "God rested on the seventh day from all his works." The second text is Psalm 95:11, which our author has open before him (or at least has called to mind). It repeats God's declaration about Israel's unbelieving and rebellious generation in the wilderness: "they shall not enter my rest."

4:6-7 God always intended for some to enjoy his rest with him. The ancient Jews to whom he first sent good news forfeited the invitation through unbelief manifested in *disobedience*. A few hundred years later, God offered his rest again to those living in the time of David. Like their ancestors in the desert, they were admonished to hear God's voice and not to harden their hearts (Psalm 95:7-8). On God's salvation calendar, his day for saving is always *today*—every time that day arrives. The day of salvation is every day that someone hears God's word and receives it in faith.

4:8 God again offered his rest to Israel in Psalm 95, which proves that the "rest" of which he speaks was still available to the people of God. The logic is elementary: If Joshua (KJV has "Jesus," the Greek form of "Joshua") had given them rest in the land, God would not have spoken later about another day. Yet that is precisely what he did.

4:9 Our author concludes that a Sabbath rest remains even today for those who trust in Christ. The words "a Sabbath rest" represent a single Greek word found only here in the New Testament. In non-biblical Greek, this word was associated with joyful celebration.

4:10 This is no ordinary human rest which one enjoys briefly and then returns to work. Those who have entered God's rest have "rested from their works" just "as God did from his" at the end of Creation Week. This is a rest of labor completed and purpose accomplished. The Sabbath which God graciously gave to Israel does not fulfill this rest. That weekly rest-day was followed by six more days of labor. Further, the weekly Sabbath was mandated by the Fourth Commandment, but God's "rest" is always promised (Matthew 11:28-30; Revelation 14:13).

4:11 The joys inherent in this rest will more than justify every effort expended to enter it. Such effort includes looking out for each other, so that no one repeats Israel's unbelief and disobedience.

God's Piercing Word

4:12 The theme of God speaking and people listening has run through this book from its start. God has spoken to us through his Son (Hebrews 1:2) and we must pay close attention (Hebrews 2:1) to the message of the Lord (Hebrews 2:3). This means hearing his voice and not hardening our hearts through unbelief (Hebrews 3:7-8, 12). We have received good news (Hebrews 4:2), but that very word penetrates, discerns and judges the hearts of those who hear it (Hebrews 4:12).

It is a perilous thing to interact with the word of God, which our author now reminds us is living (archaic: *quick*) and active, energetic or powerful. It is sharper, therefore more facile, than any two-edged sword.

Clearly this is metaphorical language. There is no actual border line at which one can divide soul from spirit. Words cannot literally separate physical joints from marrow. This verse is not about anthropological theories, and our author is not listing our various parts. He is emphasizing the entirety of the whole self, all of which God sees and knows. Inward belief or unbelief is always visible to God. It is therefore profoundly important that we receive God's word in faith (see verse two).

4:13 God knows whether each heart is good or evil and he will not be misled. All things are naked and exposed or opened before God's eyes. These words may reflect three diverse scenarios. The first concerns priestly ritual under the Torah. The second comes from the criminal law system of the first-century Roman world. The third is borrowed from the practice of medicine and surgery. The first two metaphors suggest warnings; the third produces encouragement.

- The Law of God given to Moses on Mount Sinai demanded that sacrificial animals brought for sacrifice be physically perfect. To ensure that this requirement was met, the priest thoroughly inspected every creature brought to him for sacrifice. No blemish could pass this official inspection. Similarly, our hearts are exposed moment by moment to the scrutiny of God, before whom we daily stand responsible and to whom we must finally give account.

- Roman legal procedure sometimes called for criminals to be shamed by public display. Then their heads were pulled backward and their faces exposed. Nothing in our hearts or lives can escape God's clear gaze. He sees us through and through.

- The surgical room offers a third arena in which everything is naked and open to the eyes of another (Smillie, 347-348). Aulus Cornelius Celsus, a first-century Roman medical encyclopedist, wrote of "the need to have everything open and exposed" before a surgeon could do his work. The patient lies stretched out before the surgeon who, seeing the problem clearly and without obstruction, administers the scalpel (the word here translated "sword" is also used in the Greek Old Testament for the circumcision knife) to remove whatever threatens the patient's life and well-being. So too the word of God "operates" on the heart to remove the "hardness" against which our author has just warned.

HEBREWS 4:14–16

Jesus, Our Perfect High Priest

¹⁴ Therefore, since then we have a great high priest who has passed through the heavens, Jesus the Son of God, let us hold fast to our confession. ¹⁵ For we do not have a high priest who is unable to sympathize with our weaknesses, but one who has been tempted in every way as we are, yet without sin. ¹⁶ Let us therefore approach the throne of grace with boldness, so that we may receive mercy and find grace to help in time of need.

WHY & WHEREFORE

We began this epistle with a majestic view of the Son of God, who became the man Jesus in order to bring human beings to their place of intended glory. Now, by the merits of the faithful human life lived in his body and sacrificed in his death on the cross, Jesus represents his people before God as their high priest. Throughout his life on earth, Jesus himself suffered and was tempted. Because of that personal experience, he can now assist those who are tempted, and he can provide timely mercy and grace equal to every need. Our author highlights three realities about Jesus as our high priest. He is *in heaven* (v. 14) as glorified *man* (v. 15) on *our behalf* (v. 16). In other words, Jesus the Son of God is now (and until his final appearing) *our man in heaven.*

UNPACKING THE TEXT

4:14 Because Jesus, the Son of God made *man*, has passed through the heavens to God's right-hand place of honor, and because he is there as our representative or high priest, we have every reason to hold fast to our confession and profession of faith in him (see also Hebrews 3:1).

4:15 Jesus Christ can sympathize with our weaknesses because in every way he also has been tempted or put to the test. To "sympathize" is literally to "feel with." More than a psychological reaction, this is an intentional sharing of feelings. Yet, unlike us, Jesus emerged from every test without committing any sin against God or man. Now at God's right hand, Jesus continues to represent us by his very presence as *man* in heaven. There he is, *glorified* man, and our names are inscribed on his heart (Exodus 28:29).

4:16 Because Jesus is our sympathetic high priest in heaven, we are encouraged to approach God's throne boldly in times of need. Because of Jesus, God promises to show us mercy and to give us the grace we need. "Mercy" here translates a word which the Greek Old Testament regularly uses for God's mercy or loving-kindness to his covenant people. Because God's people had received his divine mercy, they were also expected to share it with each other (see also Ephesians 5:2).

HEBREWS 5:1-10

Jesus' Path to This Position

⁵:¹ Every high priest taken from among men is appointed on behalf of men to represent them in things pertaining to God, to offer gifts and sacrifices for sins. ² He is able to deal gently with the ignorant and wayward, since he himself is subject to weakness. ³ Because of this he must offer sacrifices for his own sins as well as for those of the people.

⁴ No one takes this honor upon himself, but only when called by God, just as Aaron was. ⁵ So also Christ did not glorify himself to become a high priest, but he who said to him,

"You are my Son,
today I have begotten you."

⁶ just as he says also in another place,

"You are a priest forever,
according to the order of Melchizedek."

⁷ In the days of his flesh, he offered up prayers and supplications, with loud cries and tears, to him who was able to save him from death, and he was heard because of his reverence. ⁸ Although he was a son, he learned obedience through what he suffered. ⁹ And having been made perfect, he became the source of eternal salvation to all who obey him, ¹⁰ being designated by God a high priest according to the order of Melchizedek.

WHY & WHEREFORE

The Levitical priest identified with his people, including in his sinfulness. He could therefore deal gently with those who stumbled and erred, whether through ignorance or carelessness, and who then came to him seeking reunion with God. Throughout his entire human life of approximately 33 years, Jesus pleased the Father every moment of every day. Jesus also experienced fully every uncertainty of human life. He endured the full gamut of human suffering. He faced the human reality of utter dependence on God. Yet Jesus did not appoint himself to be high priest, even as Aaron had not assumed that office by his own presumption. God designated both Aaron and Jesus as high priests. He confirmed both their appointments by bringing life out from death.

UNPACKING THE TEXT

A Priest Who Understands

The high priest in the Levitical system served as mediator between God and the people of Israel. He was himself a man, one of the people, appointed as their representative to offer gifts to God and also sacrifices for sins.

Used together as here, "gifts and sacrifices" stand for the full range of priestly offerings (Hebrews 8:3; 9:9). If we distinguish between these categories, the difference lies in their purposes. Gifts are thank-offerings in response to God's grace (eucharistic) and sacrifices are sin-offerings as appeals for God's grace (expiatory). The descriptive phrase "for sins" refers to the sacrifices alone. Some interpreters see the distinction as between offerings that are bloodless and those that involve bloodshed, but that is inconsistent with other usage of the same terms (LXX Genesis 4:3-4).

5:2 The high priest is appointed to intercede for the people by offering sacrifices, not to judge them for their sins. As advocate and intercessor, the high priest must be able to deal gently with those who are ignorant of God's laws and those who are wayward with respect to the knowledge they do possess. Knowing their situation, the high priest literally "measures his feelings"—a picturesque expression that means to show compassion. No Levitical high priest ever had room for self-righteousness, for every one of them experienced the same weaknesses that surrounded the people whom they served.

The word translated "subject to" involves a play on words, since it can also mean "clothed." The priest, and especially the high priest, wore vestments that identified his office and set him apart from common men (Exodus 28:1-43). However, despite his holy uniform, the high priest was also "clothed" with moral weakness like every other citizen of Israel. The essence of Jesus' priesthood is his difference from other priests in this regard: God appointed Jesus as high priest precisely because of his sinless life of faithful obedience.

5:3 Because he also was a sinner, the Levitical priest was required to offer a sacrifice for himself as well as one for the people. Although he was called by God and was appointed to sacred office, he personally fell short of God's standard. He therefore needed God's mercy and forgiveness, along with his fellow-Israelites. It remained for Jesus to become a priest without sin, in a priesthood defined by moral character and not by physical qualifications.

By Divine Appointment Only

5:4 The Jews learned very early that no one arbitrarily claimed the office of high priest. God himself selected the family to wear this honor, and he divinely appointed Aaron as Israel's first high priest (Exodus 28:1). God then confirmed Aaron's appointment through a miracle of new life. On one occasion, a large group of mutinous Israelites led by Korah, Dathan and Abiram challenged Aaron's exclusive privilege. God consumed the rebel company with fire, then he swallowed the leaders' families with an earthquake (Numbers 16:1-3, 31-35). The next day, God selected Aaron's rod from all the tribal rods, then confirmed Aaron's priesthood by making his rod (a piece of dead wood) come to life, sprout buds, grow blossoms and yield almonds (Numbers 17). Aaron did not grasp the priestly office for himself. He was called by God to be high priest.

5:5-6 Christ did not presumptuously glorify himself to become a high priest. He also was chosen by God—who confirmed that appointment by raising him from the dead. Our author quotes from two Psalms, which New Testament writers commonly understood to refer to the Messiah, and which our author included in his opening bouquet of scripture quotes (Hebrews 1:5, 13). In the first quotation, God calls Jesus "my Son" (Psalm 2:7). In the second quotation, God declares Jesus to be "a priest forever, according to the order of Melchizedek" (Psalm 110:4; LXX 109:4). Unlike the Levitical high priest, whose own life required a sin offering for forgiveness, Jesus' priesthood rests on the moral quality of his life.

Jesus lived a life perfectly pleasing to God. He offered his faithful life to the Father in his dying body on the cross. The Father was pleased with *this* human life and raised Jesus from the dead. Jesus' passage through death to resurrection vindicated him from every human charge of wrongdoing, and it exhibited the Father's unrestricted approval of Jesus' life throughout.

Because he was without sin, Jesus possessed the power of an indestructible life. With such a verdict from God, it was impossible for death to retain him. A life so faithful and sinless could not remain dead. Jesus is therefore *high priest forever,* because he *lives forever* to *save forever* those who approach God through him (Hebrews 7:23-25). In chapter seven, our author will again pick up this theme to explain how Jesus' priesthood is "according to the order of Melchizedek."

God Heard Jesus' Prayer

5:7 "The days of his flesh" could be translated as "his fleshly days" and refers to the earthly life of the Son of God made man. It is the time when he shared in flesh and blood (Hebrews 2:14) and was made like his brothers and sisters (Hebrews 2:17). The agony of Jesus' soul might refer to events throughout his earthly life. However the description given in this verse is generally understood as a portrayal of Jesus' agony on the night before his death. "Prayers" and "supplications" both focus on asking. "Loud cries" and "tears" point to the intensity of the act. The Gospels do not mention Jesus' tears, but they do describe his agony of soul (Matthew 26:36-44; Mark 14:32-42; Luke 22:39-46).

But for what did Jesus pray with such intensity? On that occasion, according to the common interpretation, Jesus prayed to avoid the experience of death by crucifixion. Yet we must ask how that could be, since Jesus' prayer was "heard"? One answer might be that "heard" does not mean God did what Jesus asked. Another answer might be that the prayer that God "heard" and answered was the prayer that God's will be done. Numerous other explanations have been offered (summarized by Omark, "Saving of the Savior . . .").

Perhaps there is a better approach, one suggested by the metaphor in Jesus' Gethsemane prayer involving the cup of God's wrath. Though tempted throughout his earthly life, surely Jesus' temptations came to a crushing climax in the olive grove whose name Gethsemane means "winepress." There, pressed between the human fear of endless darkness and the knowledge of his faithful God, Jesus exuded sweat resembling drops of blood and stared straight into the face of death. If he went to the cross, could God be trusted to bring him out of death's domain?

In this hour of agony, Jesus prayed to the Father who alone was able to rescue him from death. He did not pray to avoid the experience of dying, as the Gethsemane prayer is often interpreted. He knew that was inevitable, and he had already committed himself to suffer it (John 12:23-33). Jesus prayed that God would save him "from death" as a final destiny–the Greek phrase is literally "out of death." Jesus knew that God was able to save him from the cross by twelve legions of angels, if necessary (Matthew 26:53). But he also knew that was not the Father's will and that it was not what the Scriptures had stated was to occur (Matthew 26:54).

This gives meaning to Jesus' request that the cup of God's judgment "pass from" him (Matthew 26:39). The goblet of poisonous wine is an established Old Testament metaphor for a divine judgment (Psalm 75:8; Isaiah 51:17-20; Jeremiah 25:15-26). This picture may have either of two endings. Sometimes the cup results in permanent destruction. Those who drink it fall and never rise again (Obadiah 16; Jeremiah 25:27). At other times, the cup represents a passing judgment. Its recipient staggers and reels, then recovers to thrive again. In this second scenario, God takes back the cup which passes from the one who drank it (Isaiah 51:21-23).

Even in Gethsemane, Jesus expected to drink the cup. His prayer was that after he had drunk it, the cup would pass (Matthew 26:42). Our author immediately underscores that God answered Jesus' prayers ("he was heard") because of his reverence or piety or godly life. Jesus entrusted his faithful life to the Father. The Father proved himself faithful by saving Jesus "out from" death. A human life entirely pleasing to the Father cannot remain long dead!

God's rescue of Jesus from death was a direct answer to Jesus' prayers. Yet it was necessary that Jesus share with us the actual experience of dying. Through his sinless life given to the Father on the cross, Jesus conquered the devil and liberated humankind from the paralyzing fear of death forever (Hebrews 2:14-15). By obedience to the Father in life and in death, Jesus was perfected to serve as our empathetic high priest and to become the source of our own deliverance by God (Hebrews 5:7-9).

5:8-9 Although he was the Son, Christ "learned obedience" by experiencing the full range of human suffering. The phrase speaks of on-the-job training, learning by experience, a subjective kind of learning which goes beyond the intellectual transfer of information and produces profound, life-long effects. The word translated "learned" is related to the words usually translated "disciple" and "discipline." Our author actually writes "*the* obedience," which simply adds emphasis to the word *obedience.*

This obedience perfected or completed Jesus as the source or cause of eternal salvation. His obedience qualified him to be the Savior. It is appropriate that those whom he saves should also obey him. Throughout Hebrews, the words translated "obedience" and "obey" contain a root word meaning "to hear." Our author has already discussed Psalm 95 which emphasizes the importance of "hearing" God's voice each "today" (Hebrews 3-4). He will reflect on Jesus' obedience again in considering Psalm 40 (Hebrews 10:5-10).

5:10 Christ's saving vocation is as high priest. The nature of his priesthood is "according to the order of Melchizedek." The basis of his priesthood is his designation by God.

HEBREWS 5:11–6:3

Call to Sharpen Dull Ears

[11] About this we have much to say, and it is hard to explain since you have become dull of hearing. [12] For though by this time you ought to be teachers, you need someone to teach you again the basic principles of the oracles of God. You need milk, not solid food. [13] For everyone who lives on milk is unskilled in the word of righteousness, being still an infant. [14] But solid food is for the mature, for those whose senses have been trained by practice to distinguish good from evil.

[6:1] Therefore leaving the elementary teaching about Christ, let us go on to maturity, and not laying again the foundation: repentance from dead works and of faith toward God, [2] instruction about baptisms, laying on of hands, the resurrection of the dead and eternal judgment. [3] And this we will do if God permits.

WHY & WHEREFORE

Our author introduced Melchizedek but does not discuss him yet. Before he can do that, he says, he must further prepare his readers, who lack the maturity to hear what he will say. So he pauses momentarily, and urges them to grow into spiritual adults.

UNPACKING THE TEXT

Spiritual Infancy a Problem

5:11 Our author warns that his intended discourse on Melchizedek is both lengthy ("much to say") and difficult to communicate clearly ("hard to explain"). The author can express himself well enough. The problem is that his readers are presently unable to grasp all that he would like to tell. They previously have become dull of hearing (literally "sluggish in ears") and the condition continues. They have not renounced their profession of faith in Jesus, but our author fears they might be drifting into indifference. He pauses now to point this out, hoping to energize their sluggish ears.

5:12 Considering the amount of time that has passed since they became believers, one might expect his readers now to be teachers. To the dismay of our author, they need remedial instruction instead. Their learning deficiency is not in advanced material. They need tutoring in elementary materials, in the first principles, in spiritual ABC's. In view of the advanced teaching our author already has given in this book, one wonders whether he is using irony here or is expressing a serious appraisal.

5:13 The spiritual infant who lives on milk is unaccustomed to digesting the message of righteousness and is therefore unskilled in its use. Just as an infant who takes only milk never gains experience in utilizing strong food, so the believer whose only spiritual diet consists of "baby food" will forever remain inexperienced in teaching others.

5:14 Solid food is intended to nourish the mature person. Maturity here describes one who through much practice has trained the moral senses to distinguish good and evil. To "discern good and evil" is to make independent moral choices by discerning the Lord's will in each circumstance. The ability to do that is one mark of spiritual maturity (see Romans 12:2; Ephesians 5:10, 17). Such moral discernment requires spiritual "senses" (our word "aesthetics" comes from the Greek word here). These senses may be "trained" (from a Greek root word that gives our word "gymnasium").

Instead of referring to spiritual adults "whose senses have been trained *by practice*," the clause might be translated as "who *because of their mature state* have their senses trained." So argues one scholar, who researched the pertinent Greek word in the Septuagint and in non-biblical Greek, and concluded that Bible translators and Greek lexicons since at least the year 1814 have misunderstood its actual meaning (Lee, "Hebrews 5:14 and 'EXIS' . . .").

Going Beyond ABC's

6:1 The elementary teaching about Christ includes first principles which our author identifies in this verse and the next. His readers have had instruction in such matters. However, they have not progressed beyond these ABC's. Our author encourages them to leave this elementary teaching. He is not asking them to reject its value or to doubt its authenticity. He is urging them to move on to more advanced material. Their goal is perfection or maturity or completion.

A solid building begins with a good foundation. Yet one does not lay the foundation time and time again. If a man decides that the foundation of his house is faulty and for that reason abandons the house, he will not be persuaded by re-reading original sales literature to move back in. Similarly, those who profess faith in Jesus and later renounce that faith will not be reclaimed by repeating the gospel message as if for the first time. Such persons have rejected what they know and there is no place in their hearts for re-conversion.

Our author enumerates six aspects of elementary teaching, which have been interpreted at least two ways. Some see them as elements of Old Testament teaching. Others think they are fundamental elements of Christian instruction. Our author refers to all six aspects as part of "the elemental word of Christ" (literally). This leaves open the question whether this is teaching *from* Christ or teaching *concerning* or *related to* Christ. The larger context of Hebrews and the six topics themselves seem to favor the second alternative. We will consider them to be fundamental elements in Christian instruction.

Repentance and faith are certainly Old Testament topics as well as Christian subjects. The New Testament mentions them twice elsewhere, always in this order (Mark 1:15; Acts 20:21). They are foundational in the process of coming to Christ, where repentance indicates a reversal of mental direction and faith indicates trust in God who is always faithful. Our author later speaks of repentance from "dead works," which are either sinful works leading to death or what appear to be good works that do not spring from supernatural life (Hebrews 9:14). For our author, to have faith toward God means believing that God exists, expecting him to reward those who seek him (Hebrews 11:6) and persisting in trusting and obeying him as long as one lives.

6:2 Baptisms (literally "washings") and laying on of hands are also topics that predated the coming of Jesus Christ. Old Testament rituals included purification rites for which the Greek word was the same one here translated "baptisms" (Hebrews 9:10; see Mark 7:4). Laying on of hands had a place in Old Testament ordinations. Instruction about baptisms would likely involve teaching the difference between ritual washings to purge ceremonial uncleanness and the work of Jesus required to cleanse the conscience—the inward purification to which gospel baptism points.

The earliest Christian communities exercised laying on of hands in connection with healings, blessings, ordinations, bestowing spiritual gifts and perhaps (when performing baptisms) to invoke God to bestow the Holy Spirit.

Resurrection of the dead and eternal judgment appear in the Old Testament (Daniel 12:1-2), but the concepts remain generally undeveloped there. Christian teaching says more on both topics. The form of the word "judgment" tells us the author here is thinking of the *outcome* of God's final judgment rather than the *process* of judging. For those who steadfastly wait for Jesus' appearing, that outcome will be *salvation* (Hebrews 9:27-28; 10:39). Our author expects them to rule in the world to come, when God will give them a lasting city and a lasting country. For disbelievers, especially disbelievers falsely professing to be believers, this judgment's outcome will be *destruction* in the consuming fire (Hebrews 10:27; 12:29).

6:3 In this teaching effort, as in all things, our author is subject to the will of God.

Willful Apostate Cannot Repent

⁴ For it is impossible for those who have once been enlightened, and have tasted the heavenly gift, and have shared in the Holy Spirit, ⁵ and have tasted the goodness of the word of God and the powers of the age to come, ⁶ and then have fallen away, to renew them again to repentance, since they are crucifying again for themselves the Son of God and holding him up to open shame.

⁷ For ground that drinks in the rain often falling on it, and that produces a crop useful to those for whom it is cultivated, receives a blessing from God. ⁸ But if it produces thorns and thistles, it is worthless and near to being cursed. Its end is to be burned.

⁹ Even though we speak in this way, beloved, we are confident of better things in your case, things that accompany salvation. ¹⁰ For God is not unjust; he will not forget your work and the love that you have shown for his name in serving the saints, as you still do. ¹¹ And we desire each one of you to show the same diligence so as to realize the full assurance of hope until the end, ¹² so that you do not become sluggish, but imitators of those who through faith and patience inherit the promises.

WHY & WHEREFORE

Again our author interrupts his teaching to issue a warning. He frames the warning in terms of individuals who to all appearances seem to be genuine believers, but who finally abandon everything they once professed and experienced. For all that it matters to them, Jesus can be crucified *again*. Because they now openly reject every spiritual reality to which they were temporarily attracted, they cannot *again* be renewed to repentance. These apostates are like a worthless field. The farmer cultivates it, the rain falls on it, but it produces only thorns and thistles and is finally burned. His readers are not like that, our author says. They belong to Christ and he expects their lives to manifest the fruit of salvation. Having warned and encouraged the readers, our author urges them to follow through diligently to the end. Faith and patience inherit the promise.

UNPACKING THE TEXT

When Repentance is Impossible

6:4 Our author warns that it is impossible to renew again to repentance a person who has experienced certain spiritual realities and who then falls away from Jesus Christ. The person in this scenario was once enlightened, which is a metaphor for being converted (Hebrews 10:32). It is often said that this figure of enlightenment was a symbol for baptism in the early church, but such usage is not documented before the second century.

The background of these verses 6:4-6 might well be the stories of the Israelites in the wilderness. There they were enlightened with a pillar of cloud/fire, tasted the heavenly gift of manna, and 70 of their leaders briefly experienced an outpouring of the Holy Spirit (Exodus 13:21-22; 16:15, 31-35; Numbers 11:24-25). Yet they distrusted God and finally perished without entering the promised land (Mathewson, "Reading Heb 6:4-6 in Light of the Old Testament"; Emmrich, "Hebrews 6:4-6—Again!").

To "taste" is to experience (see Hebrews 2:9). The "heavenly gift" is probably the Holy Spirit, with whom the people in this illustration have shared or partnered—however briefly. Throughout Hebrews, the "heavenly" realities transcend what is worldly both as a present higher order (Hebrews 3:1) and as an order that will endure forever (Hebrews 11:16).

6:5 Those who have "tasted the goodness of the word of God" have sampled the message of God and experienced at least some benefits and blessings from it. The "powers of the age to come" likely describes miraculous manifestations (see Hebrews 2:3-4). Readers would think of the messianic era of which such works are a sign. The "age to come" is literally the Coming Age, which is how the New Testament often speaks of the final, everlasting state of the saved (see notes at Hebrews 1:2).

6:6 In our author's hypothetical scenario, those just described later 'fall away" from all that they previously experienced. They abandon, reject and lose all interest in the gospel light, the Holy Spirit as God's gift, everything good in the word of God and the supernatural powers associated with the Coming Age. More than that, in their hearts they crucify the Son of God again.

As if that were not enough, they then "hold him up to open shame." Actually, that is putting it mildly—the Greek here could be translated loosely as: "they disgrace him by exhibiting his dead body in a public show." This same verb is used in the Greek Old Testament to describe a public hanging (Numbers 25:4). No wonder our author considers it impossible to "renew again" such people "to repentance." They have tasted God's blessings and have rejected everything God has to offer. For such a person Jesus Christ and his salvation simply hold no appeal.

Warnings in Hebrews: Two Views

Throughout this epistle, our author warns his readers of a spectrum of dangers ranging from neglect to mentally re-crucifying Jesus himself. Beginning with the least conspicuous errors and concluding with the most obvious, these warnings include:

- neglecting salvation (Hebrews 2:3),
- shrinking back (Hebrews 10:39),
- growing weary and losing heart (Hebrews 12:3),
- drifting away from the gospel (Hebrews 2:1),
- coming short of God's rest (Hebrews 4:1),
- failing to obtain the grace of God (Hebrews 12:15),
- deliberately going on sinning (Hebrews 10:26),
- becoming hardened by the deceitfulness of sin (Hebrews 3:13),
- falling away (Hebrews 6:6),
- hardening the heart instead of hearing God's voice (Hebrews 3:7-8),

- having an evil and unbelieving heart (Hebrews 3:12),
- regarding as unholy the blood of the covenant (Hebrews 10:29),
- insulting the Spirit of grace (Hebrews 10:29),
- trampling the Son of God (Hebrews 10:29),
- crucifying the Son of God again (Hebrews 6:6),
- holding Jesus up to open shame (Hebrews 6:6).

Two Interpretations

Based on their general study of Scripture as a whole, evangelical Christians of equal scholarship and piety understand these warnings in two different ways.

Believer cannot lose faith. Some Christians conclude that every true believer will inevitably persevere in faith to the end. Christians holding this view are convinced that those who fall away were never genuine believers, otherwise they certainly would not have fallen away. Those who believe that a true believer *cannot* become an unbeliever review the list of warnings in Hebrews and explain them somewhat like this:

> Outward appearances of piety and verbal claims of faith are notoriously unreliable as indicators of the true inner state. One person can better ascertain the presence or absence of saving faith in another person by observing that person's entire course of life. The true believer will persevere in faith and good works. The individual who falsely claims to be a believer will eventually manifest the heart's real unbelief and so contradict the counterfeit professions of faith.
>
> This manifestation often starts subtly and without fanfare. At first, the false "believer" begins to neglect salvation (Hebrews 2:3), shrinks back (Hebrews 10:39) or grows weary and loses heart (Hebrews 12:3). Next that person often drifts away from the gospel (Hebrews 2:1), comes short of God's rest (Hebrews 4:1) and fails to obtain the grace of God (Hebrews 12:15). The heart's true state

becomes even more apparent as the individual deliberately goes on sinning (Hebrews 10:26) and gradually becomes hardened by the deceitfulness of sin (Hebrews 3:13).

However, the real problem is in the heart as it has been from the beginning. In reality, those who fall away (Hebrews 6:6) have hardened their hearts instead of hearing God's voice (Hebrews 3:7-8). Their hearts are evil and unbelieving, which is why they turn away from God (Hebrews 3:12). Despite external appearances and vocal professions of faith, those who possess such evil and unbelieving hearts actually regard as unholy the blood of the covenant and eventually insult the Spirit of grace (Hebrews 10:29). In the worst cases, they eventually trample the Son of God (Hebrews 10:29), crucify him again in their hearts and hold him up to open shame (Hebrews 6:6). This tragic scenario reminds us once again that just as true believers are recognized by their perseverance (see notes on 3:6), so counterfeit "believers" are recognized by their absence of the same. By the "bridle" of this warning, John Calvin explains, "the Lord keeps us in fear and humility; and we certainly see how prone human nature is otherwise to security and foolish confidence" (Calvin, 138).

Believer can lose faith. Other Christians conclude that genuine believers can become unbelievers, so that people who are truly saved can finally become lost. Christians holding this view are convinced that those who fall away were genuine believers at one time, but that for some inexplicable reason and to the blame of no one but themselves they lost their faith and with it their hope of final salvation. Those who believe that a true believer *can* become an unbeliever review the list of warnings in Hebrews and explain them somewhat like this:

God does not wish for anyone to perish. No one can pluck a believer out of God's hand and nothing can separate the believer from God's love. Yet God does not force anyone to believe—or to keep on believing. In the case of those who lose their faith, there is a slippery slope that ends in destruction.

The slide begins subtly and without fanfare. At first, the believer begins to neglect salvation (Hebrews 2:3), shrinks back (Hebrews 10:39) or grows weary and loses heart (Hebrews 12:3). Next that person often drifts away from the gospel (Hebrews 2:1), comes short of God's rest (Hebrews 4:1) and fails to obtain the grace of God (Hebrews 12:15). The descent into unbelief becomes even more apparent as the individual deliberately goes on sinning (Hebrews 10:26) and gradually becomes hardened by the deceitfulness of sin (Hebrews 3:13).

The real problem is in the heart, which is always subject to the individual's power of choice. In reality, those who fall away (Hebrews 6:6) have hardened their hearts instead of hearing God's voice (Hebrews 3:7-8). Their hearts were once pure, but became evil and unbelieving, which is why they turn away from God (Hebrews 3:12). As these individuals move from bad to worse, they actually regard as unholy the blood of the covenant and may eventually insult the Spirit of grace 10:29). In the most extreme case, the person who falls from grace might finally even trample the Son of God (Hebrews 10:29), crucify him again in their heart and hold him up to open shame (Hebrews 6:6). This tragic scenario reminds us once again that while no one else can snatch a believer from God's hand, any believer has the power at any moment to renounce faith in Christ and to leave God's protection voluntarily by the exercise of his or her own free will.

Most Important Agreement

Despite this difference of understanding, both groups of Christians agree that those who fall away, who renounce their faith in Christ, or who live a life of unrepentant sin, are not saved and cannot rightly claim comfort from the many portions of Scripture which provide assurance to people of faith. In either scenario the peril is equally real. Either believers can become unbelievers, or unbelievers can mistakenly suppose themselves to be believers. "In the last analysis only perseverance can demonstrate the reality of Christian faith" (Hagner, 92).

Both situations described above call on the professed believer to examine self, to look intently at Jesus, and to recommit to follow through to the end. From a practical standpoint, therefore, the response is the same given either point of view. Responsible teachers on both sides of this discussion take seriously all scriptural warnings and sincerely admonish their respective audiences to heed their exhortations.

Like a Worthless Field

6:7-8 We pronounce God's blessing on a field or piece of ground that "drinks" or absorbs frequent-falling rain, then produces a crop useful to those for whose benefit it was cultivated. However, if a field receives the farmer's labor and drinks God's generous rain, then produces nothing but thorns and thistles, it *is worthless.* It *fails the* only *test* that matters regarding a field and *is disapproved* (the three italicized phrases all represent a single Greek adjective which is used three times in a very similar passage (2 Corinthians 13:5-7).

Such worthless ground is fit only for burning, which might at least prevent thorns from spreading to adjoining land. Our author clearly intends a double meaning, for such unproductive people will also face the burning of hell (see also Matthew 3:10, 12; 13:30; John 15:6). These two verses remind us of Isaiah's parable of the unfruitful vineyard and God's judgment on the unfaithful (Isaiah 5:1-7).

Confident of Better Things

6:9 Our author is persuaded or convinced that his readers will not fall away or resemble the worthless field. He looks for the character

What is The Danger That Prompts This Warning?

In these verses, our author is warning people who see themselves as belonging to Jesus Christ and as members of the household of God. Why, in fact, does he issue this warning, and what, exactly, is the meaning of the warning he issues? Is he concerned that people might mistakenly think they are true believers when they are not, although he is sure that genuine faith will persevere to the end? Or is he concerned because true believers can become unbelievers, so that they either forfeit salvation or fall short of reaching it in the end? To put the question another way, were the people whom our author hypothetically describes in verses 4-6 ever truly regenerated in the first place?

Although I did not always understand the matter this way, I now believe that the first answer above is correct and that the people described in verses 4-6 only thought themselves to be genuine believers, a confidence which their future course revealed to be a delusion. Among the considerations that nudged me to that conclusion are the following four from Hebrews itself, including two from this immediate context.

Earlier our author observed that those who comprise God's house make that plain by remaining steadfast throughout life (Hebrews 3:6). Here is the other side of the coin. Those who are not God's house, but are only apparent believers, also show that by falling away.

This passage itself points to the same conclusion. The portrayal of the two fields (v. 7-8) illustrates and clarifies the hypothetical situation that frames the question just before (v. 4-6). And the worthless field which finally is cursed and burned was worthless from the start, although that was not revealed until later. Good ground, when cultivated and watered, produces a good crop. Worthless ground, no matter how carefully cultivated and watered, produces thorns and thistles. Considered from this perspective, the bad ground here and the story it illustrates both remind us of the rocky ground in Jesus' Parable of the Soils (Mark 4:16-17).

Further, having asked his hypothetical question about those who fall away (v. 4-6), then clarifying it with the illustration of the worthless field (v. 7-8), our author immediately issues a disclaimer assuring his readers that he does not believe either of these portrayals accurately describes them (v. 9-10). On the contrary, he expresses confidence of "better things" from them, indeed such things as accompany or go together with *salvation*. Falling away is not something that goes with salvation. It accompanies an unregenerate state. People who enjoy salvation are accompanied—as his readers are—by ongoing good works, love for God and service to others (v. 9-10; Hebrews 10:32-34).

Finally, this epistle closes (followed only by personal greetings) with this stirring benediction: "Now may the God of peace, who brought up from the dead our Lord Jesus, the great Shepherd of the sheep, through the blood of the everlasting covenant, equip you with everything good to do his will, working in us that which is pleasing in his sight, through Jesus Christ, to whom be glory forever and ever. Amen." (Hebrews 13:20-21).

The everlasting covenant is the "new covenant" which our author will discuss in chapter 8. It is God's arrangement for saving his people through the life and death of Jesus Christ as their representative. Jesus lived his earthly life of faithful obedience to God and offered that life to the Father in his body on the cross. God approved of Jesus and his offering, and he displayed his approval by raising Jesus from the dead and awarding him the place of honor at his own right hand in heaven.

Because God views Jesus' people through the life and death of Jesus their representative, he accepts and receives them exactly as he accepts and receives Jesus himself. Based on this covenant, God has bound himself to empower his people and to produce in them lives that please him. It is certainly not pleasing to God for any who belong to Jesus to fall away, to denounce the Savior and lose their salvation. As certainly as God is faithful to his everlasting covenant, therefore, it is just as certain that no one who belongs to Jesus will ever be found in that situation. (See also John Piper, "When is Saving Repentance Impossible?" Sermon for October 13, 1996, at www.desiringgod.org.)

transformation and the charitable deeds that accompany salvation. His readers have manifested such lives and works before. The author encourages them to persevere now and not to drop out.

6:10 God is not unjust. He will remember every detail of work performed out of love for him, every deed of service to fellow-believers. The original readers had served their brothers and sisters before, and they are still serving when the author writes them this sermon (see 10:32-34).

6:11 Our author wants all his readers to continue serving God with the same diligence that has marked their lives until the present. A strong assurance that Jesus has made one welcome in God's presence produces energetic faithfulness. In turn, diligence in serving God corresponds to that assurance and confirms that is effective. Throughout this sermon, the author repeatedly warns of the danger of stopping short and encourages perseverance to avoid that situation.

6:12 Rather than becoming sluggish ("dull" in Hebrews 5:11), the readers are encouraged to imitate the faithful perseverance of those who went before them. God's people have always been commended for their faith, which manifests itself in trusting reliance and perseverance.

HEBREWS 6:13-20

God's Double Seals Guarantee His Promise

[13] For when God made a promise to Abraham, because he had no one greater to swear by, he swore by himself, [14] saying,

"I will surely bless you and multiply you."

[15] And so Abraham, having patiently waited, obtained the promise.

[16] Men swear by someone greater than themselves, and an oath given for confirmation puts an end to every dispute. [17] In the same way, when God wanted to show even more clearly to the heirs of the promise the unchangeable character of his purpose, he confirmed it with an oath, [18] so that by two unchangeable things, in which it is impossible for God to lie, we who have fled for refuge might have strong encouragement to hold fast to the hope set before us. [19] We have this hope as a sure and steadfast anchor of the soul, one that enters the inner sanctuary behind the curtain, [20] where Jesus has entered as a forerunner for us, having become a high priest forever according to the order of Melchizedek.

WHY & WHEREFORE

Now our author points to Abraham as an example of patient waiting. God confirmed his promise to Abraham with an oath, providing

110

double assurance—his trustworthy word underscored by his oath—that he would fulfill what he promised. We have the same basis for confidence based on "our man in heaven," Jesus our high priest. As our representative, he perfectly pleased the Father in our name; now he invites us to approach the Father in his name.

This relationship we have with Jesus—the *man* with whom God is thoroughly pleased—provides strong encouragement for us to hold fast to our hope and follow through.

God appointed Jesus as high priest of a particular kind—"according to the order of *Melchizedek*." And, as we will see in the next chapter, God not only gave his word that he would receive Jesus' people because Jesus perfectly pleased him in their stead. God also underscored his determination with an *oath.* Psalm 110:4 reports in advance for all posterity the Father's oath to the Son: "The Lord has sworn and *will not change his mind; '*You are a priest *forever,* according to the order of Melchizedek."

UNPACKING THE TEXT

God's Reinforced Promise

6:13 God made many promises to Abraham on various occasions. Here our author refers to God's promise to Abraham after he began to offer Isaac and was stopped by God (Genesis 22:15-17a). God swore to be true, on his own honor. Because there was no person anywhere greater than God by whom he could swear, so God swore on his own reputation and honor.

6:14 The Hebrew text of the Genesis passage uses an idiom which simply means "I will surely bless you and multiply you." God also promised that Abraham's descendants would occupy their enemies' territories and that through Abraham's descendants he would bless the world (Genesis 22:17b-18). Those promises do not interest our author at this time.

6:15 So it was, in this manner, that Abraham patiently waited. By waiting, he eventually obtained the promise of Isaac's birth and the beginning of his posterity. Although Abraham died without seeing everything that God had promised, he died in faith, fully confident that what God had promised he would perform (Hebrews 11:13, 39).

6:16 Human society respects a formal oath, made in the name of God or in the name of someone or something greater than the one swearing. Among men, an oath serves two purposes. Negatively, it puts an end to strife or dispute. Once an oath is taken, there is nothing more to say. Positively, it confirms. When someone signs a jurat (a written oath) or raises his or her hand and is placed under oath, there is nothing more that person can do to provide assurance of truthfulness. (For a summary of judicial oath practice in the Greco-Roman world, see Worley, "Fleeing to Two Immutable Things, God's Oath-Taking and Oath-Witnessing . . .")

6:17 God confirmed his promise to Abraham by an oath to show or demonstrate to the heirs of promise the unchangeableness of his own character, and therefore of his counsel or purpose and design as well.

Reason for encouragement

6:18 God doubly ensured his promise by two things that are unchallengeable and incontrovertible. He gave his word—and God cannot lie. He gave his oath--taken in his own name, formally putting his honor at stake. Any human viewing the situation can draw strong encouragement and confidence from God's promise to Abraham and later to Jesus.

When we sin, we need not lose hope. That is the occasion for crying out in hope to God, claiming the salvation which Jesus accomplished for sinners. The adjective "strong" is emphatic here. Believers in Jesus can appreciate such strength, because in their own weakness they have "fled for refuge" to the merciful and all-powerful Son of God. The Greek Old Testament uses the same word for a fugitive fleeing to the cities of refuge. Unlike the ancient Jewish fugitive who found safety in a city of refuge, believers are not waiting for a high priest to die. Jesus is our high priest and he lives forever—after the order of Melchizedek. By his twice-sure word of promise, God encourages every true believer to cling to the hope inspired by his promises and to wait patiently for their fulfillment.

His oath moves us to sing:

> "The God of Abraham praise, who reigns enthroned above; . . .
> He by himself hath sworn: I on His oath depend; . . .
> I shall behold his face, I shall his pow'r adore,
> And sing the wonders of his grace for evermore."

(From *The Yigdal* of Daniel ben Judah, ca. 1400;
Paraphrased by Thomas Olivers, ca. 1765.)

6:19 This hope is the soul's anchor—both sure or unfailing and stead-fast. In stormy seas, a ship's giant anchor provides stability and inspires confidence. We can have strong confidence in our hope's object, which is firmly secured within the true and heavenly Most Holy Place. In both the tabernacle and the Temple, that holiest compartment was located "behind the curtain" that separated it from the Holy Place. Only the high priest entered this inner sanctum, and only on one day each year—on *Yom Kippur,* the solemn Day of Atonement.

The earthly sanctuaries symbolized God's presence, which no *man* could enter unhidden and expect to live. For that reason the high priest entered the Most Holy Place shrouded by a cloud of incense smoke. How-ever, the *man* Jesus Christ has gone into the heavenly sanctuary where he now sits in honor in God's immediate presence.

6:20 Into this heavenly sanctuary, hallowed by God's personal presence, Jesus our "forerunner" has already entered (Hebrews 4:14). The Greek word translated "forerunner" sometimes referred to a scout, an advance person who led the way (see notes on "source" at Hebrews 5:9). Jesus has entered into God's presence *for* us, as our high priest. He has also entered into heaven *before* or in front of us, as our forerunner. He is both the object and the model of our faith. By his own persistent faith he opened the path into heaven. His entrance there guarantees that the way is clear for us to follow in persistent faith of the same sort as his.

HEBREWS 7:1-3

Melchizedek and Abraham: The Encounter

[1] For this Melchizedek, king of Salem, priest of the Most High God, who met Abraham returning from the slaughter of the kings and blessed him, [2] to him Abraham gave a tenth part of everything. First his name means "king of righteousness," and then also king of Salem, meaning "king of peace." [3] Without father, without mother, without genealogy, having neither beginning of days nor end of life but resembling the Son of God, he remains a priest forever.

WHY & WHEREFORE

As we come to this discussion of Melchizedek, we are like a mountaineer who is nearing the very summit of his range. No other character in the history of humankind is more honored by comparison with the Son of God made man. Yet, strangely, we know almost nothing about this ancient priest-king whose unique ministry is memorialized forever in the priesthood of Jesus who will never die. We first meet Melchizedek about 2,000 B.C.. in what appears to be a chance encounter with the great patriarch Abraham, then known as Abram. The details are reminiscent of a worship service in a liturgical church. Melchizedek produces bread and wine which presumably they share. He then pronounces a blessing over Abraham, who responds by giving Melchizedek a tithe. Then like a phantom, Melchizedek disappears. Scripture does not mention him again for another thousand years.

The next time we meet Melchizedek he is sitting silently in a single verse of the Psalms, written by David in approximately 1,000 B.C. In this verse the psalmist quotes God saying to someone:

> "The Lord has sworn
> and will not change his mind;
> 'You are a priest forever
> according to the order of Melchizedek'"
> (Psalm 110:4; LXX 109:4).

The psalmist does not identify the person to whom God says these words. For a biblical identification we must wait 1,000 years more, when another unidentified person writes this epistle that we call "Hebrews." Finally we get our answer: The person whom God designated "priest forever according to the order of Melchizedek" was none other than the Messiah—the Christ (Hebrews 5:5-6)—the *man* Jesus of Nazareth (Hebrews 5:7, 10; 6:20). Our author will name Melchizedek five more times in chapter seven (Hebrews 7:1, 10, 11, 15, 17). And with that, Scripture pulls the shades on Melchizedek and never mentions him again.

UNPACKING THE TEXT

Melchizedek the Mysterious

7:1 The Bible mentions Melchizedek in only three passages (Genesis 14, Psalm 110 and Hebrews 5-7). But he was very much a subject of Jewish speculation. Josephus makes Melchizedek the founder of temple worship in Jerusalem, while Philo associates him with reason and virtue. Some rabbinic traditions identify Melchizedek as Noah's son Shem; one rabbinic source has him conveying the priesthood to Abraham.

One of the Dead Sea Scrolls presents him as an End-Time figure who proclaims God's year of Jubilee in fulfillment of Isaiah 61:1ff and releases the debt of sin by forgiving the people (11QMelch). The scroll does not refer to Genesis 14 or Psalm 110, however, and it does not identify Melchizedek as a priest. A pseudepigraphal work perhaps written between Malachi and Matthew makes Melchizedek a descendant of Noah who perpetuates a priestly line (2 Enoch 71-72). If our author was familiar with any of these traditions he clearly does not follow them in his own discussion.

Scripture presents Melchizedek as the priest-king of the Jebusite city-state of Salem, an ancient name for Jerusalem (see Psalm 76:2), and a contemporary of Abraham (ca. 2,000 B.C.). A millennium later (ca. 1,000 B.C.) David conquered the Jebusites and made their city his capital of a united Israel (see comments at 12:22).

Melchizedek is priest of the "Most High God" *(El Elyon)*. Although this Hebrew term was also the name of a Canaanite god, it is reasonable to believe that Melchizedek served the God of Abraham. Indeed, Abraham recognized Melchizedek's God as his own (Genesis 14:22).

Bread & Wine, Blessing, Tithe

Genesis 14 relates the encounter between Abraham and Melchizedek. Abraham and his private militia of 318 fighting men are returning home with their booty after rescuing Lot and other captives from a confederation of four Canaanite warlords. These chieftains had recently attacked and plundered five other city-states in the region, including Lot's hometown of Sodom. As Abraham's entourage passes by the mountainous city of Salem, its priest-king Melchizedek comes out personally to greet them, bringing bread and wine. Acting in his priestly role, Melchizedek then honors Abraham with a sacred blessing.

7:2 Abraham responds by giving Melchizedek a tenth of all his spoils of battle and continues on his way home. This unplanned rendezvous of patriarch and priest passed largely unnoticed in its own day. However, it was destined to gain enormous significance 2,000 years later when the author of Hebrews would depict Melchizedek's unique priesthood as a Christian archetype for the priesthood of Jesus Christ.

Melchizedek's Priesthood

Our author now analyzes the separate components of Melchizedek's name. While this strikes our Western minds as odd and perhaps even dangerous, it was not an unusual way to interpret Scripture when Hebrews was written. The Jewish apologist Philo followed a similar approach, as did several later Christian theologians from Alexandria in Egypt, notably Clement and Origen.

The name "Melchizedek" combines two Hebrew words that mean "king" and "righteousness" respectively. Together they suggest "king of righteousness," a concept our author spotted earlier in Psalm 45:6-7 and handily applied to Jesus (Hebrews 1:8-9). In Genesis, Melchizedek wears the title "king of Salem" (from *shalom,* the well-known Hebrew word for "peace"). In Hebrew idiom, to describe a sovereign as "king of righteousness" and "king of peace" is to call him a righteous and peaceful king.

It is tantalizing to consider that Melchizedek has a Semitic name although he lives in Salem of the Jebusites. The Jebusites were non-Semitic descendants of Ham whose language was related to Hittite (Genesis 10:6, 15-16). This raises the interesting possibility that Melchizedek himself was of a different race from the residents of Salem whom he served as priest and king. If that were the situation, his priesthood becomes even more mystifying.

What is certain is that Melchizedek's priesthood was wholly unlike that of the Levitical priesthood in Israel. The Jewish priest held his office based on family tree, prescribed term and physical examination. Melchizedek's priesthood depended on none of those factors, but rather rested solely in his moral character. He was a man of the sort people believed God would hear. Our author turns our thoughts in that direction now with verse three.

7:3 So far as Scripture tells us, no fleshly relative of Melchizedek served in his priesthood—either before him or after. How unlike the Jewish priests, who had to establish their genealogy to qualify for service! (Nehemiah 7:63-64; Ezekiel 44:22). This man neither received his office by hereditary right nor passed it on to a physical descendant. In terms of his *priesthood,* he was "without father, without mother, without genealogy."

The Levitical priests by law served from age 25-50 and not a day less or more (Numbers 8:23-25), Melchizedek's priesthood had no threshold age upon which he entered it ("no beginning of days") and no mandatory retirement age requiring his exit from it ("nor end of [priestly] life"). Lacking any limitations of age, Melchizedek remains a priest forever. Our author does not use the phrase normally translated as "forever." He rather uses a word that means "for the duration," "perpetually," or "without interruption."

'Resembling the Son of God'

Throughout Christian history some interpreters have considered Melchizedek to be more than a mere man—perhaps even an incarnation of the Son of God. Yet our author does not develop that notion and the points which he does develop do not require it (Koester, 339-340; Attridge, 191-193). Every specific statement about Melchizedek in these verses can be understood adequately and legitimately in terms of his priesthood as a mortal man.

In this matter of personal immortality, Melchizedek differed from Jesus. Later in this chapter our author will explain, step-by-step, the specific causal relationships between Jesus' moral character, his indestructible life, his permanent priesthood and his ability to "save forever" all those who approach God through him.

Many facets of Melchizedek's priesthood remain a mystery after 4,000 years. His priesthood had no known date of origin or time of termination. It involved no priestly family tree. Its only foundation was the moral character of the man himself, although he was also a sinful mortal who finally died. But there is absolutely no mystery concerning his spiritual dignity and greatness, as our author will demonstrate next.

HEBREWS 7:4-14

Melchizedek and Abraham: The Implications

[4] Consider how great he was, to whom even Abraham the patriarch gave a tenth of the spoils. [5] And those descendants of Levi who receive the priestly office have a commandment in the law to collect tithes from the people, that is, from their brothers, though these are descended from Abraham. [6] But this man, whose genealogy is not traced from them, collected tithes from Abraham and blessed him who had the promises. [7] It is beyond dispute that the lesser is blessed by the greater. [8] In the one case, mortal men receive tithes, but in the other case, one of whom it is testified that he lives. [9] One might even say that Levi himself, who receives tithes, paid tithes through Abraham [10] (for he was still in the loins of his father when Melchizedek met him).

[11] Now if perfection could have been attained through the Levitical priesthood (for under it the people received the law), what further need was there for another priest to arise according to the order of Melchizedek, rather than according to the order of Aaron? [12] For when there is a change of the priesthood, there is necessarily a change also in the law. [13] For the one of whom these things are spoken belonged to another tribe, from which no one has ever served at the altar. [14] For it is evident that our Lord was descended from Judah, of which tribe Moses said nothing about priests.

WHY & WHEREFORE

Because Melchizedek *blessed* Abraham and Abraham gave a *tithe* to Melchizedek, our author concludes that Melchizedek held a position superior to Abraham. Melchizedek's position was also superior to the positions of unborn Levi and his unborn priestly descendants—all of whom were represented in the proceedings that day through their ancestor Abraham.

God gave his people the priesthood before he gave them the Law. When the Law was given, and the people broke it, the priesthood and its sacrifices were there waiting to provide forgiveness. Neither the Law nor the priesthood could make anyone perfect by removing the memory of sin from their minds and from God's. That remained for Jesus to accomplish—as a priest of the kind like Melchizedek. And that technicality required a change in the Law that regulated priests. The Law said that priests must come from Levi's tribe, but Jesus descended from Judah.

UNPACKING THE TEXT

Levi's Tithes

7:4 We know what happened that day when Abraham and Melchizedek met. But what does it signify to us? To understand that, our author asks us to consider Melchizedek's greatness as compared to Abraham. We read that Abraham gave a tithe or tenth of his war spoils to Melchizedek. This was not just any "Abraham," mind you. It was the very patriarch himself. Nor was his tithe some mediocre or second-rate portion of the booty. It was the choicest tenth of all, literally "off the top of the heap."

7:5 The Law of Moses provides for Levi's priestly descendants to receive tithes from their fellow-Israelites. Jews who read this provision understand from it that the Levites enjoy a privileged position, even though all the tribes trace their ancestry from Abraham.

7:6 Melchizedek's genealogy is not only unremarkable. It is entirely unknown. Under the later Mosaic law, he would have enjoyed no legal status or standing requiring anyone to pay him tithes. Yet he collected a tenth from Abraham. Not a tenth from some anonymous traveler or common stranger, but from Abraham. What is more, Melchizedek the priest then blessed Abraham—the very Abraham who on more than one occasion received special promises from God.

7:7 We all recognize that an individual holding lower position is blessed by one of higher position. Abraham was blessed by Melchizedek so it follows that Melchizedek was a "better" man than the patriarch in terms of rank and office. Melchizedek acknowledged this relative position by blessing Abraham. Abraham acknowledged it by paying tithes to Melchizedek.

7:8 In the case of the Levitical priesthood, mortal men who must eventually have a successor receive tithes (Numbers 18:21-28). In Melchizedek's case, one received them who had no successor.

7:9 Through his priestly descendants, Levi received tithes from his Jewish brothers. However, even Levi paid tithes to Melchizedek through the person of his grandfather Abraham.

7:10 If someone points out that Levi was not even born when Abraham met Melchizedek, our author observes that Levi was nevertheless present genetically (to use our word for it) in the physical body of his great-grandfather Abraham on that occasion. Just as Levi *received* tithes in the person of his priestly descendants, so he *paid* tithes in the person of his ancestor Abraham. As forefather of the Levitical priests, Levi's spiritual act of subordination (through Abraham) to Melchizedek also signified the superiority of Melchizedek's priesthood over the Levitical priesthood.

Change the System

7:11 If the Levitical priesthood could have achieved perfection (an important word in Hebrews) there would have been no further need for another priest (Jesus) after a different order (Melchizedek's, not Aaron's). The purpose of a priesthood is to remove impediments that block fellowship between the people and God. The weakness of the Levitical sacrifices and priesthood was that they could not bring about this result. That regime had to be replaced by a perfect order which could fulfill these purposes.

Our author notes that the law depended on the priesthood, although we might easily assume the opposite. Law cannot make people good—it can only tell them what "good" looks like. Because people always break law, it also points them to the reality of sin and to the fact that they are sinners. With this recognition, people turn to the priesthood with its sacrifices as the divine provision for removing sins. The priesthood provided a foundation for the law.

It was always God's plan to designate a better kind of priest who would offer a greater and more effective sacrifice for sin. This sacrifice would "perfect" God's people forever (Hebrews 10:14), an accomplishment which neither the Levitical priesthood (Hebrews 7:11) nor the Mosaic Law (Hebrews 7:19) was able to bring about.

7:12 Levitical priesthood was changed to make room for a priest after the order of Melchizedek. This perfect priest, foretold in Psalm 110:4, serves in a perfect priesthood whose sacrifice also perfects his people.

7:13-14 Our author is speaking about Jesus Christ as the next verse will state, and he belongs to the tribe of Judah, not of Levi. It is clear that under the Law of Moses, no one from the tribe of Judah ever served at the priestly altar. Jesus' genealogies (Matthew 1; Luke 3) reveal that he descended from Judah, a tribe about which the Law of Moses said absolutely nothing concerning priestly service or appointment.

Jesus' Perfect Life Secures God's Oath

[15] And this becomes even clearer if another priest arises in the likeness of Melchizedek, [16] who has become a priest, not on the basis of a legal requirement concerning physical descent, but by the power of an indestructible life. [17] For it is attested of him,

"You are a priest forever, according to the order of Melchizedek."

[18] For, on the one hand, there is a setting aside of a former commandment because it was weak and useless [19] (for the law made nothing perfect), but on the other hand there is a bringing in of a better hope, through which we draw near to God. [20] And it was not without an oath. For others became priests without an oath, [21] but he with an oath by the one who said to him:

"The Lord has sworn
and will not change his mind;
'You are a priest forever.'"

[22] So Jesus has also become the guarantee of a better covenant.

WHY & WHEREFORE

Jesus is not called a priest according to the order of *Judah* (his tribe), but according to the order of *Melchizedek.* Under the Levitical system, one qualified as priest on the basis of bloodline, birth date and a flawless body. Jesus qualified as a priest like Melchizedek on the basis of moral character, a quality of life that merited God's approval and won unbroken access to his immediate presence.

In his human body, the *man* Jesus lived a flawless and faithful life. Unstained by sin, Jesus could not be held by death. Because God appointed Jesus as priest based on his sinless (therefore "indestructible") life, God could solemnly swear that Jesus would be priest *forever* and know that he would never change his mind.

UNPACKING THE TEXT

An Indestructible Life

7:15-17 Both the priesthood and the law that regulates it have been changed, most importantly regarding the quality and qualifications of its priest. That a change has occurred has become even clearer since Jesus is not from the tribe of Levi, a fact that would immediately prevent any priestly appointment to the Levitical priesthood as regulated by the Mosaic Law. Jesus is an *other* kind of priest. His priesthood does not resemble that of the Levitical priests at all. Instead, it is "after the likeness of Melchizedek."

Jesus' priesthood is independent of any legal requirement concerning physical ancestry. It is based instead on the moral power or dynamic of a life that will never break down. The Levitical priests were selected by virtue of a legal technicality that had nothing to do with their character or personal morality. In contrast to that, God selected Jesus to be priest according to the order of Melchizedek because Jesus possesses an inherent power—an attribute of Jesus himself, inherent in his righteous person, that fits him for that position. Unlike any Levitical priest who ever lived, Jesus possesses within himself the power of an indestructible life (Acts 2:24).

Although Jesus was thoroughly tempted, he never yielded to sin. Because Jesus was without sin, Satan could not hold him in death (see comments at 2:14). Sin is the means through which death gains power over humankind—including the Levitical priests who all died. A sinless life has no point of weakness; for that reason Jesus' priesthood is firmly grounded in the inherent power of a life that will never end. Our author will return to this wonderful thought a bit later in verse 25. The messianic proclamation of Psalm 110:4, which our author has discussed earlier, confirms our author's present point when it says: "You are a priest forever according to the order of Melchizedek."

7:18-19 Our author frames these two verses by two tiny words in Greek that mean "on the one hand/on the other hand." First he mentions the setting aside or disannulling of a previous commandment regulating priests because it was inherently weak and useless or unprofitable (see also vs. 5, 16). The former legal system regulating priests was weak and ineffective because it could not bring perfection (v. 11), its regulations of priestly qualifications were physically based (v. 16) and it produced weak and imperfect priests (vs. 27-28).

The Mosaic Law made nothing perfect—not worshipers, not priests—because the priesthood it provided could not perfect (Hebrews 7:11). God has now provided a better hope through the doing, dying and exalting of Jesus Christ (Hebrews 6:18-20).

This hope actually enables us to approach God with confidence. When God gave Israel the Law at Sinai, he specifically ordered the people *not* to "draw near." The Greek Old Testament expresses that prohibition with the same verb used here (LXX Exodus 19:21). The contrast reflects a change in the grounds of access. Israel was forbidden to approach God because they all were sinners who never conformed to God's desire for faithful, loving lives. Those who approach God through Jesus Christ may do so freely, based on Jesus' offering to God on their behalf. That offering was the sacrifice and presentation of a human life that pleased God in every way, the life of one who lived and died as the representative of his people.

Priest By an Oath

7:20-22 Jesus' priestly appointment, ratified by God's divine oath, greatly surpassed the oathless appointment of the Levitical priests in dignity and intensity. Similarly, the covenant (or arrangement of relationships) of which Jesus himself personally is God's guarantee, exceeds in certainty and permanence the covenant represented by those priests.

Indeed, Jesus did not became priest without an oath, although those other priests descended from Levi were inaugurated without any oath by God whatsoever. As evidence, our author again calls on Psalm 110:4 which he cited just above to confirm that Jesus is a priest *forever* (vs. 15-17). This verse from the messianic Psalm 110 also attests that Yahweh has *sworn* to Jesus and will never change his mind for having told him: "You are a priest forever."

The older English versions said that God "will not repent," introducing unnecessary confusion since by nature God cannot sin. The majority of contemporary versions more accurately say that God "will not change his mind." The verb so translated, which our author copies directly from Psalm 110:4 (LXX 109:4), is not the word normally translated as "repent," which also refers to a general change of mind. This verb is more specific and emphasizes the thought of remorse involving a change in affection.

Another form of the same verb root describes God's reaction to the Israelites who broke his covenant ("disregarded" in Hebrews 8:9). God will never change his mind about Jesus' priesthood based on remorse or because of some afterthought or later concern. This is an important declaration because in the past God has taken back his gift of a permanent priesthood for that exact reason.

That situation is described in 1 Samuel 2:27-36. God sends an unnamed prophet to Eli, the elderly priest and judge, with his message that can be paraphrased like this. "I did choose the house of your ancestors Levi and Aaron to be my priests," God acknowledges, "and I promised them the priesthood forever. But that was before your wicked sons came along and disgraced the very office of priest by their thoroughly evil character." Eli's immoral sons have filled God with remorse and regret that he promised their ancestors his priesthood permanently. "Now I have changed my mind," God informs Eli. "The day will come when none of your descendants will be serving as my priests. In their place, I will find myself some faithful priests who take seriously the moral obligation of their office."

Jesus' Priesthood is Secure

This story will never be repeated with Jesus. Indeed, God has not only declared him to be priest *forever;* he has underscored that declaration with an oath. Eli's sons were priests by accident of birth without regard for personal character. Jesus was selected as priest precisely because of his personal character. His priesthood is grounded in his life-record of faithful, loving obedience to God—his desire and determination to *do God's will* in his human body every new "today" that came.

Jesus' priesthood rests not on a family tree or some legal term. It rests on his holy character and his obedient life. From the beginning, his priesthood has been energized and sustained by the inherent dynamic of an *indestructible life.* For that reason Jesus' priesthood is permanent—Jesus is priest *forever.* God declared it to be so, swearing to it by his own name and honor. And precisely because all the above is true, God is certain that he will never change his mind!

Because God's appraisal of Jesus is fixed and he will never have second thoughts on the subject, Jesus has become the guarantee of a better covenant. The word translated "guarantee," "guarantor" and "surety" is a noun form of the verb translated "draw near" in verse 19. Jesus' faithful life (that opens the door and invites us to draw near to God) will never change and will never fail. Nor will God change his mind about that life, which Jesus gave as an offering in his body on the cross, as we have just seen. Jesus is therefore himself the guarantee of God's covenant.

By his own presence in heaven, the risen and exalted Jesus guarantees that God has accepted his perfect sacrifice made once for all time. Jesus perfected his sacrifice in his living, performed it in his dying, and presented it in his resurrection and exaltation—all on behalf of his people and as their representative. Jesus' presence in heaven now guarantees his people full access to God through him. Because Jesus' people relate to God, and because God relates to them, through the very Jesus who lived and died as representative of them both to the other, Jesus is also the guarantee of the covenant or relationship arrangement which is both new and better than any arrangement that has ever existed before.

The word "covenant" (or "testament") appears here for the first time in Hebrews, and our author will discuss it in the chapters that follow. Throughout the Bible this word regularly refers to a one-sided arrangement of relationship between God and someone he chooses to bless. It never refers to a bargain between God and humans made as if between equals.

HEBREWS 7:23-28

Jesus Lives Forever to Save Forever

²³ The former priests were many in number, because they were prevented by death from continuing in office. ²⁴ But he holds his priesthood permanently because he continues forever. ²⁵ Therefore he is able to save forever those who come to God through him, since he always lives to make intercession for them.

²⁶ Such a high priest was fitting for us: holy, innocent, undefiled, separated from sinners, exalted above the heavens. ²⁷ Unlike those high priests, he does not need daily to offer sacrifices, first for his own sins and then for those of the people. He did this once for all when he offered himself. ²⁸ For the law appoints as high priests men who are weak; but the word of the oath, which came after the law, appoints the Son, who has been made perfect forever.

WHY & WHEREFORE

All Levitical priests needed replacements because they all eventually died. Jesus lives forever with a permanent priesthood. Because the ever-living Jesus always intercedes for his people, he forever *saves* and he saves *forever.* Jesus is exactly the high priest we need—one appointed because of his sinless character and constant obedience, now exalted by God in honor at his own right hand.

The Mosaic Law provided an imperfect priesthood. That priesthood presented imperfect sacrifices. Those sacrifices resulted in imperfect people. When all this imperfection had become undeniably clear, God provided another priest, a perfect priest—Jesus, the Son of God made *man.* As his single sacrifice, given once for all time, he offered himself—the only human who ever lived who could present to the Father the gift of a faithful and flawless life.

UNPACKING THE TEXT

A Permanent Priest

7:23 The Levitical priests who served under the Mosaic Law were numerous because they all died and had to be replaced. Although their anointing was said to admit them into a perpetual priesthood, each individual participated only during his generation (Exodus 40:15). The first-century Jewish historian Josephus says that 83 high priests officiated from Aaron to the destruction of the Temple in A.D. 70. Our writer simply observes that they all died.

7:24 By contrast, Jesus continues forever and holds his priesthood permanently. Because he will never die, he will never require a replacement or successor.

7:25 For this reason Jesus is able to save forever. "Forever" here translates a prepositional phrase in Greek that sometimes designates *extent* (completely, fully, wholly) and sometimes designates *time* (forever, for all time). Both ideas fit here. Jesus mediates this complete and eternal salvation for all that come to God through him.

Jesus made only one sacrifice for sins, but he always lives to make intercession on the basis of that sacrifice. He prepared that sacrifice by living a faithful life. He performed that sacrifice by giving his body (himself) as an offering on the cross in the shedding of his blood. He presented that sacrifice to God in his blood (metaphorically) in heaven. Jesus now applies the benefits of that sacrifice by interceding for his people.

Those who come to God through Jesus Christ rest their right standing with God and all that it involves on the perfect obedience, vicarious death, mighty resurrection and glorious ascension of Jesus their high priest. As high priest, Jesus represents his people and he carries their names over his heart (Exodus 28:29-30).

The Priest We Need

7:26 Jesus is just the kind of high priest human beings need. He is holy, innocent, undefiled and separated from sinners. Indeed, those are the very qualities that qualified him to be high priest after the order of Melchizedek. Jesus is exalted above the skies at God's right hand in heaven, where he makes intercession for his people.

7:27 Jesus does not need to offer a sacrifice daily or for himself. Instead he offered himself once for all time. His self-offering was the offering of a human life perfectly pleasing to God. A perfect offering needed to be offered only once.

7:28 The law regulating the Old Testament priesthood appointed men as high priests who were physically spotless but morally weak. In contrast to this, God fulfilled his oath by making the Son a priest—and he is perfect forever.

The beautiful images that make Hebrews 6:13-7:28 so powerful also find expression in the following hymn, written by Edward Mote in 1834.

> My hope is built on nothing less
> Than Jesus' blood and righteousness.
> I dare not trust the sweetest frame,
> But wholly trust in Jesus' Name.
>
> When darkness seems to hide his face,
> I rest on his unchanging grace.
> In every high and stormy gale,
> My anchor holds within the veil.
>
> His oath, his covenant, his blood,
> Support me in the whelming flood.
> When all around my soul gives way,
> He then is all my hope and stay.
>
> When he shall come with trumpet sound,
> O may I then in him be found.
> Dressed in his righteousness alone,
> Faultless to stand before the throne.
>
> *Refrain:*
> *On Christ the solid rock I stand,*
> *All other ground is sinking sand;*
> *All other ground is sinking sand.*

HEBREWS 8:1-6

Our High Priest Is in Heaven

[1] Now the main point of what we are saying is this: we have such a high priest, one who sat down at the right hand of the throne of the Majesty in the heavens, [2] a minister in the sanctuary and the true tabernacle that the Lord set up, and not man. [3] For every high priest is appointed to offer gifts and sacrifices; so it is necessary for this priest also to have something to offer. [4] Now if he were on earth, he would not be a priest, since there are priests who offer the gifts according to the law. [5] They serve as a copy and shadow of the heavenly things, as Moses was warned when he was about to erect the tabernacle: "See that you make everything according to the pattern shown you on the mountain." [6] But now Jesus has obtained a more excellent ministry, and to that degree he is the mediator of a better covenant, which is enacted on better promises.

WHY & WHEREFORE

Of all that can be said on the subject, this is the highlight and conclusion: *Jesus Christ is exactly the kind of high priest we need, and he is working for us in heaven.* Holy, innocent and without sin, he is perfectly pleasing to God who appointed him for that very reason. At the same time, he is *man*, one of us, experienced in our temptations and struggles and perfectly able to understand every difficulty we encounter.

Jesus is also the mediator of God's new covenant, the arrangement of relationship between God and his people. In this new relationship, everyone knows God personally, God writes his laws in their hearts and he forgives and forgets their sins.

UNPACKING THE TEXT

A Heavenly Priest

8:1 Rarely does a biblical writer conclude a discussion by specifically identifying the "main point" of what he has just said, but our author does that here. (The word translated "main point" can also refer to a summary or a heading, inappropriate in this context, or to a main point or conclusion, which both do fit.) The main point and conclusion is that Jesus Christ is the exact high priest just described, that he occupies a position of enormous influence with God in the heavenly sanctuary where, at this very moment, he is working on our behalf. His presence at God's right hand in heaven fulfills Psalm 110:1, and that scene of the Son of God so honored dominated the first chapter of Hebrews (Hebrews 1:3, 13). "The Majesty" is a reverent euphemism for God.

8:2 Jesus' presence in heaven is related directly to his ministry as our high priest. There by God's own appointment, Jesus is minister (literally "public servant," from which comes our word "liturgy") in the heavenly sanctuary (literally "holies"). This is the "true" or authentic tent, later contrasted with the tabernacle (Hebrews 9:24) that was constructed by God and not by man.

8:3 High priests are appointed to offer gifts and sacrifices (Hebrews 5:1), and Jesus is no exception. Our author told us in the previous chapter that Jesus offered himself (7:27) and that as high priest he is "holy, innocent, undefiled." As sacrifice, Jesus was all those things as well, which our author later sums up by saying that Jesus offered himself "without blemish" (9:14).

8:4 It is significant for many reasons that Jesus' priesthood is in heaven. Indeed, if he were on the earth he could not be a priest at all, because there are other people who have that job and who offer sacrifices as required by the law. This statement is the first part of a contrast that our author will complete in verse six, as indicated by two Greek words here and in verse six meaning "on the one hand" and "on the other hand."

A Heavenly Sanctuary

8:5 The Levitical priests minister on earth in a system based on and even copied from the heavenly order. The heavenly system is the true, substantial and original one. The earthly tabernacle, ordinances, high priests and rituals were shadows and copies of the heavenly counterparts.

We see this in God's instructions to Moses about building the sanctuary on earth. God admonished Moses to make all things according to the pattern (literally something struck from a die or stamp) which he was shown in the mountain (Exodus 25:40). Rabbinical lore included a story about the Archangel Gabriel coming down from heaven dressed in a workman's apron with models of the tabernacle furniture which he presented to Moses to copy. Scripture says only that Moses was shown a pattern by which he was instructed to build.

Our author and his original readers were impressed by the antiquity of competing religious systems. If his readers were tempted to turn from Jesus to Judaism because Moses' law predated Jesus' birth by more than a millennium, our author here notes that Jesus ministers in a heavenly sanctuary that existed before Moses. Further, Moses built his sanctuary by tracing the shadows of that older, heavenly sanctuary.

Some scholars have read these verses against a background of Platonic philosophy. However, we do not need to go that far for background material. One Jewish writer who lived just before Jesus had said to God concerning Solomon's temple: "You gave command to build a sanctuary in your holy mountain, and an altar in the city of your habitation; a copy of the holy tabernacle which you prepared previously from the beginning" (Wisdom of Solomon 9:8).

8:6 This verse completes "the other hand" of the contrast begun in verse four. Although Jesus cannot be high priest on earth, God has installed him in high-priestly ministry that far exceeds the earthly ministry that he could not enter. To the same extent, Jesus mediates a covenant that exceeds and surpasses the former covenant. His covenant rests on better promises than the promises supporting the Mosaic covenant.

Under the Mosaic covenant, God's continued blessings depended on the people's obedience to God's laws (Leviticus 26:3-12). Under the covenant that Jesus mediates and administers, God promises to bless his people because of Jesus' faithfulness as their representative. A pseudepigraphal writing known as the Testaments of the Twelve Patriarchs expressed one Jewish hope for a world-wide Messiah and the coming of a mediator who would intercede for the righteous (Testament of Dan 5-6). The Qumran community shared a similar dream, reflected in the Dead Sea Scrolls, that God would send either two or possibly three Messiahs to bless his people. Not even the most imaginative dreamer known to us anticipated a Messiah whose personal faithfulness to God would be unflawed.

Jesus Ensures 'New Covenant' Benefits

⁷ For if that first covenant had been faultless, there would have been no place for a second one. ⁸ But finding fault with them, he says:

> "Behold, the days are coming, says the Lord,
> when I will make a new covenant
> with the house of Israel and with the house of Judah—

> ⁹ "Not like the covenant that I made with their fathers,
> on the day when I took them by the hand
> to lead them out of the land of Egypt;
> for they did not continue in my covenant
> and I disregarded them," says the Lord.

> ¹⁰ "For this is the covenant that I will make
> with the house of Israel after those days," says the Lord:
> "I will put my laws in their minds, and write them on their hearts,
> and I will be their God, and they shall be my people.
> ¹¹ And they shall not teach each one his neighbor
> and each one his brother, saying, 'Know the Lord,'
> for they all will know me, from the least of them to the greatest.
> ¹² For I will be merciful to their iniquities,
> and I will remember their sins no more."

¹³ In speaking of a "new" covenant, he has made the first one obsolete. And what is obsolete and growing old is ready to disappear.

WHY & WHEREFORE

Through the prophet Jeremiah, God promised to make a new covenant or arrangement of relationship with his people in the future. Under that new arrangement, God promised that his people will know him personally, for he will be their teacher. He will write his laws in their minds and on their hearts and give them a new nature. When his people sin, under the new arrangement God will forgive them—and he will forget that the transgression ever occurred.

UNPACKING THE TEXT

Problem With the First Covenant

8:7 Clearly the first covenant or arrangement of relationship between God and his people was faulty, inadequate and came short of perfection, otherwise there would have been no place or room for a second arrangement. However, God long ago spoke of making a new covenant. The conclusion, our author says, is that the first covenant was faulty in some respect.

8:8 The problem with the first covenant was with the people: they did not fulfill their obligations under its arrangement. Covenant blessings depended on the people's faithfulness. Instead, they were disobedient and unfaithful. Because their faults could break the covenant, God promised through Jeremiah to establish a new covenant with his people that would avoid this problem (Jeremiah 31:31-34; LXX 38:31-34). Our author quotes this passage from Jeremiah from this point through verse 12. The Greek version of Jeremiah has God saying he will "covenant a new covenant." Here our author changes verbs to say that God will "finish" or "complete" or "fulfill" a new covenant (but in verse 10 he quotes the Septuagint's verb for the verb "to covenant").

Jeremiah prophesied during King Josiah's great reform (2 Kings 23). The people of Judah turned back to God after generations of disobedience and neglect. They capped the reformation with a great Passover celebration led by the king himself (2 Kings 23:21-23). Their zeal soon cooled, however, and the people forgot the promises they had made to God.

"New" signifies fresh in quality and not merely recent in time. (For "new" in a chronological sense, see Hebrews 12:24 which uses a different word.) Through the representative life (doing) and death (dying) of Jesus Christ, God established relationship with his people based on a new and fresh arrangement.

8:9 This new covenant will differ from the covenant that God had given to Israel at Sinai. Speaking through Jeremiah, God described his attention to little Israel in terms of a doting father and his still-wobbly toddler son. God took his people by the hand, he says, and led them out of the land of Egypt (see Hosea 11:1-3).

Despite God's tender love for Israel, his people did not respond in faithful obedience. And because the former covenant linked God's future blessings on the people's obedience, that covenant could not overcome their faulty and inadequate performance. Accordingly, God "disregarded" (the same Greek verb translated "neglect" in Hebrews 2:3) the people.

A New Kind of Covenant

God tells Jeremiah that his future covenant will surpass the former covenant in at least three significant ways. Our author calls attention to these three promises now in verses 10-12.

8:10 *Internal conformity will replace external compulsion.* Under the former covenant, God inscribed his laws on tablets of stone—"chains from without." Under the new covenant, God promises to write his laws on his people's hearts and place them in their minds—"change from within." Paul also contrasts this difference in the two covenants (2 Corinthians 3:1-18).

God gives his new-covenant people a new nature from above (John 3:1-16). This new nature, believers happily discover, corresponds to and agrees with everything that God wants his people to do and to become. Their fallen nature is still present and believers must continually be putting it to death. However, in their new nature they delight in the laws of God and find them perfectly suited to their higher inclinations. Believers have become partakers of the divine nature—to which nature God's laws are exactly suited.

8:11 *All God's people will know* him *and not just know* about *him.* Under the new covenant, all of God's people will know him personally. This promise is universal in scope and it has no exclusions or exceptions.

After the first generation of Israelites who personally experienced God's deliverance from Egypt, later Jews all learned about the God who had done exploits for their ancestors. Many people born within Israel grew up knowing about God, but not knowing God themselves. Under the new covenant everyone knows God because God himself is their savior and teacher (see John 6:44-45; Matthew 11:25-27).

8:12 *God will forgive sins and forget those sins when forgiven.* Under the new covenant, God will mercifully forgive his people's iniquities and forget their sins. Our author will discuss this in more detail in chapter 10.

8:13 Our author contemplates all that he has said and makes a final observation. Speaking through Jeremiah, God talked about a future covenant that he labeled "new." By contrast to that future "new" covenant, the covenant then in effect thus became "old" (our word "geriatric" is kin to this word) or even "obsolete" (the *paleo* part of "paleolithic"). And whatever is "obsolete" and getting "old" is ready to disappear. The old covenant, writes one commentator, is "tottering with senility" and is "like an old, old man who is sinking into his grave" (Lenski, 272).

HEBREWS 9:1–10

Rituals Couldn't Perfect the Conscience

[1] Now even the first covenant had regulations for worship and an earthly sanctuary. [2] For a tabernacle was prepared, and in the first part were the lampstand, the table, and the bread of the Presence. This is called the Holy Place. [3] Behind the second curtain was a part called the Most Holy Place, [4] having in it the golden altar of incense and the ark of the covenant covered with gold on all sides, in which there was a golden jar holding the manna, Aaron's rod that budded, and the tablets of the covenant. [5] Above it were the cherubim of glory overshadowing the mercy seat. Of these things we cannot speak now in detail. [6] When these things had been so prepared, the priests regularly entered the outer part of the tabernacle to perform their ritual duties. [7] But only the high priest entered into the second part, and he but once a year, not without taking blood, which he offered for himself and for the sins of the people committed in ignorance. [8] The Holy Spirit indicates that the way into the Most Holy Place had not yet been disclosed as long as the outer part was still standing. [9] This is a symbol for the present time, during which gifts and sacrifices are offered that cannot perfect the conscience of the worshiper, [10] but deal only with food and drink and various baptisms, physical regulations imposed until the time of reformation.

WHY & WHEREFORE

Under the Mosaic law, there was an earthly sanctuary with two compartments. The priests ministered in the first section. Only the high priest went into the second section, only on the Day of Atonement, and only carrying blood for his own sins and for the people's sins. The sacred furniture and fixtures in the sanctuary all pointed to the difference—and the distance—between sinful Israel and Israel's holy God.

UNPACKING THE TEXT

9:1 The first covenant involved numerous regulations for worship. These ritual details, the sacrifices they involved, the priests who offered the sacrifices and the tabernacle where they offered them all were part of the visible earthly system of worship under the first covenant. That system with all its arrangements symbolized an invisible heavenly system, a system now in operation through Jesus Christ, of which the former system was a copy.

An Outer Compartment

9:2 From the outside, the Mosaic Tabernacle looked like two tents fastened together in the shape of a rectangle, with the first larger tent providing access into the second smaller one. The first tent contained the lamp stand (Exodus 25:31-40; Leviticus 24:1-4) and the table (Exodus 25:23-30; Leviticus 24:6) on which the priests daily placed the "loaves of presentation" (Exodus 25:30; Leviticus 24:5-9) or bread of the Presence. This first tent was also called also the Holy Place, which is the meaning of the word "sanctuary" (although "sanctuary" sometimes refers either to the entire structure or to the second tent alone).

9:3 A linen curtain or veil (Exodus 26:31-33) hung between the Holy Place and the Most Holy Place or the Holiest of All (literally, "holy of holies"). This linen curtain is called the "second" one because a priest entering the Tabernacle from the outdoor courtyard would have passed through one curtain already to enter the Holy Place before coming to this curtain (Exodus 26:36-37).

The Inner Sanctum

9:4 The Old Testament clearly places the golden altar of incense in the first compartment outside the second curtain (Exodus 30:1, 6). Our author puts it inside the second, inner compartment, as do a variety of non-canonical Jewish sources and also the Samaritan scriptures. Incense smoke from this altar filled the Most Holy Place on the Day of Atonement, hiding God's symbolic presence from the high priest's clear view (Exodus 30:1-10; Leviticus 16:12-13). Assuming the textual accuracy of the Old Testament description, it is likely that this close association with the Most Holy Place accounts for our author's different descriptive location.

The inner tent also contained the sacred chest known as the Ark of the Covenant, now familiar to even the secular public through the 1981 adventure movie, *Raiders of the Lost Ark* (Exodus 25:10-15). Made of wood covered over with gold, the chest held three relics commemorating divine encounters in Israel's history to that point. Again, the Old Testament record seems to place two of the three in front of the Ark rather than inside it (Exodus 16:32-34; Numbers 17:10-11).

The golden jar holding the manna (Exodus 16:32-34) memorialized God's extraordinary provision of food through the wilderness years. In the Hebrew Old Testament (and English translations), the jar is made of wood. Our author follows the Septuagint, which has the jar made of gold.

The exclusive right of Aaron and his descendants to hold the priesthood was symbolized by Aaron's shepherd rod. This item was significant because God had once selected it from other representative tribal rods and then had caused it to sprout overnight, to bud with blossoms and to produce almonds (Numbers 16-17; Hebrews 5:4-6).

The tablets of the covenant, which the Septuagint calls the plaques of the testimony, were the only items stated by the Old Testament to have been inside the Ark of the Covenant. On these tablets were inscribed the Ten Commandments or Decalogue. This was the second set of stones, replacements cut by Moses after he angrily destroyed God's original handwritten pair following Israel's idolatrous sexual orgy at Mount Sinai (Exodus 32:19; 34:1-4, 28-29).

This *set* of tablets might reflect an ancient Near-Eastern practice involving conquering kings and their vassal subjects. Archaeologists have uncovered details of what they call "suzerainty treaties"—agreements imposed by a victorious suzerain or sovereign on a conquered people. It was customary for each party to retain a copy of this relation-defining treaty, often storing it in their respective temples. Israel considered its own sanctuary to be also God's place of residence among his people and therefore stored both copies in the Most Holy Place. If the suzerainty treaties did provide the background, the two stone tablets likely contained two identical copies of the Commandments, rather than the Commandments divided into two parts as often pictured.

By the time Solomon built the Temple 300-500 years later, the ark contained only the two tables of stone (1 Kings 8:9; 2 Chronicles 5:10). Assuming that it originally housed three sacred relics, two had since gone missing. The fact that the Philistines held the ark for seven months in the time of David suggests one possible explanation (1 Samuel 4:11; 6:1). Three centuries after Solomon, according to one ancient Jewish tradition, the prophet Jeremiah hid the tabernacle, the ark and the altar of incense in a cave on top of Mount Pisgah, "until God shall gather the people again together, and mercy come . . . and the glory of the Lord shall be seen, even the Cloud" (2 Maccabees 2:1-8).

9:5 The lid of the ark, made of solid gold, was called the mercy seat (Exodus 25:17). The Greek word translated "mercy seat" in Exodus appears in the New Testament only here and in Romans 3:25, where it is traditionally translated as "propitiation." However, in the Septuagint, to "make propitiation" is the same as to "make atonement" (for which the Hebrew verb means "to cover"), and it results in "purification" from sins (LXX Exodus 30:10; LXX Leviticus 15:30). Jesus Christ himself is our "mercy seat" or "place of atonement." In him our sins are covered, we are purified or purged from sin, and we enjoy at-one-ment with God.

Joined to the ends of the mercy seat were two golden angels—the cherubim of glory—facing each other and overshadowing the mercy-seat with their outspread wings (Exodus 25:18-20). Another form of the verb translated "overshadowing" describes the miraculous act by which the virgin Mary conceived (Lk 1:35) and also the effect of the cloud that covered Jesus at his transfiguration (Matthew 17:5).

This hallowed space was thought of as God's throne (1 Samuel 4:4). From here, God would issue additional commands as needed (Exodus 25:22; Numbers 7:89). This was preeminently the place where God and the high priest "met" at the apex of the ceremonies for the Day of Atonement (Leviticus 16:2, 13-15).

This is all our author says about the tabernacle and its furniture and fixtures, although he indicates that he might have spoken in more detail.

Other Christian expositors through the centuries have felt free to elaborate at length on these topics, often using allegorical interpretation.

God the Unapproachable

9:6-7 Having listed and located the furniture and fixtures used by the Levitical priests, our author turns now to their sacrificial rituals. In these two verses, our author approaches a single theme under three heads. The theme is the inaccessibility of the Most Holy Place under the Levitical system. The three approaches view the Tabernacle and sacrifices, particularly on the Day of Atonement, in terms of "who?" "where?" and "how?"

- *Who?* All priests served in the Holy Place, but only the high priest entered the Most Holy Place.

- *Where?* The Holy Place furnished a continuous spectacle of priests performing their ritual duties. The Most Holy Place was off-limits to all except the high priest, who could enter it on only one day each year.

- *How?* While priests entered the outer tabernacle for many purposes, the inner tent could be entered only with blood. The high priest carried that blood into the Most Holy Place on that annual Day of Atonement, where he sprinkled it—first for himself and then for the sins of the people (see Hebrews 5:3; 7:27; Leviticus 16:6, 11, 15).

"When these things had been so prepared" refers to the Tabernacle in the time of Moses. The phrase offers no help in dating the writing of Hebrews.

9:8-9 By emphasizing this very restricted access to the Most Holy Place, the Holy Spirit indicated that the roadway to God was not yet available to fallen humans. The two tents of the Tabernacle—one off-limits to laymen, the other open only to the high priest and only on one day each year—signified God's inaccessibility. Later our author will explain that Jesus' sacrifice now provides his people free access into God's very presence (Hebrews 10:19-20).

The details of the Levitical priesthood and sacrifices were symbols, reminding worshipers that their offerings could not perfect the conscience.

This perfecting required a cleansing of the conscience that removed the burden of guilt. That result would be achieved by Jesus' sacrifice (Hebrews 10:22). It is the subjective counterpart in the worshiper to God's forgetting sins that he has forgiven—an objective hallmark of the new covenant, as we saw in the previous chapter.

9:10 The offerings made by Levitical priests cleansed only externally. Ceremonial laws and rituals were only for the interim, until Jesus would come and make a reformation. "Physical regulations" cannot accomplish spiritual or internal cleansing. "Reformation" translates a word meaning a "straightening," and "the time of reformation" is a reference to the present era within salvation history when God, through his Son made man, puts sinful humankind right with himself and fulfills all the shadows and symbols of the old covenant system in Jesus Christ. The "time of reformation" is the same period known as the Last Days (Hebrews 1:2).

HEBREWS 9:11-17

Jesus' Blood Obtains Eternal Redemption

¹¹ But when Christ appeared as high priest of the good things that have come, then through the greater and perfect tabernacle not made with hands (that is, not of this creation), ¹² not with the blood of goats and calves, but with his own blood, he entered the Most Holy Place once for all, having obtained eternal redemption. ¹³ For if the blood of goats and bulls, and the ashes of a heifer sprinkling those who have been defiled sanctifies for the purifying of the flesh, ¹⁴ how much more will the blood of Christ, who through the eternal Spirit offered himself without blemish to God, cleanse our consciences from dead works to serve the living God? ¹⁵ For this reason he is the mediator of a new covenant, so that those who are called may receive the promise of the eternal inheritance, because a death has taken place for the redemption of the transgressions committed under the first covenant. ¹⁶ For where a will is involved, the death of the one who made it must be established. ¹⁷ For a will takes effect only at death, since it is not in force while the one who made it is alive.

WHY & WHEREFORE

Then came Christ, the Son of God made *man* in the person of Jesus of Nazareth. In his human body and as representative of his people, Jesus lived a life perfectly pleasing to God which he gave to God as an offering in his body on the cross. On the cross Jesus shed his blood, again as high priest representing his people. Jesus' sacrifice cleanses our consciences and qualifies him as the mediator or go-between who reconciles God and man. Jesus' people relate to God on the basis of Jesus' perfect doing and dying as their representative. This is the essence of the new covenant, the new relational arrangement between God and the new, now-ransomed, humankind.

UNPACKING THE TEXT

Christ Entered Heaven's Inner Sanctum

9:11 Christ our high priest has now appeared—first on earth and now in heaven—ushering in the time of reformation and dispensing the "good things" that belong to the era of messianic fulfillment. The Greek participle translated "coming," "to come" or "that have come" speaks of fulfillment both as "already" and as "not yet." With Christ's doing and dying, with his rising and exaltation, the "coming" Age has begun. Christ's people already enjoy its good things (see also Hebrews 6:5). However, they have not yet entered the "coming" city (Hebrews 13:14), or the "coming" world (literally "inhabited earth") of which that city is the centerpiece (Hebrews 2:5).

As high priest, Christ passed through the outer tent of the greater and perfect tabernacle or sanctuary, which is his humanity typified by his body. In that humanity he has now entered the Most Holy Place of heaven itself. Human beings did not construct the divine sanctuary where Christ serves (see Hebrews 8:2). Indeed, they could not construct it because its materials are not found within this physical creation that humans now inhabit.

9:12 Like the Levitical high priest on the Day of Atonement, Christ entered the Most Holy Place carrying blood. The Levitical high priest went into the Tabernacle's inner compartment with the blood of a goat for himself and the blood of a calf (or bull) for the people. Christ entered into heaven with his own blood, a symbol for the merits of his faithful and sinless life which he offered to the Father, once, in his human body on the cross.

The Levitical high priest repeated the Atonement ritual every year. Christ entered into heaven's Most Holy Place "once for all" time and "once for all" people. Because he had by his perfect sacrifice "obtained eternal redemption," there was no reason for Christ to offer it again (see comments at Hebrews 1:3). The death of the sin offering and the presentation of its blood were viewed as a single process. For this reason, the fact that Jesus entered heaven with his own blood does not detract from the uniqueness and unrepeatability of his single offering. (This disagrees with Morris, 86).

Our author envisions reality in terms of an eternal realm presently invisible to our earthly senses, and a temporary realm we can now see and touch but that will soon pass away. The author of Hebrews expresses this perspective when he mentions:

- eternal salvation (Hebrews 5:9),
- eternal redemption (Hebrews 9:12),
- the eternal Spirit (Hebrews 9:14),
- eternal inheritance (Hebrews 9:15) and the
- eternal covenant (Hebrews 13:20).

Benefits of His Offering

9:13 Again our author invites us to make a comparison. He has just observed that Christ as high priest offered a sacrifice superior to any sacrifice offered by Levitical priests. To the same degree, our author now notes, Christ's ministry also results in benefits far better than theirs.

Whether we think of sin-offerings involving blood of goats and bulls, or purification rituals using the ashes of a sacrificed red heifer (Numbers 19:1-22), the effects are only ceremonial and external.

9:14 Our author hammers his point home with a rhetorical question. In contrast to Levitical ceremonial cleansings, the blood of Christ cleans our internal consciences from "dead works." Our fundamental problem is not uncleanness incurred through touching a dead body (Numbers 19:11-16). Our most basic problem consists of our thoughts and deeds that result in guilt, separate us from God, and finally end in death. Jesus' blood purges his people from sin's death-oriented defilement. It frees them to serve the living and life-giving God. By his single sacrifice, once offered and now accepted forever, Jesus liberates, cleanses, purifies, sanctifies and perfects his people. In this way he prepares them to become his royal nation and his holy priesthood sent out to serve the world.

Christ offered himself without blemish to God. God did not take Jesus' life from him. Jesus freely gave (offered = as an "offering") God his sinless life of faithful, loving obedience (John 10:17-18). In keeping with the eternal plan, the Father and the Son cooperated in a dance of perfect love to accomplish the redemptive goal determined by the Father and accomplished by the Son (Hebrews 2:9-10; 5:7-10; 10:7; 12:2-3).

Christ made his offering (literally) "through eternal spirit." This expression might mean that Jesus was led and empowered by the Holy Spirit to make this offering, just as he was led and empowered to live his entire life in trusting faith. Or the expression might call attention to the interior result of Jesus' sacrifice in contrast to the "fleshly" outcome of blood-letting under the first covenant. We lose nothing by holding to both ideas.

9:15 The same sacrificial death of Jesus that cleansed the conscience also inaugurated the new covenant. Our author has previously identified Jesus as the guarantee (Hebrews 7:22) and the mediator (Hebrews 8:6; see also Hebrews 12:24; 1 Timothy 2:5) of the new covenant. Here we learn that Jesus also benefited those who lived and died under the old covenant. By his life and death, his doing and his dying, Jesus redeemed everyone whom God called to himself under the old covenant—the very people who violated and broke that covenant by transgressions for which the old covenant provided no effective remedy.

Jesus' atonement extends to all who trust God as he revealed himself to them—people of the sort our author will chronicle in chapter 11. This includes people who never personally heard of Jesus, many of whom died before Jesus was even born. So great is the scope of God's saving purpose and the enormous breadth of his love. The "eternal inheritance" awaits them all.

Covenant or Will?

9:16-17 In verses 12-14 our author compares the blood of animals with the blood of Christ, which he does again in verses 18-26. For three verses between these two sections, he moves the focus from blood in particular to death in general. Interpreters are sharply divided concerning the meaning of verses 16-17. The controversy arises because the Greek word translated "covenant" in verse 15, which our author repeats in verses 16 and 17, can refer to a testamentary will as well. Which legal instrument is intended in verses 16-17, a covenant or a testamentary will?

Either answer has its problem. Verses 16-17 state that some sort of legal instrument takes effect only upon the death of the person who makes it, and that the maker's death must therefore be confirmed. This *description* clearly fits a testamentary will as we know it now. However, the *discussion* surrounding verses 16-17 concerns a covenant, and nothing in the context suggests that our author intends to change the topic in verses 16-17. On the other hand, the observations made in verses 16-17 easily fit a testamentary will, but describe a covenant only by what seems to be stretching the language. Both views have scholarly advocates who offer serious explanations for each.

The majority of commentators and translators believe that our author shifts the topic from "covenant" in verse 15 to "testamentary will" in verses 16-17, then back to "covenant" in verse 18. These interpreters offer an explanation like the following. When our author used the words "inheritance" and "death" in verse 15, those words triggered the thought of a testamentary will. Since the Greek word for this instrument is the same as the word for a covenant, our author simply goes down a side trail for two verses before returning to his regular usage (Attridge, *Commentary,* 255-256).

It is also plausible to interpret the Greek word with its regular meaning of "covenant" in verses 16-17 along these lines. In the Old Testament, a covenant between two parties was often sealed with the death of a sacrificial animal. We might think of it as a dramatic way of saying "cross-my-heart-and-hope-to-die" multiplied times one-hundred. The person making the promise put himself under the same fate as the slaughtered animal if he broke the promise. We see an example of this ritual in God's covenant with Abraham to give his descendants the land of Canaan (Genesis 15:9-21). Until the sacrificial animal was slaughtered and butchered, the covenant was only a proposal. The (symbolic) death of the covenanter was necessary for the covenant to take effect (Lane, *Commentary* II, 242-244).

However, animal sacrifices were not always required for the establishment of a covenant. Yet one can still make a case for "covenant" throughout verses 16-17, with a slightly different explanation. In this interpretation, the passage is speaking of the old covenant which the Jews broke, bringing on themselves the penalty of death. Until the covenant-breakers are dead, the covenant's penalty-provision is not enforced. Jesus therefore dies for the forgiveness of the covenant-breakers, and so validates the covenant itself (Hahn, "A Broken Covenant and the Curse of Death").

In the end, nothing is lost by either view. If we think of a testamentary will, Jesus' death released the benefits which Jesus, now alive again at God's right hand in heaven, administers to his people. If we think of a covenant, Jesus' life performed and satisfied all of its stipulations. His death sealed the covenant and exhausted all its curses. Now alive at God's right hand in heaven, Jesus guarantees to his people all the covenant blessings and benefits.

HEBREWS 9:18-23

Blood, Blood, Blood—
Everywhere We Look

[18] Therefore not even the first covenant was inaugurated without blood. [19] For when every commandment had been proclaimed to all the people by Moses according to the law, he took the blood of calves and goats, with water, scarlet wool and hyssop, and sprinkled both the book itself and all the people, [20] saying, "This is the blood of the covenant that God has commanded for you." [21] And in the same way he sprinkled with the blood both the tabernacle and all the vessels used in worship. [22] Indeed, according to the law almost everything is purified with blood, and without the shedding of blood there is no forgiveness. [23] Therefore it was necessary for the copies of the things in the heavens to be purified with these sacrifices, but the heavenly things themselves with better sacrifices than these.

WHY & WHEREFORE

In a sacrificial system focused on forgiveness it is *blood, blood, blood* everywhere we look. God's first covenant with Israel established at Sinai was sealed with a blood-sprinkling ritual. That ceremony included the pronouncement: "This is the blood of the covenant," which Jesus later repeated and filled with new meaning when instituting the Eucharist or Lord's Supper. The tabernacle and its vessels also were dedicated with blood. In fact, under the Mosaic Law, one can scarcely imagine either ceremonial purification or spiritual forgiveness apart from blood-letting.

The heavenly realities (which the earthly priests and sacrifices copied) were also purified by blood—the self-sacrificed blood of Jesus Christ.

UNPACKING THE TEXT

Covenant Ratified With Blood

9:18-20 Having moved briefly from the idea of a covenant to discuss a testamentary will (both represented by the same Greek word), our author's thoughts now return to the first or Mosaic covenant and the place of blood in its inauguration (Exodus 24:1-8). When God had finished giving Israel the law, Moses read it in the hearing of the people. They promised to do everything that God had commanded. Taking blood of sacrificial animals, Moses sprinkled half against the altar and half on the people. "Behold, the blood of the covenant," he intoned. The blood sealed the people's acceptance of the covenant and it sealed God's acceptance of the people based on the terms of the covenant.

Hebrews mentions several details that the Exodus story does not include. Exodus makes no mention of goats in the ceremony. It does not mention the use of water, scarlet wool or hyssop in the sprinkling. It makes no mention of the Book being sprinkled. On the other hand, it says that the altar was sprinkled, a fact that Hebrews omits.

We may assume that Moses or his assistant mixed water with blood for the sprinkling and that he used wool wrapped around hyssop to perform the sprinkling ritual. These details were standard requirements in the case of the Passover lamb (Exodus 12:22), the purification ceremony for one cleansed of leprosy (Leviticus 14:1-9, 49-53), or the cleansing of someone who had touched a dead body (Numbers 19:17-18).

Our author quotes Moses as saying, "This is the blood of the covenant that God has commanded for you," a slight change from "Behold the blood . . ." reported in Exodus. It is possible that he is paraphrasing what Moses said. It is also possible that he is matching Moses' language to Jesus' words of institution at the Lord's Supper (Matthew 26:28).

The new covenant was also sealed with blood, formalizing Jesus' successful obedience to all that God had spoken in his ear. Jesus spoke of "the new covenant in my blood" when instituting the Lord's Supper (Luke 22:20) and Paul repeated his words (1 Corinthians 11:25).

Sanctuaries Dedicated With Blood

9:21 When the tabernacle was completed and ready for sacred use, Moses sprinkled it and all its vessels used in priestly ministry. Our author includes details beyond those given in the Old Testament story. On the other hand, he does not mention that the tabernacle and its furnishings were sprinkled with oil (Exodus 40:9-11; Leviticus 8:10-11; Numbers 7:1) and that the altar was sprinkled with blood as well (Leviticus 8:15). Josephus adds that the entire tabernacle and furnishings were purified with incensed oil and with blood of bulls and rams *(Antiquities* 3:8:6).

9:22-23 The expression "shedding of blood" represents one Greek word which in all biblical literature is found only here. Without such blood-letting, our author says, there is no "forgiveness." With one exception, this is the only time the New Testament uses this Greek word for "forgiveness" in such a setting without adding the explanatory words "of sins." The other such usage is in Luke 4:18, which quotes the Septuagint version of Isaiah 61:1-2. There, standing alone in elegant splendor, the word usually translated "forgiveness" means "deliverance" in a general sense. Based on that precedent, we may read "forgiveness" here with the same meaning of "deliverance" in general (Attridge, 195).

The Levitical sacrifices and ceremonies were shadowy copies of the eternal or heavenly realities accomplished by Jesus Christ (Hebrews 8:1, 5). Under the Law of Moses, intentional sin affected both the sinner and the sanctuary. It stained the sinner with guilt but it also defiled the Most Holy Place. The "sin offerings" (or "purification offerings") made by the high priest on the Day of Atonement provided *forgiveness* for the sinners' guilt and provided *purification* for the sanctuary's defilement. (See comments at Hebrews 1:3.) Corresponding to that, Jesus purified the heavenly sanctuary by sprinkling his own blood which he shed in the one offering of himself.

HEBREWS 9:24-28

Christ's Life, Death and Judgment

[24] For Christ did not enter a sanctuary made with hands, which was a mere copy of the true one, but into heaven itself, now to appear in the presence of God for us. [25] Nor was it to offer himself again and again, as the high priest enters the Most Holy Place every year with blood that is not his own; [26] for then he would have had to suffer again and again since the foundation of the world. But now, once at the end of the ages, he has appeared to put away sin by the sacrifice of himself. [27] And just as it is appointed for men to die once, and after that the judgment, [28] so Christ, having been offered once to bear the sins of many, will appear a second time, not to deal with sin, but to bring salvation to those who are eagerly waiting for him.

WHY & WHEREFORE

Although unique in many respects, there is one way in which the sacred history of the Son of God made *man* follows the trail that humankind in general is ordained to walk. For God has appointed that each human being should live *one life,* die *one death* and pass through *one judgment* for the life once lived. Therefore Jesus Christ also lived one life, died one death and God judged the life Christ had lived. Finding it pleasing in every respect, God certified his verdict by raising Christ from the dead. Because of Jesus' *one life, one death* and *one judgment,* God accepts the "many" who now eagerly wait for him to return bringing salvation.

154

UNPACKING THE TEXT

Christ's One Appearance in Heaven

9:24-26 Like the high priest on the Day of Atonement, Christ has made an atoning offering for sin. However there are important differences.

- Christ encountered God in heaven;
- The Levitical high priest met God in a hand-made sanctuary.

- Christ offered his sacrifice once;
- The Levitical high priest offered his sacrifice every year.

- Christ offered himself as his sacrifice;
- The Levitical high priest offered blood not his own.

- Christ put away sin by his sacrifice;
- The Levitical high priestly sacrifice could not put away sin.

Seven times in chapters 7-10 our author speaks of Jesus Christ himself as the "offering" or as the one who "offered" himself (Hebrews 7:27; 8:3; 9:14, 28; 10:10, 12, 14). This metaphor calls attention to the life of faithful obedience which Jesus lived and which he then offered as a gift to the Father in his body on the cross. In contrast, our author speaks of Jesus as a "sacrifice" only twice (Hebrews 9:26; 10:12), although he specifically refers to Jesus' death in terms of the suffering involved (Hebrews 2:9; 9:26; 13:12; perhaps also in 2:10, 18; 5:8).

Interestingly, our author never speaks of Jesus as the Lamb of God, a figure employed by John the Baptist (John 1:29, 36), Philip the Evangelist (Acts 8:32), Peter (1 Peter 1:19), Paul (1 Corinthians 5:7) and especially John of Revelation who portrays Jesus as the Lamb:

- whose sacrifice God has accepted (Revelation 5:6; 13:8);
- who is with God in heaven (7:9);
- whose blood has washed his people's robes (7:14);
- who has redeemed his people (14:4);
- who is praised and is worthy of praise (5:8, 12-13; 7:10; 15:3);
- through whose blood the martyrs conquer (12:11);
- who is victorious over his enemies (14:1; 17:14);
- who will come in judgment (6:16; 14:10); and

- who finally will be his people's
  - shepherd (7:17),
  - groom (19:7, 9),
  - temple (21:22) and
  - light (21:23).

Christ's offering is once for all; it occurs at the end of the ages; it results in the abolition of sin. When sin is abolished, redemption history has reached its goal and no further sacrifice is needed. Jesus came at the decisive time. Indeed, it was his coming that made that particular time decisive. (See notes on Hebrews 1:2 and on Hebrews 9:10-12.)

One Life, Death & Judgment

9:27-28 The Bible does not teach reincarnation or the immortality of the soul. Instead, it portrays the human being as God's creation who depends on God for life. In these two verses our author sums up humankind's appointed journey. Each person lives one life, dies one death and then faces God the judge. In becoming the *man* Jesus Christ, the Son of God placed himself under the same regimen. Christ also lived one human life, died one death and faced God in judgment.

Throughout his one life, Christ faithfully and lovingly did the Father's will without deviation and without exception. The life-record of his human experience is now permanently preserved and secured in his own glorified humanity. Christ's human life has been lived. It will never be repeated and its record will never change. It is what it is, forever.

In his single death, Christ laid down his faithful and sinless life, offering it as a gift to the Father. As we will learn in the next chapter, it was the gift God had always wanted from human beings. It was the offering to end all offerings. For any person who might give God the sacrifice of an obedient life, no other sacrifice would be needed. Jesus Christ gave this gift to God by offering himself bodily on the cross. He will never die again. His death has passed into history—on earth and in heaven.

In his death Jesus was "offered up." As high priest Jesus offered himself (Hebrews 7:27; 9:14, 25; 10:12) and as sacrifice he was offered (9:9, 2:28). The verb "bear/bore" in these verses describes the priestly work of lifting up an offering on the altar, whether it involves blood (Hebrews 7:27) or not (Hebrews 13:15). Jesus' self-sacrifice was for sins. Not for his own sins, for he was sinless. He died for "our sins," a personal and precious truth that lies at the heart of the gospel (1 Corinthians 15:3). But the truth is greater than that. Jesus also died "to bear the sins of many," and so fulfilled the declared task of the Suffering Servant of prophecy (Isaiah 53:12).

The next phrase in the Septuagint adds: "and on account of their sins he was delivered up" (Isaiah 53:12). Paul quotes that phrase in saying that Jesus "was delivered up on account of our transgressions" (Romans 4:25), changing "their sins" to "our transgressions" and moving the verb from the end to the beginning for emphasis.

Like all human beings, Christ was judged by God. God examined, inspected, "judged" (the Greek word for "judgment" can be spelled in English as *crisis)* the life Christ had lived, and declared that it pleased him precisely in every respect. To signify his acceptance of Christ's life, God raised him from the dead (death cannot long hold anyone who lives a spotless and sinless life!) and seated him at his right-hand place of honor in heaven.

Christ was judged once-for-all, never to be judged again. Because God's judgment of Christ's unrepeatable life is also unrepeatable, the outcome of that judgment will never change. Because of Christ's perfect doing and perfect dying in their name, his people approach God on the basis of Christ's life-record and God relates to them accordingly.

When the Priest Comes Out

When the high priest had completed the ritual for the Day of Atonement, he came out of the sanctuary and joined the waiting people. His successful exit signified to them that his sacrifice had been accepted by God. For that reason his appearing assured them that *they* were accepted by God. One intertestamental writer describes that thrilling moment when the high priest rejoined his people: "How glorious he was when the people gathered round him as he came out of the inner sanctuary!" (Sirach 50:5).

Our author recalls that happy scene as he completes his sentence. When God is ready, he tells us, Christ will appear a second time. In that appearance he will not deal with sin, for he dealt with it decisively by his one life, death and judgment. When he appears the next time, Christ will be bringing the fullness of salvation to his people. Buoyed by that hope, they eagerly wait and confidently confess:

Christ has died.
Christ has risen.
Christ will come again.

HEBREWS 10:1–4

Amoral Blood Reminds, Not Removes

¹ Since the law has only a shadow of the good things to come and not the true form of these realities, it can never, by the same sacrifices which they offer continually year after year, make perfect those who draw near. ² Otherwise, would they not have ceased to be offered, since the worshipers, having once been cleansed, would no longer have any consciousness of sins? ³ But in those sacrifices there is a reminder of sin year after year. ⁴ For it is impossible for the blood of bulls and goats to take away sins.

WHY & WHEREFORE

The Mosaic Law was imperfect because it qualified priests on the basis of genealogy and physical fitness, not on the basis of character. The priesthood was imperfect because it could not remove the consciousness of sin and give a clear conscience. Even when the High Priest entered the Most Holy Place on the great Day of Atonement, the blood he presented reminded the people of their sins committed during the past year. For reasons soon to be made clear, it was impossible for the blood of bulls and goats to take away sins. Our author now explains the third of four psalms from which he tells the salvation story.

UNPACKING THE TEXT

10:1 The law could only foreshadow the heavenly realities yet to come, the true forms that Jesus Christ would bring into reality at the time of messianic fulfillment. That included its pattern for a sanctuary, its provision for a priesthood, and its regulations for the sacrifices the priests would offer (see comments at Hebrews 9:11).

Perfection characterizes the new order that Jesus represents, not the former order with its earthly sanctuary and Levitical priests. Our author has told us already that worshipers under the former system were not made perfect. This is demonstrated by the repetition of offerings involving the same sacrifices continually, year after year.

10:2 If those offerings had cleansed or purged the worshipers, the consciousness of sins committed would have disappeared with the smoke of those sacrifices. A clean conscience and sins forgotten are blessings that only Jesus provides (Hebrews 9:14).

10:3 Levitical sacrifices not only failed to erase the consciousness of sins. They actually had the opposite effect. Even the sacrifices offered on the Day of Atonement reminded of past sins (Leviticus 16:21). The yearly repetition of these sacrifices highlighted the fact that they did not remove either the guilt or the memory of sin. The word translated "remembrance" or "reminder" in this verse is the same word translated "remembrance" or "memorial" in connection with the Lord's Supper (1 Corinthians 11:24-25).

10:4 The conclusion is inescapable. Animal blood lacks the moral quality necessary to remove either sin's accursed guilt or its accusing memory. That is why the blood of bulls and goats cannot take away sin.

HEBREWS 10:5-10

God Receives What He Always Wanted

⁵ Consequently, when Christ came into the world, he said,

"Sacrifice and offering you have not desired,
  but a body you have prepared for me;
⁶ in burnt offerings and sin offerings
  you have taken no pleasure.

⁷ Then I said, 'Behold, I have come—
  in the scroll of the book it is written of me—
  to do your will, O God.'"

⁸ When he said above, "You have neither desired nor taken pleasure in sacrifices and offerings and burnt offerings and sin offerings" (which are offered according to the law), ⁹ then he said, "Behold, I have come to do your will." He takes away the first in order to establish the second. ¹⁰ And by that will, we have been sanctified through the offering of the body of Jesus Christ once for all.

WHY & WHEREFORE

The problem was in the sacrifices. However flawless the animal, however perfect a specimen in species and gender and age, its life record remained only the accumulated daily history of an amoral creature. Such a life record could never give God what he had always wanted from his human creatures—a life of faithful, loving obedience. With this in mind, our author now discusses his third great psalm. This time he looks at Psalm 40:6-8, the words of which he presents as from the mouth of Jesus.

The Son of God came into the world as the *man* Jesus to remedy this situation. He came to give God what he had always wished for but had never received—a sinless life that would perfectly reflect God's desires for human beings in fellowship with himself. To accomplish this, God gave Jesus a human *body.* Jesus fulfilled all God's will or wishes in that human body. He then gave the embodied fulfillment of God's will as a gift to the Father by offering his body on the cross. By that *will-of-God-incarnated,* fully performed and given to God in Christ's body, we his people have been sanctified or made holy. So cleansed and set apart, we now offer God our own sacrifices of praise and good works.

UNPACKING THE TEXT

Animal Offerings Never the Point

10:5-6 God had always known that animal blood could not remove the guilt or the memory of sin. From eternity he had planned another offering, to which the sacrifices of animals would always point and by which they would be replaced. The discussion that follows must be seen in the light of the "consequently" or "wherefore" at the beginning of this verse. What follows makes clear why the blood of bulls and goats could never take away sin.

Verses 5-7 are a quotation from Psalm 40:6-8 (LXX Psalm 39:7-9). With these words before him, our author finally explains, directly and unambiguously, the meaning and significance of sacrificial blood. In doing so, he also explains why Jesus' self-offering was of such incredible value that it would never need to be offered again, and why it could never be supplemented or improved by any other offering.

These words from Psalm 40 tell us why the Son of God became lower than angels to become a human being. They explain the purpose of Christ's advent into the world as a man. They show God's purpose in sending Christ, and they also show Christ's purpose in coming, which motivated and shaped his entire life every day. So that Jesus Christ could give God the one thing he had always wanted, God prepared Jesus a human body.

God's First Choice From the Beginning

Our author visualizes the Son of God addressing the Father:

⁵ "Sacrifice and offering you have not desired,
but a body you have prepared for me;
⁶ in burnt offerings and sin offerings
you have taken no pleasure."

God's first choice was never sacrifices and offerings. The Law of Moses made provision for many kinds of sacrifices, but none of them was God's preference from his people. God's first choice was not a "peace offering" (expressing thanks) or a "cereal offering" (representing consecration). It was not a "burnt offering" (lifting up worship). It was not even a "sin offering" (acknowledging guilt).

God's first choice—his greatest desire both for and from his human creatures, is the very same thing he has wanted since Adam exhaled the residue dust from his nostrils and opened his eyes to see the pristine marvels of the Garden of Eden. God desires what he desired from his people Israel, but which he always desired in vain. The creator of the cosmos wants what seems most natural and right to any thinking person. He wants a human life in perfect fellowship with himself, a life reflecting his wishes and plans for the human creature, a life totally attuned to God's own will and pleasure every moment of every day.

From the offering made by Abel to the altars built by Abraham, from the sacrifice of Noah to the sacrifices of generations of Jewish priests, whatsoever the offering and whatever its purpose, not one of them ever measured up to simple obedience—God's first choice from men and women. It has always been better to maintain fellowship with God than to restore it. God always preferred a consecrated life to a dead sacrifice. From the day that God made man, his first choice was for people to love and live in fellowship with him, to do what he wanted—from pure hearts aligned with God's own wishes for human beings.

Moses, Israel's great lawgiver and its first prophet, made that plain from the beginning. "And now, Israel," he inquired rhetorically, "what does the LORD your God ask from you, but to fear the LORD your God, to walk in all his ways, to love him and to serve the LORD your God from your whole heart and your whole soul, and to keep the commandments and statutes of the LORD your God which I command you today, that it may be well with you? (Deut. 10:12-13, my trans. of LXX.) Throughout Israel's history, God's spokesmen frequently reminded his covenant people of this loving obedience which was his chief desire (1 Samuel 15:22; Psalm 51:16-17; Micah 6:6-8; Isaiah 1:11-17; Amos 5:22-24; Jeremiah 7:21-23). But to give God such loving obedience, one must be a human being with a human *body*.

Needed: One Human, With Body

10:7 And *this*, our third Psalm (40), tells us, is why the Son of God became a *man*. In the words of Psalm 40, as fulfilled by Jesus, the quotation continues:

> ⁷ "Then I said, 'Behold, I have come—
> in the scroll of the book it is written of me—
> to do your will, O God.'"

The Greek version of Psalm 40 says "a body you have prepared." The Hebrew text says, "You have dug out my ears." The Greek translators might have used "body" to include the ears and all the rest. The God who shaped each part also shaped the whole body. Or we may think of Jesus Christ (or David, originally) as saying "You have made ears that I may hear your will and do it" (see Isaiah 50:4-5).

Either explanation yields the same result. The important thing is that God was never keen on receiving pile after pile of animal sacrifices. What God really wanted was pure human fellowship and obedience. So when the Son of God came into the world he did not come as an angel but as a human baby. He came as the human baby Jesus, with a human baby *body*.

The psalm quotation continues from the mouth of Christ. "I have come," Jesus says, "to do your will, O God." The explanatory phrase, "in the scroll of the book it is written of me," is part of the quotation. It might mean, "I personally pledge to do everything the Law requires." Or it might mean, "David's psalm anticipated my own obedience." We do not have to choose one meaning at the expense of the other for both of them are true.

Two Subjects—Second is First in Importance

10:8-9 Having quoted from Psalm 40 in verses 5-7, our author now gives his own commentary on its application to Jesus Christ. Christ mentioned

'Jesus' and 'Christ' in Hebrews

One instinctively wonders why our author speaks sometimes of "Jesus," at other times of "Christ" and three times of "Jesus Christ." At almost every point in the story what is said of "Jesus" is said also of "Christ."

- The one who became the man Jesus once was higher than angels (Hebrews 2:9) and Christ appeared (Hebrews 9:11).
- Jesus (Hebrews 3:1-2) Christ (Hebrews 3:6) was faithful to God throughout life.
- Jesus suffered outside the gate (Hebrews 13:12) when Christ was offered up (Hebrews 9:28).
- Jesus Christ offered his body to God in which he had lived a faithful and obedient life (Hebrews 10:10).
- Jesus (Hebrews 10:19) Christ (Hebrews 9:14) shed his blood.
- Jesus (Hebrews 4:14; 6:20) Christ (Hebrews 5:5; 9:24) is now our high priest in heaven.
- Jesus Christ is forever the same on our behalf (Hebrews 13:8).
- Through Jesus Christ we relate to God (Hebrews 13:21).

Though we cannot draw sharp and exact distinctions in every case, it is safe to say that when our author wishes to emphasize the humanity of Jesus, whether during his earthly life or during his life now in heaven, he speaks of "Jesus." When he wants to focus on Jesus' work as the prophesied agent through whom God rescues his people, he speaks of "Christ." And when he desires to underscore that this "Jesus" and the "Christ" are one and the same, he combines that name and title.

two subjects here, he notes. *First* he mentioned the Levitical sacrificial system with its many sacrifices and offerings for sin. *Then* he mentioned a second subject—his own coming to do the will of God. As a matter of fact, our author continues, Christ took away the *first* thing he talked about—all those sacrifices and offerings prescribed by the law—to make stand or to establish the *second* topic mentioned—his personal commitment as a man to perfectly fulfill all God's wishes.

Jesus' stated life-purpose was to do the will of God. As it happens, Jewish offerings (the first thing mentioned here) had always been God's *second* choice, while simple obedience (doing God's will, the second thing mentioned here) had always been his *first* preference.

10:10 Throughout his human life Jesus Christ fully *embodied* God's will by doing everything God wished, wanted or desired. By doing this, Jesus wrapped up God's will, as it were, in his human *body*. Then he gave that *will-of-God-done* as a gift or present to God, by offering that *body* on the cross—that very body in which he had done God's will throughout life, the body in which he had fully wrapped up the fulfillment of all God's wishes, the body in which Jesus had *embodied* the fulfillment of all God's desires.

Jesus accomplished all of that for his people. For them he did the *doing* of God's will, wishes or desires. For them he did the *dying* through which he offered that present to the Father. God was totally pleased with this present, this offering, which provided everything he had ever wanted human beings to do and to be. And by this *will of God*, which Jesus had perfectly embodied throughout his life and had given to the Father as an embodied present in his death, "we" have been "sanctified" or made holy. No wonder our author has mentioned time and again, as he does here, that Jesus' offering occurred only "once for all!" (See Hebrews 7:27; 9:12, 26, 28 and 10:10.)

Made Holy by Blood of Jesus Christ

The "we" who have been made holy are all of Christ's people, every person who finally will be saved, regardless of when they lived or what revelation they were given by God.

The mention of people being sanctified or made holy takes us back to the appointment and consecration of Aaron and his sons, the original Levitical priestly family. Before they could enter the Tabernacle bringing sacrifices to God, they first had to be made holy. To accomplish this, God prescribed an elaborate consecration ceremony (Exodus 29:1-46). We also have been made holy, by the offering of Jesus' body, to qualify us to offer sacrifices to God. To be sure, we do not bring sin-offerings. We do bring offerings of praise (Hebrews 13:15) and good works (Hebrews 13:16), and for that priestly ministry we had to be sanctified or made holy.

In this verse the author speaks of our Savior as "Jesus Christ," combining his name (Jesus) and his title (the Christ/Messiah/Anointed). He uses the same double reference two other times as he nears the close of this epistle (Hebrews 13:8, 21). Besides these three references to "Jesus Christ" in Hebrews, our author refers to "Jesus" ten times (Hebrews 2:9; 3:1; 4:14; 6:20; 7:22; 10:19; 12:2, 24; 13:12, 20) and nine times to "Christ" (Hebrews 3:6, 14; 5:5; 6:1; 9:11, 14, 24, 28; 11:26).

Christ Performs His Offering and Sits Down

[11] Every priest stands day after day ministering and offering time after time the same sacrifices, which can never take away sins. [12] But when this man had offered one sacrifice for sins forever, he sat down at the right hand of God, [13] from that time waiting until his enemies are made a footstool for his feet. [14] For by one offering he has perfected forever those who are sanctified. [15] And the Holy Spirit also testifies to us, for after saying,

> [16] "This is the covenant
> that I will make with them
> after those days, says the Lord:
> I will put my laws on their hearts,
> and I will write them on their minds,"

[17] then he adds,

> "I will remember their sins
> and their lawless deeds no more."

[18] Where there is forgiveness of these, there is no longer any offering for sin.

WHY & WHEREFORE

What a tedious and monotonous job the Levitical priest had! He could never sit down because his work was never finished. And his work was never finished because his sacrifices (of amoral animals) could never take away sins. Jesus, on the other hand, offered one sacrifice one time, and sat down at God's right hand. His work of making offerings was over. By his single offering, Jesus perfected his people forever. God's new-covenant promise included the pledge not to remember his people's sins. And if God forgives his people's sins (which is the only way he could choose to forget them), there is no need for a sin offering ever again.

UNPACKING THE TEXT

10:11 Imagine a day in the life of a Levitical priest. He awakes and dresses, then grabs a handful of olives and a piece of flatbread to break the night's fast. Then, kissing his Levitical wife goodbye, he walks or rides his donkey to the Tabernacle. There he stands, all day long, offering one sacrifice after another as the people of Israel come to confess their sins and to make amends to God according to the Law. That night the priest tries to rest—finally off his aching feet! The next morning he is back at his post, standing all day, offering the same sacrifices he offered the day before. So it goes, week after week, month after month, year after year. His is a standing job because his work is never finished. His work is never finished because the people are never freed from a guilty conscience.

10:12 In contrast to that picture, consider the priestly ministry of Jesus Christ. Some 2,000 years ago, on a cross outside Jerusalem, he offered a single sacrifice for sins. Because of that sacrifice, God forgave Jesus' people and forgot their sins forever. Then, atonement accomplished, Jesus *sat down* at the Father's right hand in heaven. The picture of Christ at God's right hand comes from Psalm 110, the fourth Psalm our author uses to tell the Jesus story. He has referred to it several times, beginning with his opening paragraph (Hebrews 1:3). Now, having come almost full circle, he is ready to bring his presentation to a close.

10:13-14 Like a double picture frame, these verses bring together two images of Jesus Christ from Psalm 110. The first image shows him as the *king,* enthroned at God's right hand in heaven (Psalm 110:1). There he enjoys a position of honor second only to that of the Father, who has given him all authority in heaven and on earth (Matthew 28:18; Ephesians 1:21-22; Philippians 2:8-11; 1 Peter 3:22). The second image from

Psalm 110 presents Jesus as our *priest*, who has presented his offering in the Most Holy Place of heaven itself (Psalm 110:4). He has made the perfect sacrifice, once-for-all.

Jesus' twin roles as king and as priest both remind us that the End has already begun, but that it has not yet reached its final conclusion. Whether we consider Jesus' kingly reign or his priestly ritual, we live in the gap between the "Already" and the "Not Yet." Although Jesus is *already* the *king,* not everyone now acknowledges his authority, for all things are *not yet* visibly beneath his feet. For now, Jesus awaits the news that all his enemies have been defeated. The final enemy to be destroyed is death (1 Corinthians 15:24-26). And while Jesus is *already* the *priest,* he has *not yet* received God's signal to exit the heavenly sanctuary and rejoin his people in person. For now, Jesus remains seated in heaven's Most Holy Place in the presence of God.

10:15-17 God's new-covenant promise to Jeremiah, which our author already discussed in chapter eight, agrees with the statement that Jesus has now perfected his people. As part of that promise, God said he would forget his people's sins—the essence of genuine forgiveness.

10:18 Once forgiveness is obtained, additional sin offerings are unnecessary. Jesus has accomplished forgiveness and his sacrifice will never be repeated.

With this, our author concludes his exposition. For the rest of his sermon he will encourage, exhort and warn, based on the teaching he has already given.

HEBREWS 10:19–25

Jesus' Blood Calls for Ongoing Response

[19] Therefore, brothers, since we have confidence to enter the sanctuary by the blood of Jesus, [20] by the new and living way that he opened for us through the curtain (that is, his flesh), [21] and since we have a great priest over the house of God, [22] let us draw near with a true heart in full assurance of faith, having our hearts sprinkled clean from an evil conscience and our bodies washed with pure water. [23] Let us hold fast to the confession of our hope without wavering, for he who promised is faithful. [24] And let us consider how to provoke one another to love and good deeds, [25] not neglecting meeting together, as is the habit of some, but encouraging one another, and all the more as you see the Day drawing near.

WHY & WHEREFORE

Through the single offering of his own body and blood, Jesus our high priest has provided humankind with extraordinary blessings. He has opened the curtain that prevented access into the Most Holy Place of heaven and has given us confidence to enter. Our author now encourages us to do three things in response: Let us *draw near* to God's presence. Let us *hold fast* to our hope, and let us *consider* how to motivate each other as the people of God. These exhortations are appropriate because of who and whose we are; they are timely in view of our place in salvation history. Now is the time for intentional community—we are not isolated wanderers. Indeed, we are the fellowship of God's redeemed People.

UNPACKING THE TEXT

Confidence to Draw Near and to Hold Fast

10:19 Based on Christ's accomplishments previously discussed and summed up in verses 19-21, our author urges his readers to respond in three specific ways. As before (Hebrews 3:1, 12), "brothers" is generic and includes both brothers and sisters. "Confidence" (or "boldness") here translates a word borrowed from the world of politics and which meant freedom of speech. It does not signify audacity but rather the absence of inhibition. We can now enter boldly into the heavenly Most Holy Place. The larger phrase may also be translated "boldness for an entrance into the holiest." Jesus' sacrifice makes possible the general fact and it enables the personal act.

10:20 Our means of entry into the heavenly sanctuary is a road or way described both as "new" or recent (see Hebrews 9:8) and as "living" or life-producing. This sanctuary is the heavenly original of which the earthly Most Holy Place was a copy. Being "behind the curtain" (Hebrews 6:19-20), it was off-limits until Jesus opened the new and living way "through the curtain." Jesus did this by means of "his flesh," his blood (Hebrews 10:19) or his body (Hebrews 10:5, 10). All three expressions are symbols of his faithful and sinless life which he offered to God in his obedient death on the cross.

10:21-22 Jesus is our "great priest," here the same as high priest. Because he holds that position and because he has cleansed us inside and out, our author invites us to "draw near." This is a priestly phrase which describes the act of bringing worship to God (Hebrews 4:16; 7:25; 11:6). We are now able to do that with a true heart—one that is guileless and sincere—because it has been "sprinkled" with Jesus' blood. This image of sprinkled blood brings to mind the ceremony ratifying the covenant at Sinai (Hebrews 9:18-22). It also reminds us of the priestly installation of Aaron and his sons, which involved washing the body with water (Exodus 29:4, 21; Leviticus 8:6, 30). The statement that our bodies were "washed with pure water" likely refers to the outward rite of Christian baptism, which in the New Testament sometimes accompanies and always bears witness to inward cleansing by Jesus' blood (Acts 22:16; Titus 3:5).

10:23 Believers should also cling unwaveringly to their confession of hope, a common theme throughout Hebrews (Hebrews 3:6, 14; 4:14; 6:11). Human hope is grounded in divine faithfulness. The more intently we hope, the more we depend on God.

10:24 The third response involves mutual care for each other, a concern with two stated objectives. "Provoke" here has a positive meaning; its object is increased love and good deeds. The word it translates came into English as "paroxysm." Our responses to Christ's blessings thus include faith (v. 22), hope (v. 23) and love (v. 24).

Keep Encouraging—The Great Day is Coming

10:25 This mutual obligation to provoke or stir up each other requires that believers be together. Some house churches known to our author were in danger of dissolving through sheer discouragement. He warns them against "neglecting" meeting—not merely missing a gathering, but abandoning their coming together altogether. Based on the form of the word translated "meeting together," one commentator has raised the possibility that the original readers had been attending Sabbath services in Jewish synagogues and remaining for messianic (Christian) devotions afterward. Some were leaving before the second meeting, a practice our author urges them not to continue (Bruce, *The Epistle to the Hebrews*, 254). The word translated "meeting together" appears but one other time in the New Testament. There it refers to the gathering of all the saved to meet Jesus Christ at his return (2 Thessalonians 2:1). The thought of that great assembly remains before us as our author completes his sentence.

The encouragement should intensify as "the Day" draws near. A shortened form of "the Day of the Lord," this expression refers throughout the Old Testament prophets to an occasion of divine visitation when God will punish sin and deliver the righteous. Our author probably has in mind the final Day of the Lord—the climax of human history when Jesus will appear again to bring salvation. One might ask how readers of Hebrews can "see" that Day approaching. The answer surely is that one can "see" it the same way that we "see" Jesus (Hebrews 2:9), that the patriarchs "saw" their reward (Hebrews 11:13), and that Moses "saw" the invisible God (Hebrews 11:27). It is "seen" by faith (see also Rom 13:11-12), as we consider the End-Time events which with Jesus' first coming have begun already (see notes on Hebrews 1:2).

Some interpreters read "the Day" here as a reference to Jerusalem's destruction. In the beginning, Jesus' followers expected the end of classical Judaism also to mark the close of present human history (see Matthew 24:3; Acts 1:6-8). However, Jesus had taught his disciples that the two events would be separated by a period of unknown duration called "the times of the Gentiles" (Lk 21:24). That period began in A.D. 69-70, when the Romans destroyed Jerusalem and its Temple, and it still continues today. It will end when Jesus appears again.

The New Testament epistles suggest that first-century believers held a variety of views about the timing of Jesus' second coming and the end of present history. Paul's Thessalonian correspondence addresses certain anxieties concerning believers who already have died or who might die soon, a concern based on an expectation of Jesus' imminent return (1 Thessalonians 4:13-18). By the time of Second Peter, the epistle's recipients are troubled by skeptics who question whether Jesus will return at all (2 Peter 3:3-4).

Our author's comments here and in the remainder of chapter 10 seem to indicate that his original readers were somewhere between those two psychological states of mind. They do not expect Jesus to return at any moment, but neither have they given up hope of his return. Our author explains that Jesus, as high priest, is presently occupied in the heavenly sanctuary, but that he will certainly come again for his waiting people (Hebrews 9:24, 27-28). With no firm basis for dating the writing of Hebrews, we cannot be more precise than that.

HEBREWS 10:26-31

There Is No Other Offering

²⁶ For if we deliberately go on sinning after receiving the knowledge of the truth, there no longer remains a sacrifice for sins, ²⁷ but a fearful expectation of judgment, and the fury of a fire that will consume the adversaries. ²⁸ Anyone who has rejected the Law of Moses dies without mercy "on the testimony of two or three witnesses." ²⁹ How much worse punishment do you think one will deserve who has trampled the Son of God, regarded as unholy the blood of the covenant by which he was sanctified, and insulted the Spirit of grace? ³⁰ For we know him who said, "Vengeance is mine; I will repay." And again, "The Lord will judge his people." ³¹ It is a fearful thing to fall into the hands of the living God.

WHY & WHEREFORE

Because there is no other atoning sacrifice for sin, whoever despises Jesus' offering walks away from the only means of forgiveness available. Under the Law of Moses the penalty for breaking God's covenant was immediate capital punishment. What punishment should one deserve who consciously and permanently tramples the Son of God, dismisses as common the blood that makes us holy, and insults God's gracious Spirit? A certain and fiery judgment awaits such hubris at the hands of the ever-living God.

UNPACKING THE TEXT

10:26 The purpose for frequent encouragement among believers is to prevent their drifting away from Jesus and sliding into ultimate apostasy. That is a fearful but totally unnecessary possibility, however one explains it theologically. If a true believer *can* stop believing, the danger is obvious. If a true believer *cannot* stop believing, the danger is equally real. For it is very possible to suppose oneself to be a true believer and all the while be self-deluded (Pink, I, 604-605). Under either scenario, all those who are finally saved do trust in Christ until the end of their lives.

The Law of Moses distinguished between sins committed in weakness or ignorance, and sins committed deliberately and audaciously. It provided sin offerings for the first category of sins, but for the second kind of sin it made no provision (Numbers 15:25-31). Our author has warned

Apostasy in Practice

To go to the place of no more sacrifice, one does not have to intellectually forsake every element of Christian understanding piece by piece until nothing remains. Nor is it necessary that someone stand before the public and specifically renounce Jesus Christ and all that he has done. A person can fall to the place of no more sacrifice while supposing that he or she is a genuine believer. This is a *practical* apostasy, not necessarily an *intellectual* one. As such, it allows the greatest room for self-deception. It can occur in more ways than one.

- It can happen when someone *listens* to God speak through the Son, *professes* to believe God's promises, *claims* to rely on Jesus Christ and his sacrifice for sin, *attends* public meetings with other believers—but steadfastly continues to practice sin and immorality as a chosen and regular way of life.

- It can happen when someone listens, professes, claims and attends as just described, and even demonstrates a somewhat transformed life—but one day decides it isn't worth the effort, packs away the Bible, stops meeting with believers, quits praying, puts Jesus out of mind and, from that point forward, lives as if Jesus did not exist and if this present life were the final stop.

already that the person who forsakes Jesus Christ may finally cross a point of no *return* (Hebrews 6:4-6). Here he adds that one may also reach a place of no more *sacrifice*. No one stumbles into this place accidentally or by mistake. To go there requires intentional conscious effort.

Our author includes himself in the warning: "If *we* deliberately go on sinning . . . ." The word "deliberately" begins the sentence, a place of emphasis in Greek syntax. The participle translated "go on sinning" is present and active in form; this "sinning" is an ongoing way of life. This intentional act of rejection can be committed only by one who has first known the truth. "Knowledge" here translates an intensive word-form that suggests thorough knowledge or knowledge gained by experience. Such knowledge increases responsibility. Morally speaking, the person who truly knows Jesus cannot simply decide one day to abandon him and, with a tip of the hat and a "fare-thee-well," saunter guiltlessly away. For this individual, no further sin-offering is available.

10:27 The person who high-handedly abandons Jesus Christ becomes God's adversary or opponent, and can rightly anticipate a "fearful" or terrifying judgment. Our author borrows language from Isaiah to portray that judgment as a consuming fire that devours God's adversaries (Isaiah 26:11). The same imagery appears throughout the Bible (Deuteronomy 9:3; Malachi 4:1, 3; Matthew 13:40; 2 Thessalonians 1:8; Hebrews 12:29). The "fury" of this fire is literally its "zeal," which is the ordinary Greek word for God's fiercely-avenged "jealousy" (Psalm 79:5 [LXX 78:5]; Zephaniah 1:18).

10:28-29 Our author has already invited his readers to consider reprisals under the Mosaic Law in calculating the just punishment for neglecting Christ's great salvation (Hebrews 2:2-3). Now he encourages a similar reckoning regarding the fate of one who rejects Jesus Christ. The counterpart to apostasy under the Law was unrepentant idolatry. Its prescribed punishment was death—with no room for mercy (Deuteronomy 13:1-18). The requirement of "two or three witnesses" was a procedural safeguard to ensure due process and to prevent unjust convictions (Deuteronomy 17:6-7).

"How much worse" should the punishment be for one who abandons Christ? The question echoes in counterpoint to the earlier inquiry in 9:13-14. There, the question "How much more" contrasted the limited effects of animal sacrifices with the comprehensive benefits resulting from the blood of Christ (Hebrews 9:13-14). Apostasy is such a terrible sin because at its root it renounces the new covenant—God's arrangement of relationship with his people through Jesus Christ as their representative.

The Sin's Horrific Nature

The person who willfully turns away has "trampled the Son of God." The two syllables in the Greek verb for "trample" are literally "down" and "walk"—picture somebody lying flat on the ground while pedestrians use him as a sidewalk. It would be difficult to imagine an act of greater disdain—and for Jesus, at that, the Son of God whom we confess as our high priest in heaven (Hebrews 4:14).

An individual who willingly abandons Jesus has "regarded as unholy the blood of the covenant by which he was sanctified." Apart from Jesus' blood, we once were common and profane. Jesus' blood elevated us. By that blood, God transformed us and made us fit to serve others in his name (Hebrews 9:11-14; 10:19). Yet the person who abandons Jesus labels his blood as ordinary and unfit. Surely there can be no greater irony than this. "Regarded" involves mental calculation; the same Greek word is translated "considered" in a positive sense (Hebrews 11:26).

Whoever commits this apostasy has also "insulted the Spirit of grace." Long ago, God promised to give his people the "Spirit of grace and mercy" (Zechariah 12:10). It was through this eternal Spirit, this gracious Spirit, this Spirit that pours grace into our hearts, that Christ "offered himself without blemish to God" (9:14). The verb translated "insulted" has at its root the Greek noun which comes into English as "hubris." For the Greek-speaking world of the New Testament, this word described an act of outrage or contempt. Many people considered it the worst possible sin. How very tragic and inappropriate that anyone should behave that way toward the gentle and giving Spirit of God!

God's Judgment is Fearful

10:30 Although our author asks his readers to consider the punishment apostates might deserve, he really does not expect us to provide a final answer. Judgment belongs to God—who both claims it and to whom his people attribute it, as two Old Testament quotations make clear. The first quotation, "Vengeance is mine; I will repay," apparently comes from a lesser-known Greek text of the Song of Moses (Deuteronomy 32:35) and is also quoted by Paul (Romans 12:19). The second quotation, "The Lord will judge his people," also comes from the Song of Moses (Deuteronomy 32:36) and is repeated in the Psalms (135:14 [LXX 134:14]).

To say that God will "judge" means that he will call someone to account. However, in the Old Testament, to say that God will judge his people usually means that he will come in judgment on their behalf, vindicating them from their enemies or oppressors. That is the sense of this quotation (Deuteronomy 32:35; Psalm 135:14). Its meaning in Hebrews is either that God will vindicate his faithful people from the implied slander of those apostates who renounced faith and abandoned Christ, or that God will call to account ("judge") the apostates who are secretly intermixed among his faithful people.

10:31 Our author's point is clear, and it can be summarized in one sentence: "It is a fearful thing to fall into the hands of the living God." Elsewhere in the New Testament, God's "hands" symbolize the believer's security (John 10:28-29). Here, God's "hands" symbolize the apostate's destruction. This "fearful thing" is the "fearful judgment" mentioned in verse 27 shortly before. Again the adjective "fearful" leads the sentence, which gives it added emphasis.

On the other hand, at least one scholar interprets verses 26-31 as a warning of Jerusalem's imminent destruction by the Romans because of the covenant-breaking by the Jews (Gleason, "The Eschatology of the Warning in Hebrews 10:26-31").

HEBREWS 10:32-39

Past Commitment Spurs Endurance

32 But remember those earlier days when, after you had been enlightened, you endured a hard struggle with sufferings. 33 Sometimes you were publicly exposed to reproaches and persecution, and sometimes you were partners with those so treated. 34 For you had compassion on those in prison, and joyfully accepted the plundering of your property, knowing that you yourselves have a better and lasting possession. 35 Therefore do not throw away your confidence, which has a great reward. 36 For you need endurance, so that when you have done the will of God, you may receive what was promised. 37 For,

> "Yet a little while,
> and the coming one will come and will not delay;
> 38 but my righteous one shall live by faith,
> and if he shrinks back,
> my soul has no pleasure in him."

39 But we are not of those who shrink back and are destroyed, but of those who have faith and are saved.

WHY & WHEREFORE

Our author reminds his first readers of the original zeal which they experienced immediately after their conversion. They had willingly accepted mistreatment, and they had stood with others who were being mistreated. The commitment which they demonstrated then is the answer to their problem now. A quotation from Habakkuk reminds them

Major Warning/Encouragement Sections

These first ten chapters of Hebrews contain the author's primary exposition of Scripture and his exhortations not to abandon Jesus Christ as Savior. That material divides naturally into two main sections (Hebrews 1:1-6:12; 6:13-10:39), each of which concludes with a remarkably parallel, two-pronged message of warning and encouragement. This analysis comes from William L. Lane, but I have stated it here in my own words (Lane, *Commentary* II, 296-297).

First warning section (6:4-8)

- describes the apostate,
- recalls the readers' past experience with God,
- points out the impossibility of recovery, and
- states clearly what the apostate can expect at the End.

First encouragement section (6:9-12)

- appeals to a basis for comfort,
- recites the readers' past experiences that reflect that basis for comfort,
- urges action needed in the present, and
- closes with a reminder of the good things awaiting the believer at the End.

Second warning section (10:26-31)

- describes the apostate,
- recalls the readers' past experience with God,
- points out the impossibility of recovery, and
- states clearly what the apostate can expect at the End.

Second encouragement section (10:32-39)

- appeals to a basis for comfort,
- recites the readers' past experiences that reflect that basis for comfort,
- urges action needed in the present, and
- closes with a reminder of the good things awaiting the believer at the End.

of their two final options. They can live by faith and be saved, or they can displease God by drawing back and be destroyed.

UNPACKING THE TEXT

Remember the Past

10:32-34 In the previous paragraphs our author appealed through negative fear of future judgment. In this paragraph he motivates through positive memories from the past. The "earlier days" refer to the period immediately after they had come to know Christ ("had been enlightened"). Stirred with fresh zeal, they had "endured a hard struggle with sufferings." The two words "hard struggle" translate a Greek word used of an athlete's efforts during the contest. Our author will return to an athletic metaphor in chapter 12.

Their struggle had included bearing up under abuse that was both verbal ("reproaches") and physical ("persecution"). This abuse had been inflicted on them personally and also on their fellow-believers. The verb translated "publicly exposed" means to be made a spectacle or subjected to public ridicule. The word might suggest that they had been hauled into a theater or arena, although we later learn that these first readers had not yet shed blood for their faith (Hebrews 12:4).

Some of their company had been imprisoned; others had suffered conscription of property. The pain of losing their property might have included knowing it was soon to take place while helpless to prevent it. The verb translated "accepted" can also mean bearing something that is about to occur. These details of their suffering could describe either some type of official persecution or isolated outbreaks of mob violence. Not knowing when Hebrews was written, we cannot be more specific than that.

All this they had accepted with joy, following the instructions and the example of Jesus himself (Matthew 5:11-12; Hebrews 12:2). Their courage resulted in part from the knowledge that they personally ("yourselves" is emphatic) had a possession better than the possessions they had lost. What they had would last or endure when this present age has passed away. "Better" is a key adjective in this book. Our author uses it more than a dozen times.

10:35-36 Hopefully, the memory of their past faithfulness will stir discouraged believers to persevere again. Specifically our author urges them not to toss aside their "confidence"—that "freedom of speech" rooted in free access to God through the sacrifice of Jesus (Hebrews 3:6; 4:17; 10:19). This same "confidence" also enables the believer to bear witness to Jesus Christ freely and without inhibition. Such confidence has a "great reward." The word translated "reward" refers to the payment of wages. Our author used it negatively before (Hebrews 2:2). Here he uses it in a positive sense.

For now they need to endure. When they have done the will of God, they will receive what God has promised them. By doing the will of God, one walks in the steps of Jesus who came to do the will of God (Hebrews 10:4-10). Doing the will of God also provides the benefit of enjoying God's company and fellowship. God wishes so strongly for us to do his will that he himself equips us completely to do that very thing (Hebrews 13:20-21).

Face the Future

10:37-38 Our author supports his call to endure with words from two Old Testament prophets, which he borrows and shapes to fit his immediate need. Verse 37 opens with "a little while" (an unusually intensive phrase in the original) from Isaiah 26:20. This introduces the longer quotation from Habakkuk 2:3 which completes verse 37 and includes verse 38.

In the original context of Isaiah 26:20, the prophet heralds God's coming judgment on the world's inhabitants at the hands of the Babylonians. He calls on God's faithful people to enter their closets and hide for "a little while" until the fury has past. Habakkuk also announces a vision of coming judgment by the Babylonians. It is certain, he says. If it delays, wait for it. The invader is haughty and wicked. In contrast to the invader, God's faithful remnant ("my righteous one") will find life through faith(fulness). Either God's faithfulness will preserve that one, or that one will find rescue through trusting in God. In both cases, faith results in life, a life shaped by faith shown by obedience and holding fast to God.

It is not absolutely clear whom our author identifies as "the coming one." Based on Habakkuk's judgment context, it might refer to the Roman armies that would destroy Jerusalem. (Since we have no date for Hebrews, we cannot know that for sure). It might refer to Jesus Christ, who will come in judgment against unbelievers when he brings salvation to his people.

Our author borrows the words "a little while" from Isaiah, and adds "Yet" at the beginning to create an affirmative statement. He then quotes Habakkuk 2:3, adding "the" to make "the coming one" and reversing the order of the two statements that follow. Adding the definite article to the "coming one" suggests that Jesus is in view. Mentioning "my righteous one" who will "live by faith" before the statement about shrinking back allows our author to present his readers with two options in their own lives.

Considering all these elements individually and together, it is reasonable to understand that Christ's coming or appearing (Hebrews 9:28) is certain. Because the "last days" have already begun (Hebrews 1:2), the Day of the Lord (Hebrews 10:25) will not be long in coming. Facing that prospect, our author encourages his readers to persevere (perhaps faith's greatest indicator in Hebrews) and find life at Jesus' coming. He warns them not to "shrink back" by forsaking Jesus (Hebrews 10:26, 39), thereby incurring God's displeasure.

10:39 "We," the author continues, placing his readers in the same category with himself, do not fit the category of those who "shrink back" and are "destroyed" (Hebrews 10:27, 31). We are rather among those who "have faith," who persevere by "holding fast," and who finally "are saved."

Introducing the Hall of the Faithful

With this, we might imagine our author leading us outdoors and down a shady path to a low-slung square building situated just beyond the gardens. This is the Hall of the Faithful, he says, and he invites us to browse as long as we wish. Those whom we will see honored here, he explains, are a sampling of God's faithful people who lived before Jesus was born. As we make our way through this Hall, we will see in everyday terms what faith looks like in real life—the kind of faith that perseveres to the saving of the soul.

The Hall of the Faithful has four wings, each devoted to an era of world history. The first wing celebrates faithful people from the beginning through the Flood. It contains three exhibit rooms, one each for Abel, Enoch and Noah. The second wing highlights patriarchal faith as demonstrated by Abraham (with his wife Sarah), Isaac, Jacob and Joseph. It has two rooms—a large one housing the Abraham exhibit, and an undersized room that contains the three other displays.

In the third wing we will find three areas but without any dividing walls. The first area occupies most of the wing, and it features the faith of Moses as seen throughout his life. That flows into the second area which focuses on the Exodus. The third area contains a model-size reproduction of the walled city of Jericho. In an upper-story window of the model, a tiny figure of a woman stands beside a red rope. The fourth wing is actually a single room, in which a giant screen fills an entire wall. This area will feature a powerful video that pays tribute to a cross-section of faithful men and women from the time of Israel's judges until shortly before the birth of Jesus.

HEBREWS 11:1-3

Faith Sees the Invisible and Assures

[1] Now faith is the assurance of things hoped for, the conviction of things not seen. [2] For by it the people of old obtained approval. [3] By faith we understand that the universe was framed by the word of God, so that what is seen was not made from things that are visible.

WHY & WHEREFORE

The faith that endures to the end assures its possessors that their hope is well-founded. It views the invisible world of spiritual realities, and it holds with strong conviction to what it sees there. The invisible realities predated the visible universe which the invisible God spoke into being by his word. These are not mere theories, generalities or platitudes. They are living principles which first animate, and then describe, God's faithful people throughout history.

UNPACKING THE TEXT

11:1 We enter the foyer to the Hall of the Faithful and immediately spot an inscription above the door. "Now faith is the assurance of things hoped for," it announces; "the conviction of things not seen." The word translated "assurance" reflects the sense of the Hebrew word for "believe," from which Hebrew verb our word "Amen" is ultimately derived. Such faith is convinced that God is faithful. This conviction in turn gives substance to all of God's promises. The same word can also refer to the evidence or proof of a thing, and therefore to the conviction based on that proof. Godly faith is convinced of spiritual realities which the physical eye cannot see. For the believer, faith is an organ of spiritual perception more dependable than the physical senses of hearing and of sight.

11:2 By such faith, honorable men and women of the past obtained God's approval and also approval from God's faithful people. Our author is about to name an honor roll of believers from throughout the entire Old Testament and for 200 years beyond. Interestingly, none of the biblical stories featured here expressly mentions the faith of the characters. Indeed, actions speak louder than words.

Both before and after our author wrote Hebrews, Jewish and Christian writers promoted particular virtues by pointing to outstanding individuals who modeled them. The intertestamental book of Sirach (or Ecclesiasticus) begins such a passage with the words, "Let us now praise famous men" (Sirach 44:1). Mattathias, the godly patriarch of the Maccabean heroes, encouraged his sons from his deathbed by reminding them of great men in Jewish history: "Now therefore, my sons, be zealous for the law, and give your lives for the covenant of your fathers. Call to mind what deeds our fathers did in their times" (1 Maccabees 2:50). The early Christian writer Clement of Rome clearly had Hebrews 11 in mind when he wrote the passage beginning: "Let us also be imitators of those who went about in goatskins and sheepskins preaching the coming of Christ" (1 Clement 17:1 – 19:3).

Although our author is not alone in his method of encouragement, his list of heroes is unique in highlighting people who through faith saw the invisible God, trusted his promises and patiently endured until the end.

11:3 For faith, seeing and grasping what is invisible provide an adequate basis for understanding. For example, it is by faith that we "understand" the origin of the universe to be God who speaks. That is a reality that science, which by definition analyzes and categorizes observable phenomena, can neither discover, confirm nor disprove. Paul also uses "understanding" in this way when talking about the creation (Romans 1:20). Our author does not expressly affirm here that the creation was made from nothing. He does deny that it was made from raw materials of the visible kind.

HEBREWS 11:4-7

God Honored Faithful Abel, Enoch and Noah

⁴ By faith Abel offered to God a better sacrifice than Cain, through which he obtained testimony that he was righteous, God showing approval of his gifts; and through his faith, though he is dead, he still speaks. ⁵ By faith Enoch was taken away so that he did not experience death, and he was not found because God had taken him. For before he was taken, he was commended that he pleased God. ⁶ And without faith it is impossible to please God, for whoever comes to him must believe that he exists and that he rewards those who seek him. ⁷ By faith Noah, being warned by God about things not yet seen, in reverent fear built an ark to save his household. By this he condemned the world and became an heir of the righteousness that comes by faith.

WHY & WHEREFORE

Our first exemplars of faith are the pre-Flood trio consisting of Abel, Enoch and Noah. Abel's faith led to his death. Enoch's faith kept him from seeing death. Noah's faith resulted in escape from a particular death. In response to their faith, God declared both Abel and Noah to be righteous, and for the same reason he commended Enoch as one who pleased God.

UNPACKING THE TEXT

Abel

11:4 Leaving the foyer now, we move into the first wing of the Hall of the Faithful and into the first of its three rooms. This room clearly honors the faith of Abel, whose story is told in Genesis (Gen. 4:3-8). An exhibit highlights three points about Abel:

- By faith Abel offered a better sacrifice than his brother Cain.

- Through his sacrifice (or his faith) he obtained testimony that he was righteous, God showing approval of his gifts.

- Through his faith, Abel still speaks from the dead.

Why did God consider Abel's sacrifice "better" than Cain's? The Hebrew text reports only that Cain brought his offering from the fruit of the ground and Abel from the firstborn of his flock. In the Greek translation of Genesis, God rejects Cain's sacrifice because he "did not divide it correctly" (LXX Genesis 4:7). Jewish literature suggests many possible reasons why God favored Abel's sacrifice, including the quality, quantity, content (blood) and procedure (cut up correctly). The best explanation probably lies in the difference between the attitude and character of the men themselves. In short, Abel was a man of faith and Cain was not, as Jesus suggested (Matthew 23:35; 1 John 3:12).

Most likely, God indicated his choice of offerings by sending fire, which consumed Abel's gifts but left Cain's offering untouched. One Greek version of Genesis adds this explanation, which is also supported by analogy with other Old Testament sacrificial stories (Leviticus 9:23-24; Judges 6:21; 1 Kings 18:30-39; 2 Chronicles 7:1).

Through his faith, dead Abel "still speaks." His blood cries out to God for vengeance (Genesis 4:10) as our author notes later (Hebrews 12:24). That is probably not the point here, however, since our author says that Abel "speaks" rather than "cries out." Through Abel's faith which God approved, Abel still speaks to us about our enjoying God's approval also by faith.

Enoch

11:5 We leave Abel's room and move into the next. This room honors Enoch, who also obtained God's approval through faith. He "walked with God" (Genesis 5:24) and, in the Greek Old Testament, "pleased God." The Hebrew text says that Enoch "was not, because God took him." The Greek translation says he "was not found, because God translated him." Our author summarizes both by saying that Enoch "did not experience death." Non-biblical Jewish writings honor Enoch as a man of repentance (Sirach 44:16) and as a preacher of righteousness (1 Enoch 91-105). Our author focuses on the statement that Enoch "pleased God" (LXX Genesis 5:24) which he develops in the following sentence (Hebrews 11:6).

11:6 We know that Enoch was a man of faith because he pleased God, and "without faith it is impossible to please God." Any time anyone anywhere comes to God, it must be by faith. The idea of approaching or coming to God is important throughout Hebrews, and this same verb regularly expresses that idea (Hebrews 4:16; 7:25; 10:22; 12:22). Here "faith" also includes specific intellectual content—that God *exists* and that he *rewards* those who seek after him. These two elements correspond to the attributes of faith in verse one: by faith the believer is convinced that the unseen God exists. Faith gives substance to the reward for which one hopes, but which has not yet been received.

Noah

11:7 The final room in the Hall's first wing features Noah's faith as its theme. The Genesis story (Genesis 6:8—9:17) says that Noah (like Enoch) pleased God, although it does not specifically mention his faith. Yet Noah illustrates a variety of faith's dimensions as our author points out. He received a word from God ("being warned," the same verb used in Hebrews 8:5; 12:25). Although the oracle concerned a future reality then still invisible, Noah responded in action. This exemplifies the firm conviction that faith supplies concerning "things not seen" (Hebrews 11:1). In building the ark, Noah was moved by his piety or reverent fear, the same interior quality that motivated Jesus (Hebrews 5:7) and which ought also to move us (Hebrews 12:28).

Noah is the first person whom Scripture identifies as "righteous" (Genesis 6:9; 7:1), a description repeated in Jewish literature (Ezekiel 14:14, 20; Sirach 44:17). Our author follows Habakkuk in associating righteousness and faith, with an emphasis on the obedience and steadfastness that faith produces (Hebrews 10:38-39). By his own faithful conduct Noah condemned the faithless world—either by contrast with his own life or verbally as a preacher of righteousness (2 Peter 2:5). Through his faith, he became an "heir" of God's promised reward (Hebrews 6:17).

HEBREWS 11:8-12

Abraham Persevered in Faith

⁸ By faith Abraham obeyed when he was called to go out to a place that he was later to receive as an inheritance. And he went out, not knowing where he was going. ⁹ By faith he lived in the land of promise as in a foreign land, living in tents with Isaac and Jacob, heirs with him of the same promise. ¹⁰ For he was looking forward to the city that has foundations, whose architect and builder is God. ¹¹ By faith Sarah herself received power to conceive when she was past the age, since she considered him faithful who had promised. ¹² Therefore from one man, and him as good as dead, were born descendants as many as the stars of the sky in multitude and as innumerable as the sand by the seashore.

WHY & WHEREFORE

Abraham the great patriarch moved out into an unseen future based only on God's word. Then for decades he persevered, in obedience to the invisible God who makes promises concerning things that do not yet exist.

UNPACKING THE TEXT

11:8 We enter the second wing of the Hall which is divided into a larger and a smaller room. The large room is devoted entirely to Abraham, the great patriarch of the Jews and father of the faithful for believers in Jesus. And little wonder, since he illustrates so vividly at least four aspects or themes that are associated with faith throughout Hebrews.

- When God called Abraham, he immediately obeyed.
- Abraham was a pilgrim en route to an inheritance.

191

- His reward was invisible and waited in the future.
- Motivated by God's promises, Abraham patiently persevered.

Man Without a Country

The saga begins with God's call to Abraham to leave all that was famil-iar (land, kin, home) and to go to a destination which only God him-self then knew (Genesis 12:1-5). The patriarch's response was immediate and straightforward—"when called, Abraham obeyed." Jesus also learned obedience and became the source of salvation for those who obey him (Hebrews 5:8-9).

Abraham left home, not knowing his destination, because faith pro-vides conviction of things not seen (Hebrews 11:1). Genesis calls his end-goal "the land." Our author changes that to "a place" that God would identify when the time was right. We know that this "place" was a per-manent homeland (Hebrews 11:14) consisting of a heavenly city and a heavenly country (Hebrews 11:10, 16).

11:9 Abraham's faith motivated a lifetime of trust. From his perspective, daily existence was that of a foreigner or stranger, although lived on real estate that God had promised to give to his descendants (Genesis 17:8; 23:4). Although we can read the Genesis account in a matter of minutes, Abraham lived a nomadic life in tents for a full century (Genesis 25:7). Our author previously has described Abraham as a man who lived from God's promise (Hebrews 6:15; 7:6). So, for that matter, do faith-pilgrims in every age (Hebrews 4:1; 6:12, 17; 10:36; 11:33, 39).

11:10 Faith in God's promised future can sustain the believer because faith gives assurance based on physically-invisible realities (Hebrews 11:1). That is the significance of the "for" that begins this verse. Abraham was not wandering aimlessly. He had some understanding of a well-es-tablished city ("that has foundations"). It was a city not of this creation, but one designed and constructed by God. This is the eschatological or End-Time destination of all people of faith (Hebrews 12:22; 13:14).

Abraham, Sarah and an Heir

11:11 The majority of standard modern English versions say that by faith Abraham's wife Sarah was enabled to conceive a son although past the normal age. In this case, the minority NIV and NRSV are almost certainly correct. The Greek phrase translated "conceive" in this verse literally means to "throw down seed." That expression normally and naturally describes the father's part in conception and not the mother's. Additionally, when God promised Abraham and Sarah a son, Genesis portrays Sarah's reaction as laughter and not faith (Genesis 18:12-15).

The verse is better translated to say that "By faith Abraham, even though he was past age—and Sarah herself was barren—was enabled to become a father because he considered him faithful who had made the promise" (NIV). Although the prospect of descendants was impossible by human power or calculation, Abraham judged it possible because God promised it. Abraham stands as a model of that faith which considers the faithfulness of God and lives accordingly.

11:12 Because of his faith in God's word and the action that it inspired, Abraham eventually had descendants as numerous as the stars at night, as many as the grains of sand that line the seashore (to use the very graphic, pre-scientific biblical hyperboles). Our author is not quoting any specific passage here; he is paraphrasing several Old Testament statements (Genesis 15:5; 22:17). Yet for purposes of starting a family, Abraham was the same as dead. Paul makes the same point in Romans 4:19, where he insists that the God in whom Abraham's faith (and ours) is placed is a God well able to raise the dead.

HEBREWS 11:13-16

Faith Creates Pilgrims With Passion

¹³ All these died in faith not having received the promises, but they saw and greeted them from a distance. They confessed that they were strangers and foreigners on the earth, ¹⁴ for people who say such things make it clear that they seek a homeland. ¹⁵ If they had been thinking of that country they came from, they would have had opportunity to return. ¹⁶ But as it is, they desire a better country, that is, a heavenly one. Therefore God is not ashamed to be called their God, for he has prepared a city for them.

WHY & WHEREFORE

Because faith gives substance to intangible hope and provides conviction concerning invisible realities, it enables the believer to stake everything on God's promised future. Abraham and his near descendants did not live to see the fulfillment of God's promises. They were still clinging to those promises when they died. In this faith, they willingly gave up their homeland to live as displaced sojourners on the earth. God is pleased to be known as their God.

UNPACKING THE TEXT

11:13 The first readers of Hebrews knew what it meant to feel like strangers in their own homeland while waiting for something better and abiding (Hebrews 10:32-34). Such were the lives of the patriarchs also. They died unfulfilled, but they did not die discouraged. Their faith had peered into the approaching future and had seen and greeted everything

194

God had promised. The vision of the heavenly homeland inspired them to confess that this present world was not their home (Genesis 23:4; 47:4, 9; Leviticus 25:23). The imagery of a home-bound traveler "greeting" or "saluting" his city as it comes into view was common in classical Greek literature and is also familiar in our own experience.

11:14-16 Such a confession identifies its maker as one in search of a homeland which this earth cannot provide. Their search is deliberate rather than drastic. After all, these pilgrims chose the sojourner life. At any moment they could have stopped the journey, reversed their course and returned to the country from which they had begun. They have made their choice—they seek a heavenly country, and they will not be content with anything less. An unknown writer 300 years after Christ described believers in just such terms:

> They live in their own homelands, but as foreigners. They share in everything as citizens, but endure everything as aliens. Every foreign country is their homeland, but every homeland is a strange country to them. . . . They spend their time on the earth, but their citizenship is really in heaven (Epistle to Diognetus 5:5, 9, my translation).

God is pleased to be identified with such people of faith (Exodus 3:6, 15-16).

HEBREWS 11:17–22

The Patriarchs Trusted God for Their Future

[17] By faith Abraham, when he was tested, offered up Isaac; and he who had received the promises was offering up his only son, [18] of whom it was said, "In Isaac your descendants shall be called." [19] He considered that God was able to raise him from the dead, from which he did receive him back, figuratively speaking. [20] By faith Isaac blessed Jacob and Esau regarding things to come. [21] By faith Jacob, when he was dying, blessed each of the sons of Joseph, and bowed in worship, leaning on the top of his staff. [22] By faith Joseph, when he was about to die, made mention of the Exodus of the Israelites and gave instructions concerning his bones.

WHY & WHEREFORE

When God commanded Abraham to offer Isaac as a sacrifice, he was asking the patriarch to destroy the child on whom God's promise of Abraham's descendants depended. Trusting God in both his command and his promise, Abraham concluded that God could and would raise Isaac from the dead.

In his own old age, Isaac expressed faith in God by pronouncing blessings on his sons in defiance of the future, both as unknown and as foretold in part by God to Abraham. Jacob demonstrated the same faith and blessed his grandsons. Joseph exemplified such confident trust in God by his dying request to be reburied eventually in the land of promise.

UNPACKING THE TEXT

Trusting God Who Raises the Dead

11:17 Abraham had left Ur—and given up his past. Now God was asking him to give up his future as well. Nevertheless, when he was tested (Genesis 22:1), by faith Abraham offered up Isaac his son. Never mind that an angel stopped him in the act before the deed was done. Already Abraham had offered Isaac as a sacrifice in his own mind and heart (Genesis 22:1-14). According to Jewish tradition, Isaac was a grown man of 23, 25 or even 37 years old at the time, and he possessed faith equal to his father's. However, the Hebrew and Greek words alike in the Genesis account portray Isaac as a "lad" or "young man."

Jesus himself was tempted and so are his people (Hebrews 2:18; 4:15). In the offering of Isaac (the Jews call this event "The Binding of Isaac"), Abraham was "tested" or tempted on multiple levels. The command to offer his son Isaac defied sanity, strained human emotion to the breaking point and required the blind sacrifice of godly conscience on the altar of divine sovereignty. Any person who claimed to receive such a revelation today would be committed to an institution for the mentally ill. Anyone who attempted to obey such a command would face criminal charges of the most serious sort. In fact, this story elicits such moral incredulity from the pious reader that he or she easily misses the essence of the faith-test involved, namely that God seemingly asks Abraham to destroy the very son on whose survival the fulfillment of God's own covenant promises depended.

11:18 This command created a crisis of faith as well as of will. God had promised Abraham a multitude of descendants—through Isaac, his only freeborn son. Abraham seemingly must choose between God's promises (which presuppose Isaac's future) and God's command (which results in his death). What does one do when God's promises and his commands seem irreconcilable? Abraham responded to such a dilemma by faith, which meant proceeding in obedience to God's unambiguous command, confident that God was both able and faithful to carry through on his promises.

11:19 However, faith does not preclude thinking, reasoning or even imagining. The text literally says that Abraham did some calculating or accounting and reached a conclusion. Against all odds, God had empowered Isaac's conception through two parents who by age were both dead for purposes of procreation. The same God was certainly able now, if need be, to raise Isaac from among those literally dead to fulfill his promises and to accomplish his purposes (Romans 4:17-22). Abraham considered the situation and decided that God would do that very thing (Genesis 22:5). And figuratively speaking, God did.

In Abraham's faithful mind Isaac was already dead. At the last moment, God interrupted the real-time action and Abraham received his son back, as it were, from the dead. The second blessing of the "Eighteen Benedictions," a traditional Jewish prayer from before the time of Christ, perpetuated the conviction which sustained Abraham on this occasion. "Blessed are thou, O Lord," it says, "who revives the dead."

Our author's comment here about "figurative" language literally says "in a parable" (as at Hebrews 9:9). For that reason some have seen Isaac as a figure or prototype of Jesus who was to come. Indeed, several parallels spring to mind. Isaac was Abraham's only son. He was conceived by supernatural intervention. He was born as a child of promise to become a man through whom God would bless the world. Before the world was blessed, Isaac carried the wood for his own death. In the end, his father received him back from the dead.

The stories of Isaac and of Jesus do include certain similarities. Most important, though, is the dissimilarity. So that Isaac would not die, God *provided* a sacrificial ram, caught in a thicket by his horns. So that we would not die, Jesus *became* the Lamb of God and died with a crown of thorns on his head.

Trusting God Who Provides a Future

11:20 By faith this same Isaac, now both old and blind, blessed his sons Jacob (Genesis 27:26-29; 28:1-4) and Esau (Genesis 27:39-40) concerning events then future. The phrase "things to come" translates a participle that appears throughout Hebrews and usually points to the time when God will finally fulfill all his promises (Hebrews 2:5; 6:5; 10:1; 13:14). Isaac's paternal blessings predicted the fortunes of two nations—Israel (from Jacob) and Edom (from Esau)—which came to pass as prophesied by Isaac. Isaac spoke these blessings by faith. He had a word from God.

Despite the unknown future, he declared it aloud, confident that God would bring it to pass. Isaac's faith was put to still another test, involving the circumstances surrounding the blessing. Jacob the cheater had reversed the positions of his two sons to deceive his father who could not see. When he later learned of the trickery, Isaac remained confident that God would still accomplish his purpose.

11:21 Jacob similarly trusted God for the future. On his deathbed, he also pronounced blessings on Ephraim and Manasseh, his grandsons by Joseph (Genesis 48:1-22). Jacob exemplified the same faith by requiring Joseph to swear to transport his bones to a cave Abraham had bought in Canaan, then bowed in worship while leaning upon the top of his pilgrim's staff (Genesis 47:29-31; Genesis 15:13-16). Our author quotes a Greek translation which has "staff" where the Hebrew text has "bed." The same Hebrew consonants stand for either word.

11:22 Joseph also trusted God for the future as he approached his death. He meaningfully recalled (rather than "made mention"; the same verb is translated "thinking of" or being "mindful of" in Hebrews 11:15) God's promise to bring Abraham's descendants out of Egypt to the promised land. Trusting that promise, Joseph left an instruction to take his bones to Canaan when the Exodus took place (Genesis 50:24-25). Generations later, the Israelites honored Joseph's faith in God's promise by taking his bones with them out of Egypt (Exodus 13:19) and eventually burying them at Shechem (Joshua 24:32).

Moses and His Parents Lived by Faith

[23] By faith Moses, when he was born, was hidden for three months by his parents, because they saw that the child was beautiful, and they were not afraid of the king's edict. [24] By faith Moses, when he had grown up, refused to be called the son of Pharaoh's daughter, [25] choosing rather to share mistreatment with the people of God than to enjoy the fleeting pleasures of sin. [26] He considered the reproach of Christ greater wealth than the treasures of Egypt, for he was looking to the reward. [27] By faith he left Egypt, not fearing the king's anger; he persevered, as seeing him who is invisible. [28] By faith he kept the Passover and the sprinkling of blood, so that the destroyer of the firstborn would not touch them.

WHY & WHEREFORE

Because we expect to discover Moses in this honor roll of faith, it ought not surprise us to find his parents here as well. By faith Amram and Jochebed flagrantly defied Pharaoh's edict to kill all male babies born to Hebrew mothers. Because they did that, Moses survived to become a man of faith himself. Inspired by his own trust in God, Moses renounced his royal adoption to identify with a race of slaves. He left Egypt without the king's permission, later confronted him in the name of God and ultimately led the Israelites as God rescued them from centuries of slavery.

UNPACKING THE TEXT

11:23 We have covered two wings of the Hall of the Faithful, and now we stop for a short rest break. After a few minutes, we resume our tour in the third wing's first room. It underscores the faith of the great deliverer and law-giver himself—Moses. Our author previously commended Moses' faithfulness in God's house (Hebrews 3:2, 5). Now he notes that the new-born Moses was hid three months by his unnamed parents. This reflects the Greek translation of Genesis which credits both parents; the Hebrew text mentions only his mother (Exodus 2:2). The infant Moses was "beautiful" or "proper," that is, he was stately or urbane in appearance (see Acts 7:20).

We learn elsewhere that Moses' parents were Amram and Jochebed, both Levites of the clan of Kohath (Exodus 6:14-20). Their act of civil disobedience violated the Pharaoh's order that Hebrew male infants should be thrown into the Nile (Exodus 1:22). Our author states that Moses' parents were unafraid of the king's edict. Exodus does not include that detail, but it does say that the Egyptian midwives feared God (Exodus 1:17, 21).

Moses' Great Choice

11:24 When Moses reached maturity he had the option to claim, or to relinquish, his identity as Pharaoh's adopted grandson, with all the rights and responsibilities that designation afforded. Drawing on his spiritual resources, he acted by faith and repudiated the privileged position. No longer would he be known as "Son of Pharaoh's Daughter," the foster mother who had adopted him as an infant (Exodus 2:9-10). Scripture is unclear whether Moses renounced his royal ranking in some public act or if he simply took his place alongside the enslaved Hebrews in a series of conflicts with Egyptian officials (Exodus 2:11-12; Acts 7:23-25).

We cannot know the identity of Pharaoh's daughter with any certainty. "Pharaoh" was a dynastic title, not a personal name. Suggestions have included Thermuthis (Tharmuth) and Meri, daughters of Rameses II (13th-century B.C.), as well as Hatshepsut, the powerful daughter of Thutmose I (15th century B.C.). In the end, when Moses lived is less important than how he lived—and we know that he lived by faith.

11:25 Naturally gifted, physically charming, well-educated and royally-adopted, Moses might have enjoyed high position in Egypt, perhaps even that of the "Pharaoh." Instead, he chose to suffer mistreatment with the en-slaved Hebrews and to forfeit the fleeting and temporary pleasures of sin.

11:26 The treasures of ancient Egypt remain legendary even today, and Moses "considered" them deliberately and with care. He then concluded that the "reproach of Christ" was of greater wealth than Egypt's riches, looking by faith at God's invisible, but certain, reward. The same verb here translated as "considered" was also translated as "regarded" in an earlier, negative, setting (Hebrews 10:29).

Moses Leaves Egypt Twice by Faith

11:27 By faith Moses left Egypt to live in Midian (Exodus 2:15). Our author adds that Moses was not motivated by the king's anger, although the Exodus account places him under a cloud of fear of some sort (Exodus 2:14). Through one crisis after another, Moses persevered by seeing the invisible God. Again we remember faith's fundamental trusting-points: it believes that God exists and that he rewards those who seek him. Moses' faith highlighted Pharaoh's unbelief by contrast.

Moses' exit from Egypt in this verse should not be confused with the later exodus of the Israelites in general. This exit occurred before the Passover, which is mentioned next (v. 28). The present verse does not mention the Israelites' faith (v. 29) which we might expect if the Exodus were in view. When the Exodus did occur, Israel did not flee Egypt in fear. Instead, the Israelites then departed orderly at the request of Pharaoh and the Egyptian population (Exodus 12:31-33).

11:28 By faith Moses celebrated the original Passover and declared it a perpetual annual celebration (Exodus 12:1-20). As part of the Passover ritual, Moses sprinkled the lamb's blood as God directed. God rewarded this faith by rescuing and freeing the Israelites when the destroyer wiped out the firstborn of all Egypt's men and animals in the climactic act of judgment (Exodus 12:21-30).

According to the Synoptic Gospels, Jesus instituted the Eucharist or Lord's Supper during a Passover meal. John's Gospel presents Jesus as dying simultaneously with the slaying of Passover lambs in the Temple (John 19:31, 36). Paul utilizes Passover symbols when he compares moral purity among believers to unleavened bread and speaks of Jesus Christ as Passover Lamb (1 Corinthians 5:6-8). Interestingly, our author draws analogies from the Day of Atonement, not from Passover, to explain the meaning and significance of the self-offering of Jesus Christ.

HEBREWS 11:29-31

Faith at the Exodus and at Jericho

²⁹ By faith the people passed through the Red Sea as on dry land; but when the Egyptians attempted to do so, they were drowned. ³⁰ By faith the walls of Jericho fell down after they had been encircled for seven days. ³¹ By faith Rahab the prostitute did not perish with those who were disobedient, because she had welcomed the spies with peace.

WHY & WHEREFORE

Later in this chapter we will hear of faithful people whose faith cost them their lives. For the moment, however, we celebrate some whose lives were saved by their faith. Trusting God, the people of Israel marched through the Red (or "Reed") Sea to freedom on a path made when God separated the water by a strong wind. The Egyptian army mimicked the Israelites' action without knowing their God, and died as a result. Years later, Israel's army spared Rahab's family in the conquest of Jericho because she had trusted God and hidden Israelite spies who scouted the city in advance of their invasion. The invasion was successful because God toppled Jericho's defensive walls in response to Israel's faithful (but highly unusual) week of otherwise-embarrassing marching.

UNPACKING THE TEXT

11:29 The next room in the Hall is dedicated to the Exodus. As the Israelites fled the pursuing Egyptian army, they came to the apparently-impassable barrier of the Red Sea. Following God's directions, Moses signaled with his shepherd's rod and God sent a strong east wind that divided the waters. By faith the Israelites marched across the mud flats. The Egyptians attempted to follow, but they lacked the faith to succeed. (Literally, they "made a trial of" the sea). Moses signaled with his rod again, the waters resumed their normal place, and the Egyptian army was wiped out (Exodus 14:21-30).

The Hebrew Old Testament calls this body of water the Sea of Reeds. The Greek Old Testament names it the Red Sea. The story of God's victory over Egypt on this occasion becomes the Old Testament "gospel," the prototype of God's future rescues in keeping with his covenant mercies (Isaiah 11:15-16; 51:10-11).

11:30 There is much to think about in this Hall of the Faithful. We walk into the third room of this third wing. A miniature of the city of Jericho fills the space before us. We remember that by faith the walls of Jericho fell after they had been encircled for seven days (Joshua 6). The entire episode required Israel to trust God's promise, move in obedience and persevere through a week of apparent divine inactivity until it was God's own time to respond. In the 1930's, an archaeologist named Garstang announced that he had discovered Jericho's walls from Joshua's time. However, later excavations by Kathleen Kenyon brought that claim into serious question. We may be glad that faith does not require validation by external evidence. When exercised, it validates itself to those who exercise it.

11:31 Rahab had heard reports of God's deeds on Israel's behalf and she had believed in God (Joshua 2:10-11). By faith she peacefully received and hid two Israelite spies. When Israel finally invaded Jericho, they spared Rahab although her disobedient neighbors perished. James also lauds Rahab for demonstrating faith that acts as well as professes (James 2:25). The second-century Christian leader Clement of Rome extolled Rahab as a model of hospitality and faith (1 Clement 12:1).

Both Hebrew and Greek Old Testaments identify Rahab as a prostitute (Joshua 2:1; 6:17, 22, 25). Through the years, some Jewish and Christian interpreters have attempted to transform her into an innkeeper or even a pagan temple prostitute. However, the biblical description is clear. The plain truth is that all God's people are sinners. Rahab is characteristic of many others, whom God redeems from lives of public or notorious sin.

Despite her former way of life, Rahab's heart and life were transformed by trusting the God who both exists and rewards those who seek him. As the eventual wife of Salmon, Rahab's descendants included King David and ultimately our Lord himself (Matthew 1:5).

HEBREWS 11:32-38

True Faith Both Triumphs and Suffers

³² And what more should I say? For time would fail me to tell of Gideon, Barak, Samson, Jephthah, of David, Samuel and the prophets. ³³ Who through faith conquered kingdoms, enforced justice, obtained promises; stopped the mouths of lions, ³⁴ quenched raging flames of fire, escaped the edge of the sword; from weakness were made strong, became mighty in battle, put foreign armies to flight. ³⁵ Women received back their dead, raised to life again. Others were tortured, refusing to accept release, so that they might obtain a better resurrection. ³⁶ Others suffered mockings and flogging, and even chains and imprisonment. ³⁷ They were stoned, they were sawn in two, they were killed by the sword. They went about in sheepskins and goatskins, destitute, afflicted, mistreated, ³⁸ of whom the world was not worthy. They wandered in deserts and mountains, and in caves and holes in the ground.

WHY & WHEREFORE

Heroes and heroines of faith experience both triumphs and tragedies, whether we think of their life circumstances or their earthly outcomes. In the world's eyes, they include winners and losers, victors and victims. In this section our author summarizes apparent successes and failures alike. Like the Son of God, Jesus Christ himself, these valiant men and women looked by faith to the God who is invisible. They risked everything on the confidence that he will always be faithful. They persevered— whatever the cost or the consequences. This is biblical "faith teaching," not the self-centered, humanistic philosophy that has captivated so many professing believers in our time.

UNPACKING THE TEXT

Faithful Judges and Prophets

11:32 We come now to the fourth wing in the Hall of the Faithful with its large open space and giant screen. The program begins. The pace immediately picks up. "What more shall I say?" our author asks rhetorically. "Time would fail me" to give details about all others who might be included. He names four specific men from the period of Israel's judges, one king, one prophet-judge, then mentions "the prophets" in general. Our author does not name the first four in chronological order, perhaps reflecting his rushed presentation.

Gideon, also called "Jerubbaal" (Judges 6:32), defeated an enormous coalition of marauding Midianites with 300 men. Following God's instructions, Gideon repeatedly downsized an original army of 32,000 until only 300 men remained. Gideon undertook a military operation against hopeless odds. He did that by faith, in response to God's repeated promises of success. The details of Gideon's final victory left no doubt that God was due the credit (Judges 6-8).

As war commander to Deborah the judge, Barak led a successful assault against a Canaanite force which enjoyed military superiority because it possessed iron chariots. Although somewhat cowardly by nature, Barak boldly proceeded to battle after Deborah assured him of God's presence and aid (Judges 4-5).

Samson's exploits involved his personal resistance against Philistine occupation of his homeland. Despite (or perhaps because of) his own obvious moral weaknesses, Samson was keenly aware that his extraordinary physical strength was God's continual gift (Judges 13-16).

Jephthah rescued the Israelite tribes who had settled east of the Jordan River from hostile Ammonites. His military zeal was grounded in the stories of God's mighty deeds in times past and in his assurance that God would also accompany him in battle. In a moment of sincere devotion to God, Jephthah swore a misguided and poorly-worded vow. That vow eventually cost him his daughter's life. Our author does not suggest that

Jephthah's faith played any role in that horrific event. The son of a prostitute and an outcast to his half-brothers, Jephthah neither experienced nor modeled a functional and healthy family (Judges 11).

Praised by the apostle Paul as a man after God's own heart, David served God's purpose in his own lifetime (Acts 13:22, 36). His saga fills most of three biblical books and contains many anecdotes that illustrate faith and inspire it in others (1 Samuel 16-31; 2 Samuel; 1 Chronicles 11-29). Yet perhaps the Psalms provide us the clearest window into the faithful heart of Israel's greatest liturgist and king. The far-reaching influence of the Psalms on the Christian church is beyond reckoning. The Book of Hebrews itself exemplifies the depth and the extent of that influence.

Samuel was the final charismatic judge in Israel and also the first in a guild of established prophets (1 Samuel 3:19-20). From early childhood, he heard God's voice with open ears and an obedient heart (1 Samuel 3).

"The prophets" include the 16 canonical prophets as well as all the non-writing prophets (see comments on Hebrews 1:1). Their faith is evident in their words and their deeds. We remember "the mighty works of Elijah and Elisha, the patient and trying service of Hosea or Jeremiah, the holy boldness of Micaiah or Amos or Daniel, the unquestioning obedience of Ezekiel, or the confident reliance which Habakkuk expresses so beautifully in his poetic third chapter" (Fudge, 139-140). These and other individual prophets will come to mind as we read the details our author gives in the following verses.

11:33-34 The visuals on our screen now begin to overlap and the titles fade rapidly in and out. These two verses contain nine clauses divided evenly into three distinct sets. The first three clauses summarize military and governmental successes which the people mentioned in verse 32 accomplished through faith.

- *Conquered kingdoms.* Acting on their trust in God, the five named judges all experienced victories in battle (though Samson fought single-handedly without an army), but David excelled them all (1 Chronicles 18:6, 13).

- *Enforced justice.* As the last of the judges, Samuel faithfully led God's people with integrity and without scandal (1 Samuel 12:1-4). David also reigned over Israel in a manner both fair and right, producing a society marked by justice and equity (1 Chronicles 18:14). The clause translated as "enforced justice" can also refer to an individual who lived in a way that was fair, right and just.

- *Obtained promises.* God made specific promises to Barak (Judges 4:6-7), Gideon (Judges 6:16; 7:7), Samson (Judges 13:5) and David (2 Samuel 7:8-16). Each of these leaders lived with faith in God's promise, and each eventually saw God do what he had said he would do. Our author earlier made the same statement about faithful Abraham (Hebrews 6:15).

The next three clauses recall divine rescues from premature deaths by execution. These deliverances are also attributed to faith. In the original language, the three major verbs used here are pleasantly alliterative.

- *Stopped the mouths of lions.* Of those specifically named, Samson (Judges 14:5-6) and David (1 Samuel 17:33-37) both overpowered lions through divine strength which they drew upon through their faith. However, our author is clearly thinking of Daniel, one of "the prophets" (v. 32), from whose Greek Old Testament story he borrows the words "stopped the mouths of lions" (Daniel 6:22 [LXX 6:23]). The next verse in both the Hebrew and Greek texts explains that Daniel sustained no injury whatsoever "because he trusted in his God."

- *Extinguished raging flames of fire.* From intertestamental times onward, Jewish "Bible stories," like Christian ones today, featured the closely-related tales of the Lions' Den (Daniel 6:16-24) and the Fiery Furnace (Daniel 3:13-30). Before they were tossed into Nebuchadnezzar's supercharged incinerator, Shadrach, Meshach and Abednego expressed confidence that God was able to rescue them (Daniel 3:17). Following their deliverance from the furnace, the king personally explained that the three had trusted in their God (Daniel 3:28). The Greek parallel says that God rescued them *because* they trusted in him (LXX Daniel 3:95).

- The faith of Shadrach, Meshach and Abednego stands out even more in the Greek text, which inserts 67 extra verses beginning with verse 24. Most of the insert consists of songs of prayer and praise by Azariah (Shadrach) and then by the entire group as they walked in the middle of the fire. This addition begins with the words: "And they were walking in the midst of the flame, singing to God and blessing the Lord" (LXX Daniel 3:24).

- *Escaped the edge of the sword.* Our author literally says "mouth" of the sword, the same word in the earlier phrase "mouth of lions." By faith David (1 Samuel 17:45-50), Elijah (1 Kings 19:1-3, 15-18), Elisha (2 Kings 6:24-31) and Jeremiah (Jeremiah 26:12-24) all escaped the edge of the sword. Three verses later, our author will commend others who through faith were killed by the sword (Hebrews 11:37).

Our author returns in the final three clauses to the theme of victories, with emphasis on the divine source of the power that won them.

- *From weakness were made strong.* As elsewhere in Hebrews, the word here translated "weakness" refers to the limited strength of humanity in general (Hebrews 4:15; 5:2; 7:28). In this clause, our author remembers people possessing obvious natural weakness which God replaced with divine power. Gideon was commissioned by an angel who challenged him to "go in this strength of yours" and rescue Israel, drawing Gideon's response that his clan was "the weakest in Manasseh" (Judges 6:14-15). God empowered Samson's greatest feat in Samson's moment of greatest weakness (Judges 16:28-30).God still says to his people: "My power is made perfect in weakness" (2 Corinthians 12:9). To which all those who see with eyes of faith respond: "When I am weak, then I am strong" (2 Corinthians 12:10).

- *Became mighty in battle, put foreign armies to flight.* The two final clauses go together. They describe the successful outcome of nearly every military exercise conducted by God's people throughout the Old Testament and during the intertestamental period as well. First Maccabees records the adventures of 2nd-century B.C. freedom fighters from the family wearing that name. These brave and godly men (and women, in other roles) struggled for Jewish independence against the pagan Seleucid tyrant Antiochus IV. Antiochus took the title *Epiphanes* ("Illustrious One"), but the Jews mockingly nicknamed him *Epimenes* ("Madman").

11:35a In the first part of this verse our author completes his honor roll of faithful people whom God vindicated visibly by giving them victory over their enemies. In the second part of the verse he begins a recital of honored believers who appeared outwardly to be the vanquished victims of their godless persecutors and opponents.

The first list closes with women "who received back their dead, raised to life again." Biblical examples of such women include the widow of Zarephath whose son Elijah raised back from the dead (1 Kings 17:17-24) and the woman of Shunem whom God similarly blessed through Elisha (2 Kings 4:18-37). The story of the Shunemite provides our author's title for this category with its statement that the bereaved "woman . . . received her son" (LXX 2 Kings 4:37).

Faith Endures Torture and Murder

11:35b In direct contrast to these whose loved ones were received back alive out of death, others were tortured for their faith and offered release if they would renounce it. However, they refused to avoid death at such a cost, placing their hope in God to provide a "better resurrection."

The verb translated "torture" (literally "to beat to death") is behind the English word "timpani," another name for the musical instrument known as a "kettle drum." The Greek word specifically referred to a particularly horrific torture in which the victim was stretched tightly on a rack and then beaten in the stomach like a drum until dead. The meaning expanded to include torture on a wheel and then torture in general. During the 2nd-century B.C. Jewish persecution by Antiochus, a godly, 90-year-old scribe named Eleazar was beaten to death on the rack because he refused to eat pork in violation of God's commandment (2 Maccabees 6:18-31).

The Jewish writer Philo told of similar torture inflicted on Jews by the Roman official in first-century Alexandria, Egypt. Flaccus, the Roman prefect, presented the public with an all-day theater spectacle. For the morning entertainment, Jews were scourged, hung up, tortured on the wheel, sentenced to death and then dragged through the middle of the orchestra to be executed. The afternoon program continued with dancers, buffoons, flute-players and all the other theatrical "diversions" (*Against Flaccus* 85).

Many faithful Jews were offered amnesty—which they refused—in exchange for a renunciation of their faith. They refused to accept "release." The word is literally translated "redemption" and it commonly refers to freedom obtained for a price. These martyrs weighed their alternatives and evaluated the possibilities. Better to die than to pay the price of denying God, they concluded. As he was dying, Eleazar commented that he could have escaped torture, but that he chose instead to endure terrible sufferings because he feared God (2 Maccabees 6:30).

They chose "a better resurrection." That is, they preferred to die horrible deaths now and to be raised immortal by God, rather than to escape death now for a limited time, but to lose all hope of endless life. This was the clear choice of seven brothers whom Antiochus tortured to death for their faith (2 Maccabees 7). One brother said to his tormentors: "You send us from this life, but the King of the world shall raise us up who died for his laws, and he will revive us to eternal life." Another brother confessed: "I received these limbs from heaven. For (God's) name's sake I consider them as nothing. I hope to get them back from God again." After killing six brothers, Antiochus offered the youngest one wealth and political position if he would only deny God. The youngest brother responded: "After enduring brief pain, these brothers have now drunk ever-flowing life according to God's covenant. But by God's judgment you shall receive fair punishment for your arrogance. Like my brothers, I surrender my body and soul for our ancestral laws."

11:36 Others throughout history knew the sting of cruel verbal mockings or taunts. Jesus had taught his disciples to expect as much (Matthew 5:11-12), and the original readers of Hebrews already had known their share (Hebrews 10:33). Believers have been flogged, lashed and whipped; they have suffered chains, bonds and incarceration in prison. Both Joseph (Genesis 39) and Jeremiah (Jeremiah 20:2; 37:15; 38: 6) were imprisoned for their faithfulness to God. The same fate befell the prophets Micaiah (1 Kings 22:26-27) and Hanani (2 Chronicles 16:10). Some of the original recipients of Hebrews also had been imprisoned for Christ and others were still being held (Hebrews 10:34; 13:3).

11:37 We remember the first-century martyr Stephen, who was stoned to death for his testimony of faith. Centuries before that, a wicked nation of Israelites had stoned a prophet named Zechariah in the very courtyard of the Temple itself (2 Chronicles 24:20-22; Matthew 23:35). Jewish tradition says that Jeremiah also was stoned to death by Jews in Egypt after the fall of Jerusalem (Jeremiah 42-44). The Apostle Paul suffered stoning, which he survived (2 Corinthians 11:25).

Because of their faithfulness to God, others were sawn in two. According to ancient Jewish tradition, the apostate Judean king Manasseh ordered Isaiah's execution with a wooden saw. He chose that death for the prophet, the tradition says, because Isaiah had hidden in the trunk of a cedar tree after Manasseh had issued a warrant for his arrest. We can believe this of a king who sacrificed his own children to a pagan god (2 Chronicles 33:6), and who led God's people to become more evil than the nations (2 Chronicles 33:9).

Faith Perseveres Despite Other Persecutions

Here the Greek text adds that others "were tempted" or "met trial," a comment that most standard versions do not translate. Some scholars have speculated that our author wrote another verb only one letter different that meant "met death by fire." Some faithful Jews were burned to death (2 Maccabees 6:11). However, no textual evidence supports this proposed reading.

Some of God's people have been killed by the sword and others have been delivered from such a death (Hebrews 11:34; Acts 12:1ff). Elijah was spared this death when others were not (1 Kings 19:10). Uriah was murdered by the sword, but Jeremiah was delivered (Jeremiah 26:23-24). God alone knows why some are allowed to die and others are not. He will reward every faithful person regardless of the details.

Still other faithful people have been evicted from their homes and deprived of proper clothing. As a result they went about in sheepskins and goatskins. They were destitute, afflicted, mistreated—a far cry from the victories and conquests enjoyed by others who also served God well through their faith (Hebrews 11:33-35a). Anyone who suggests that authentic believers always prosper materially and enjoy worldly success reveals his or her own ignorance of biblical teaching, spiritual reality and genuine faith.

11:38 Unbelieving mobs sometimes judge God's faithful people as unfit for this world (Acts 22:22). Their conclusion is correct, although not in the way the unbelievers think. Persecuted believers are unfit for the world because they deserve a better one—and God will give it to them in his own time. Meanwhile, these people of faith sometimes live in deserts, mountains, caves and holes in the ground. When Jezebel tried to kill Elijah, the prophet fled to the desert, then to a mountain and finally to a cave (1 Kings 19:1-14). Others endured the same difficulties during the period between the Testaments as predicted by Daniel the prophet (Daniel 11:31-36; 2 Maccabees 5:27).

HEBREWS 11:39-40

Past Faithful Are Incomplete Without Us

[39] And all these, though commended through their faith, did not receive what was promised, [40] because God had provided something better for us, so that apart from us they would not be made perfect.

WHY & WHEREFORE

The faithful need perseverance only because God postpones their rewards. Yet from Abel forward God has commended his people for their faith—and commended their lives by their faith. He delays their public vindication and reward in order for others to join their ranks of faith. When the time arrives, we will all rejoice together.

UNPACKING THE TEXT

11:39-40 These all—from Abel forward—were commended through their faith and obtained a good report—directly from God (Hebrews 11:4) or by the faithful who came after them (Hebrews 11:2). Yet they did not receive the final inheritance that God had promised. They were not for this reason denied divine grace, and they will not be excluded from final glory and immortality when Jesus appears bringing salvation. Whenever faithful people live, they are justified by the merits of the one offering of Jesus Christ (Hebrews 9:15).

Faithful lives often go unrewarded now. But that does not mean that faith is useless, or that God is unfaithful. It points rather to the unity of all true believers through the person, sacrifice and mediation of Jesus Christ (Hebrews 9:15). God's unfailing plan is to allow history to run its course, then to reward all people of faith together.

"Better" is one of our author's favorite adjectives. It characterizes the new covenant and all that it represents. Our author uses "better" to describe Christ's name or position (Hebrews 1:4). It fits Jesus' sacrifice dedicating the heavenly sanctuary (Hebrews 9:23), the new testament (Hebrews 7:22) or covenant (Hebrews 8:6) and hope based on Jesus Christ (Hebrews 7:19). Our author also speaks of a "better" resurrection (Hebrews 11:35), country (Hebrews 11:16), substance (Hebrews 10:34) and message of Christ's blood (Hebrews 12:24). In turn, these blessings are expected to elicit "better" behavior from those who receive and enjoy them (Hebrews 6:9).

The verb "to make perfect" has also become familiar to us in reading this Epistle. Jesus Christ, the Son of God made man, was perfected as our high priest by all that he experienced in life and in death (Hebrews 2:10; 5:9; 7:28). Having become a perfect high priest for his people, Jesus also makes his people perfect through the offering of his faithful human life in his body on the cross (Hebrews 10:14; 12:23). Such perfection blossoms into flower through a life of faith expressed in obedience to God. This faith often accomplishes great feats. It also sometimes endures great suffering. Perhaps most of all, it is the faith that perseveres. That is what we saw in Jesus Christ. It marked the lives of the heroes and heroines of faith who preceded us. The same perseverance is foremost in our author's mind now as he comes to his final words of encouragement and exhortation.

HEBREWS 12:1-3

Jesus and Early Believers Encourage Us

¹ Therefore, since we are surrounded by so great a cloud of witnesses, let us also lay aside every weight and the sin that so easily entangles us, and let us run with endurance the race that is set before us, ² looking to Jesus, the author and perfecter of our faith, who for the sake of the joy that was set before him endured the cross, despising the shame, and has sat down at the right hand of the throne of God. ³ For consider him who endured such hostility from sinners against himself, so that you will not grow weary and lose heart.

WHY & WHEREFORE

Whether we live inconspicuously or in the spotlight of the world, our lives are far more public than we ever might imagine. Our author asks us to picture ourselves as runners in a great arena. Surrounding us in the heavenly stands are God's faithful people from the beginning of time. They know just what we are feeling, for they also have run this race. Like us, they have felt the thrill of challenge. They also have known weariness to the point of exhaustion. Despite it all, they persevered— they *finished* their race. Now we look more closely and see someone else. There, in the seat next to God himself, sits Jesus Christ! He, too, has run this race—against great opposition, at that. Now, like the others, he is here to cheer us on.

UNPACKING THE TEXT

Surrounded by a Cloud of Witnesses

12:1 As we exit the Hall of the Faithful described in Hebrews 11, our author is waiting. We walk together down a short path to what resembles an ancient outdoor theater, its moss-covered stones blending into the surrounding gardens. To tell the truth, our senses are overloaded—and for very good reason. As we moved through the Hall, absorbing each video, portrait and tableau, we had relived every thrilling exploit and escapade. What pressures, passions and persecutions they encountered and endured, these faithful men and women of centuries past!

Each exhibit had also included a recorded narrative, charged with declaratory sentences packed with past-tense verbs. Now our author leads us into the open stadium. He chooses a position a few steps in front of our little group and clears his throat to speak. A respectful hush falls over those assembled. "Therefore," he begins. Our minds focus on his voice so as not to miss a word. "Therefore, *let us . . . .*"

This "therefore" is stronger than the word usually so translated, and it appears only one other time in the New Testament (1 Thessalonians 4:8). Here, it stands emphatically at the front of the sentence, connecting the previous section with the one that follows. Since we are surrounded or encompassed by so great a cloud of witnesses, there must be an especially appropriate response on our part. This unusual word for "cloud" appears several times in the Septuagint, but only here in the New Testament. Non-biblical Greek writings also used it as a metaphor for a crowd since the time of Homer. The more common word for "cloud" has the same figurative sense in the Greek Old Testament (Ezekiel 38:9, 16).

Our tour through chapter 11 has identified some of the faces in the crowd-cloud surrounding us. They belong to people our author calls "witnesses," a word from which we get "martyr." We should think first of witnesses in a courtroom, giving their testimony to what they have personally seen, heard and experienced. However, testifying is sometimes dangerous, especially when testifying about matters involving God and ultimate loyalties. For that reason, the words for "witness" or "one testifying" came to be used in a special way to describe witnesses whose testimony cost them their lives (LXX Nehemiah 9:26; Acts 22:20). Some people in our Hall of the Faithful were martyr-witnesses in that sense. However, everyone honored there had testified by word and by walk—to a God who had encountered them, and to a value-system based on invisible realities unperceived by a faithless world. These "witnesses" are more than spectators—they *testify* as well as watch.

The Race of a Lifetime

The courtroom image fades from our minds; the scene of a stadium takes its place. This time we are poised at the running-blocks, not for a 100-yard dash or even for the quarter-mile event. This race is the marathon. In the Olympic Games of ancient Greece, the foot race was the first of five events and it was the only contest given a lengthy period of time. In this contest, the winning attribute is endurance rather than sheer speed. That is the author's word to us now: "let us run with endurance the race that is set before us."

The word translated "race" originally meant the place where an athletic competition was held, and then it came to mean the event itself. This Greek word produced our words "agony" and "agonize," which tells us something about the intensity of the exertion called for. In that vein of total commitment, our author urges us to take off and place aside every weight that might impede our best effort, particularly "the sin that so easily entangles us." Ancient athletes completely disrobed for their contests, and "lay aside" here translates a verb that sometimes means stripping off clothing (Acts 7:58; Colossians 3:8). Whatever hinders our faith-marathon is better laid aside. "The sin" mentioned here is probably the sin of quitting too soon, of giving up before we reach the end. However, in the spirit of the verse as a whole, we ought each to ask the Holy Spirit to reveal any other sin to us that especially retards our own spiritual race.

The athletic contest is a metaphor, of course, one widely used by wandering philosophers in the first-century Greco-Roman world and by preachers since. One writer roughly contemporary with Hebrews also lauded faithful Jews between the testaments using this similar language:

> Truly they were engaged in a divine contest, because on that day virtue gave out the awards and tested their endurance. The prize was immortality in endless life. Eleazar was the first contestant. His mother with her seven sons joined the competition. The other

brothers contended. The tyrant was the antagonist. The world and the human race were spectators. Reverence for God was the victor and it gave the crown to its own athletes. (4 Maccabees 17:11-15).

Finally, because our text employs a figure of speech, we should not misuse it by trying to mine literal details concerning the present state of the dead—their consciousness or lack of it, and whether they are aware of activities among those still living on the earth.

Fixing Our Eyes on Jesus

12:2 The greatest encouragement comes by looking intently at Jesus, a focused act better expressed as "fixing our eyes on Jesus." The verb is akin to the noun for a "vision." It suggests that we form a permanent and clear image of Jesus in our mind, to which we will continually return. Jesus is the appropriate vision to encourage our firm resolve. In this salvation marathon he is the champion ("author" here; "source" in Hebrews 2:10). He is our "forerunner" (Hebrews 6:20), who first completed this race without flaw and opened the track from earth to heaven. Jesus is the "perfecter" or finisher of faith, a word found only here in the Bible. There is no "our" in the Greek. As both author and perfecter of faith, Jesus personally embodies all the traits and virtues which faith includes. In Jesus himself, we see perfect faith, and also the faithfulness that it produces.

For the third time, our author calls us to intensify our view of Jesus Christ. We "see" him, the Son of God incarnate, in the position of honor for which God created men and women (Hebrews 2:9). We "consider" how he came to that position through daily faithfulness to the Father (Hebrews 3:1). Now, rewarded for his own faithfulness by the faithfulness of God, we "form a fixed image" of Jesus at God's right hand in heaven (Hebrews 12:2). Specifically, we see Jesus who ran the marathon, despite overwhelming opposition and against seemingly insurmountable odds. We see Jesus, who finished the race, now enjoying his reward beside God's own heavenly throne.

Jesus came to this reward by enduring the cross. He endured the cross by despising the shame—the shame that the cross symbolized, and that it smeared over the person and memory of every wretched soul who became its victim. Today we wear crosses as jewelry and use them to decorate our homes and churches. That was not the case in the Roman-ruled world of the first century. There the cross was a symbol of humiliation and great shame. An engine of execution, it was reserved for political insurrectionists and the lowest of criminals. One perk of Roman citizenship, in the event a citizen committed a capital offense, was the guarantee of immunity from crucifixion. Citizen Paul was therefore beheaded, while noncitizen Peter was crucified upside down. Crucifixion was considered so disgraceful that the Roman poet Cicero, who died about 43 B.C., urged his imperial neighbors not to watch a crucifixion, and to avoid either speaking or even thinking about the subject.

Jesus endured the cross, but *why* did he endure? Our author tells us that as well—Jesus endured "for the sake of the joy that was set before him." The joy that was set before Jesus likely included his delight in doing the will of God (Psalm 40:8; Hebrews 10:5-10). It also included his joy in bringing many of his human brothers and sisters to final glory with himself (Hebrews 2:10; Isaiah 53:10-12). On every "today" of his life, the man Jesus heard God's voice and received God's promise in faith. Just as regularly, he placed himself within the Father's purpose in simple and wholehearted trust. In that trust and with the confidence it inspires, he then endured every expression of hostility and every manifestation of opposition the enemy threw his way, consistently doing all the Father's will throughout his entire life.

Jesus' faith was not in vain. A few decades before our author wrote Hebrews, God had raised Jesus from the dead and seated him in honor at his own right hand in heaven (Psalm 110:1; see Hebrews 1:13; 8:1; 10:12). In saying that Jesus "sat down" there, our author uses a verb tense telling us that Jesus not only took this seat, but that he occupies it still. This was the cost for Jesus to endure, and this was his reward for doing it.

12:3 Again our author urges us to "consider" Jesus. His verb suggests that we draw an "analogy," that we compare and contrast the obstacles Jesus faced alongside the hindrances that bedevil and frustrate us. The original readers of Hebrews had endured verbal and physical hostility from sinful people (Hebrews 10:32-33). Jesus also endured the same. The words point again to the race, the runner, and the reward that is waiting at the course's end. There is no good reason to grow weary and lose heart.

HEBREWS 12:4-11

Wisdom Literature Exhorts Us

⁴ In your struggle against sin you have not yet resisted to the point of shedding your blood. ⁵ And you have forgotten the exhortation that addresses you as sons:

"My son, do not regard lightly the discipline of the Lord,
nor lose heart when you are reproved by him.
⁶ For the Lord disciplines those whom he loves,
and punishes every son whom he receives."

⁷ It is for discipline that you endure; God is treating you as sons. For what son is there whom his father does not discipline? ⁸ But if you are without discipline, of which all have become partakers, then you are illegitimate children and not true sons. ⁹ Furthermore, we had earthly fathers to discipline us, and we respected them; shall we not much more be subject to the Father of spirits, and live? ¹⁰ For they disciplined us for a short time as seemed best to them, but he disciplines us for our good, so that we may share his holiness. ¹¹ No discipline seems enjoyable at the time, but painful; but later it yields the peaceful fruit of righteousness to those who have been trained by it.

WHY & WHEREFORE

Our author now hands us three encouragement cards containing portions of Scripture. We open the first, which features proverbs about fathers and sons. Earthly difficulties, our author explains, are part of God's purposeful discipline while training us for coming glory.

UNPACKING THE TEXT

12:4 Unlike Jesus himself, the original recipients of this ancient sermon had not yet resisted to the point of shedding their blood. Now the athletic metaphor seems to move from the foot race to the boxing match, during which first-century boxers would fight barehanded until their hands were bruised and bleeding. Perhaps no metaphor is involved and this is literal language. In that case our author is simply noting that his first readers had not yet faced the threat of martyrdom, though some of their mentors and teachers seemingly had (Hebrews 13:7). For Jesus, the path of faith led straight to the cross. His followers must be faithful even if the same sacrifice is required of them.

With this verse, our author turns from the figure of the stadium filled with witnesses to consider three other scenes drawn from the three primary divisions of the Old Testament Scriptures. First, in verses four through eleven, he discusses a quotation from the Writings (Proverbs 3:11-12). Then, in verses 12-17, he makes a point from the Prophets (Isaiah 35:3). He ends with verses 18-29, in which he mentally re-enacts a scene from the Torah (Exodus 19-20) and contrasts its terror with the comforting picture projected by the gospel.

Discipline is Profitable but Not Pleasant

12:5-6 His first text is Proverbs 3:11-12, which he uses to encourage the faithful to view their difficulties as proof of God's loving, parental discipline. We tend to see such difficulties as evidence of God's disfavor. Throughout this context, "discipline" translates a word used (among other ways) for a father's training of his son. Because discipline proves the father's love (Revelation 3:19), its recipients must not lightly regard or belittle its value and purpose. God both disciplines and receives his child who undergoes this training.

12:7 To have its greatest effect, discipline/training requires endurance by believers who receive it. They have launched by faith into a process. God is aware of their suffering and it fits into his purpose. The verb here may also be translated as an imperative ("endure for the purpose of discipline"). More probably, it a simple indicative verb ("you endure for the purpose of discipline") which states the case.

12:8 Rather than becoming alarmed at the presence of discipline, believers should have concern at its absence. The son who grows up without restraint or training is suspected of being an illegitimate child. What father would fail to give his true son the discipline that will make him an honorable and responsible man?

12:9 These truths are well known through common experience. As children, most of us had physical or surrogate fathers who provided us with correction. When we became mature adults, we remembered and appreciated that discipline—and we respected our fathers who delivered it. How much more ought we to submit to God, the father of spirits, and to find life. The last phrase is reminiscent of the proverb which, in the Septuagint, says: "For a commandment of the Law is a lamp and a light, and reproof and discipline are a pathway of life" (LXX Proverbs 6:23).

12:10 If we can respect the training and discipline of our earthly fathers, which they administered with mixed motives and short-term results, how much more should we revere the heavenly father, whose discipline is to make us like himself for our eternal good?

12:11 No one enjoys being disciplined at the time. It is a painful experience. Yet, for those who are trained by it, discipline produces pleasant long-term benefits, here called "the fruit of righteousness." This summary statement combines agricultural imagery ("fruit") with athletic imagery ("trained" translates a verb related to our word "gymnasium").

Isaiah's Pilgrimage Offers Guidance

¹² Therefore strengthen your drooping hands and your weak knees, ¹³ and make straight paths for your feet, so that what is lame may not be put out of joint, but rather be healed. ¹⁴ Pursue peace with everyone, and the holiness without which no one will see the Lord. ¹⁵ See to it that no one fails to obtain the grace of God; that no root of bitterness springs up and causes trouble, and by it many become defiled. ¹⁶ See that no one is immoral or godless like Esau, who sold his birthright for a single meal. ¹⁷ For you know that afterward, when he wanted to inherit the blessing, he was rejected, for he found no place for repentance, though he sought it with tears.

WHY & WHEREFORE

Our second encouragement card features a quotation from Isaiah and a sketch of a band of travelers on pilgrimage together. Some are infirm and weak, others are simply tired. The strong travelers assist the others. Under the drawing are two rules for the road: "Seek peace with fellow travelers" and "Seek holiness with God." Our author has added his own observation that Esau is an example of someone who failed at both.

UNPACKING THE TEXT

12:12 The chapter began with images of athletes who are firm in body, strong and energetic. Now we envision a cross-section of travelers, some with drooping muscles and worn-out joints. These are weary people— their hands are slack and their knees are weak. Our author encourages the travelers who are in good physical condition to assist those who are not. The language comes from Isaiah 35:3 and Proverbs 4:26. In Isaiah, the pilgrimage consisted of Jews returning to their land from Persian dispersion. Here the travelers are moving to the New Jerusalem and the world to come.

Pilgrims Prepare The Trail

12:13 Strong travelers are admonished to make straight paths for their companions. In this way, the feet of those who are lame will not (literally) "be turned or twisted out." This might refer to one being twisted or turned out of the path, a notion supported by the Greek text of Proverbs 4:26-27. That passage urges making straight paths, then says not to turn to the right hand or to the left. Or it might refer to lame limbs being turned or twisted out of joint. Most standard English versions follow this interpretation, which more clearly contrasts with the next phrase, "but rather be healed."

The original language lends itself to either interpretation and both ideas are appropriate. Each believer is to do whatever is possible to assist weaker brothers or sisters and to prevent them from stumbling. The desired result is a path on which no one misses the trail, on which no lame pilgrim trips and injures a limb that is already weak. Speedy travelers are to bear patiently with the slower, the strong support the weak, the energetic assist the weary.

The verb form of the word translated "lame" describes the Israelites who were "limping," "halting" or "wavering" between two opinions in the time of Elijah and who, for that reason, could not decide whether they would serve Yahweh or Baal (1 Kings 18:21, Greek). Similarly, the first readers of Hebrews were indecisive regarding their spiritual commitment to Jesus Christ. In this way, they were also "wobbly" or lame.

Rules For Fellow-Travelers

12:14 As every family who has made a road trip with multiple children knows, peace is a highly-valued condition among those traveling in close company. Our author quotes Psalm 34:14 as he urges readers to pursue peace on their pilgrimage together. Peter, himself the author of another pilgrimage sermon, quotes the same verse (1 Peter 3:11).

Faith-pilgrims also need holiness if they are to see the invisible Lord. God's people have always been called to holiness—because God himself is always holy (Leviticus 11:45; 1 Peter 1:15-16). Just as peace enables relationship with fellow-travelers, so holiness enables relationship with God.

12:15 The word here translated as "see to it" or "look diligently" is closely akin to the Greek noun translated as "overseer," which evolved in English into the word "bishop." The author of Hebrews refers to spiritual leaders only generically (Hebrews 13:7, 17) and without traditional or formal titles. However, in urging his readers to "imitate," "be persuaded by" and to "submit" to those leaders, he clearly places primary responsibility on the leaders to show the way so that others can follow.

The goal of this watchfulness is that no one fails to obtain or to come short of (see Hebrews 4:1) the grace of God. We already enjoy many benefits of God's grace (Hebrews 2:9; 4:16; 10:29; 13:9). Yet we still await its fullness in the Age to Come. The person who drops out of this faith-journey, who wills to forget it and to return to prior interests and pursuits, never reaches the goal of the pilgrimage.

If we visualize a band of travelers, we might also envision them foraging for food. While doing that, it is very important to be watchful and not to gather bitter roots that could cause widespread food poisoning (Deuteronomy 29:18). Similarly, our author warns his readers to guard against any "root of bitterness" that might spread and sicken God's people.

Esau's Bad Example

12:16 Pay attention that no one becomes sexually immoral, either with fellow-travelers during the intimacy of the journey (Hebrews 13:4), or with outsiders along the way. Our author continues by warning against becoming godless or profane—that is, regarding what is holy as if it were common and therefore lacking respect or reverence for what is holy. Among the patriarchs Esau was such an individual. According to Jewish tradition, Esau also was sexually promiscuous.

By trading his birthright to his brother Jacob for a single meal, Esau demonstrated his lack of reverence for things worthy of great respect (Genesis 25:29-34). The birthright was supposed to belong to the oldest son, and it signified the right to a double portion of the father's inheritance when he died. Esau's bartering of his special inheritance revealed his cavalier attitude toward a highly-revered privilege. It also demonstrated his indifference to his own potential role in the lineage of Abraham and in God's covenant purposes and promises.

The same failure to distinguish between the common and the holy, to recognize what is truly valuable and to regard it and treat it accordingly, almost always leads one into sin. This hazard includes not only sins of irreverence or blasphemy against God, but also violations of trust (such as adultery, embezzlement and theft) and offenses against the person and name of another. On the other hand, there is no more effective preventative and defense against sin than an intuitive humility before the holiness of God, a sense of the appropriate which that reverence inspires, and a constant awareness of one's identification with the blameless Son of God.

12:17 A godless mind that is dismissive of spiritual matters today will not, apart from divine intervention, become reverent tomorrow. A profane spirit forfeits present blessings and, from a human standpoint, it also forecloses the possibility of any change or improvement in the future. One who has no regard for what is holy might possibly experience regret or even remorse, if some personal loss appears imminent. However, the godless individual lacks the moral sensitivity that can produce repentance. Esau also exemplifies this truth.

Readers familiar with the Old Testament story know already that afterward, when Esau thought about what he would be missing, he wanted to inherit the blessing. However, his remorse came too late, and he was rejected (Genesis 27:30-40). This verse has three key phrases, all somewhat ambiguous and capable of at least two meanings. *Who* rejected Esau—Isaac, God or both? *Where* did Esau find no place for repentance—in himself, in his father, or in both? *What* did Jacob seek carefully with tears—the blessing or a place for repentance?

By bequeathing the birthright to Jacob, Isaac rejected Esau's rightful claim to it as the slightly-senior twin brother. However, since the patriarchs acted for God in bestowing ancestral blessings (Hebrews 11:20), our author seems to be saying that Jacob either reflected or gave voice to God's own rejection of Esau in the process. Jacob himself believed that the blessing, once given, could not be retracted (Gen. 27:33).

Esau found no place in his own heart for a moral change of mindset. He found no place in his father Isaac for a reversal of the previously-given birthright. He sought the blessing with tears—tears no doubt for his own loss (Genesis 27:38).

HEBREWS 12:18-24

Mount Sinai and Mount Zion

¹⁸ For you have not come to a mountain that can be touched, a blazing fire, to darkness and gloom and a tempest, ¹⁹ and the blast of a trumpet and a voice of words such that those who heard it begged that no further word be spoken to them, ²⁰ because they could not bear what was commanded: "If even an animal touches the mountain, it must be stoned." ²¹ And so terrifying was the sight that Moses said, "I tremble with fear." ²² But you have come to Mount Zion and to the city of the living God, the heavenly Jerusalem, and to innumerable angels in festive gathering, ²³ to the assembly of the firstborn who are enrolled in heaven, to God the judge of all, to the spirits of the righteous made perfect, ²⁴ to Jesus, the mediator of a new covenant, and to the sprinkled blood that speaks a better word than the blood of Abel.

WHY & WHEREFORE

In this section of Scripture, we open our third encouragement card. Written on one inside panel is a quotation from Exodus. The other panel contains two small pictures. One drawing represents Israel gathered at Mount Sinai; the other portrays Mount Zion, the heavenly Jerusalem. Capping the scene in the second drawing is Jesus himself, whose portrait greeted us at the beginning of this book.

UNPACKING THE TEXT

Fearsome Mount Sinai

12:18 We peer at the first little drawing and recognize it as a portrayal of God's delivery of the Law at Mount Sinai. Our author says that this in no way resembles our own approach to God. Sinai was a horrifying scene of storm and darkness, fire and earthquake, thunder and the voice from heaven. The Israelites had assembled there to meet the God who, by a series of memorable supernatural events, had rescued them from Egyptian slavery as he had promised their ancestor Abraham. The Torah reports the fearsome details (Exodus 19:16-20; Deuteronomy 4:11; 5:23; 9:15). A blazing fire crowned the mountain's top and storm clouds shrouded the rest. From the darkness and gloom of the clouds, there burst thunderous noises and tempestuous storms.

12:19 The people had wanted to hear God for themselves. However, after a blast that sounded like a trumpet and a voice speaking words from God, they begged Moses to be their intermediary and pleaded that God not speak directly to them again (Exodus 20:18-19; Deuteronomy 5:23-27).

12:20 The assembly gathered at Sinai was both awed and terrified—and well might they be! To impress the people with his unapproachable holiness, God had decreed the mountain off-limits to every living being, whether animal or human. Violators were to be summarily executed without mercy. In the Old Testament, an animal that wandered on the mountain was to be stoned if it then returned to the people, or shot with an arrow if it remained outside the people's reach (Exodus 19:12-13).

12:21 Moses himself was so overcome by the terrifying sight as to remark, "I tremble with fear." The Old Testament account says that Moses spoke in response to the trumpet-like sound (Exodus 19:19). It does not report what he said. One verse earlier, the Greek text says that all the people (which would include Moses) were driven out of their senses for fear (Exodus 19:18).

Reassuring Mount Zion

12:22 Israel encountered God at Mount Sinai, under circumstances that emphasized his distance, transcendence and judgment. For those who approach God through Jesus Christ, the enthroned Son of God made *man*, now their representative at the Father's right hand, the contrast could not possibly be more striking. Our author describes his readers' encounter (including yours and mine) with God in terms of Mount Zion.

The verb translated "you have come" (here and in verse 18 above) is in the Greek tense which tells us that believers not only have approached God in the past, but that they continue in his presence still. Because of Jesus and his one-time offering of himself on our behalf, we *forever* encounter God in the delightful, intimate and assuring way described in verses 22-24. Our word "proselyte" comes from this same verb root.

We have come into God's presence—not at Sinai-mountain, but at Zion-mountain. In Israel's history, Jerusalem was situated on Mount Zion. As David's capital city (2 Samuel 5:6-9) and the site of Solomon's Temple, Zion had long been celebrated as God's own holy city (1 Kings 14:21; Psalm 78:68; Psalm 132-134).

Here, however, Mount Zion stands for heavenly Jerusalem—God's true city, if you please. We have met this imagery before (Hebrews 11:10, 14-16) and we will see it again (Hebrews 13:14). The metaphor of a glorified Jerusalem appears in the Old Testament (particularly Ezekiel 40-48), between the Testaments (including the Dead Sea Scrolls) and in the writings of both Paul and John (see references in comments on Hebrews 11:10). Details and emphases differ from author to author, of course. For the writer of Hebrews, "Mount Zion" and the heavenly Jerusalem portray the intimacy with God enjoyed by those who belong to Jesus and draw near to the Father through him.

Populating this Mount Zion first of all are innumerable angels, literally "myriads" or tens of thousands (Psalm 68:17; Daniel 7:10; Revelation 5:11). Our author has already told us that the angels are on call as God's messengers and servants in general (Hebrews 1:7, 14).

12:23 In the heavenly Jerusalem, however, these angels are in "festive gathering." This phrase translates a single word from which comes the English word "panegyric." In the Greek literature, this is the word for a public celebration which all the people attend, usually in honor of some notable individual. Also joining in this celebration are human beings from every time and place. Together they constitute "the assembly of the firstborn ones" (plural in the original) who already are enrolled citizens in this heavenly city.

On the earth, these faithful followers of Jesus experienced rejection, mistreatment and loss of property and freedom. Here, however, God is present—God the judge of all, persecutor and persecuted alike—and He will acquit or condemn each person. This characterization of God as judge would be particularly meaningful to readers with a Hebrew background.

"The spirits of the righteous made perfect" refers to godly people such as those described throughout Hebrews chapter 11. Although many of these died before Jesus was born, they walked by faith while they lived. God has declared them to be "just" on the basis of Christ's atonement (Hebrews 9:15). The perfection or completion they lacked when they died in faith they have now attained (Hebrews 11:39-40). Our author is describing the blessedness of those who approach God through Jesus Christ, in contrast to the fear of approaching God in the Old Testament.

12:24 Also present at this festive gathering is Jesus, the mediator of a new covenant (see Hebrews 8:6). "Jesus" is his saving name as *man*, one in true nature with his earthly brothers and sisters (Matthew 1:21; Hebrews 2:9-18). Jesus is mediator of the new covenant. In his own humanity he first established and now secures eternal relationship between God and redeemed humankind. This covenantal relationship rests on Jesus' faithful obedience to the Father as representative for his people. Jesus sealed this covenant with his blood, ensuring its benefits, and he now lives forever to administer its blessings.

The metaphor of the sprinkled blood of Jesus Christ reminds God and us alike that, by his faithful life and atoning death, Jesus has accomplished total and thorough cleansing from sin. He has purified our hearts or consciences (Hebrews 9:13-14; 10:22). Indeed, he has purified heaven itself (Hebrews 9:19-24).

Jesus' sprinkled blood speaks better or more effectively than that of Abel. This is true if we think of Abel's own blood, violently shed by his brother Cain. It is also true if we think of the sacrificial blood that Abel offered to God. Jesus' blood also speaks *of* better things than either of those. Abel's sacrifice could only speak of an atonement remaining to be accomplished, while his own blood cried out for vengeance. Jesus' blood, however, speaks of an accomplished atonement that removes every barrier between holy God and sinful human and blazes a path from earth into the inner sanctum of heaven itself.

In the final five verses of the chapter, our author looks again to the prophetic portion of his Scriptures for his closing appeal.

Final Shaking Will Remove Impermanent

²⁵ See that you do not refuse him who is speaking. For if they did not escape when they refused him who warned them on earth, how much less will we escape if we turn away from him who warns from heaven. ²⁶ At that time his voice shook the earth; but now he has promised, "Yet once more I will shake not only the earth but also the heaven." ²⁷ This phrase, "Yet once more," indicates the removal of what can be shaken—that is, created things—so that the things that cannot be shaken may remain. ²⁸ Therefore, since we are receiving a kingdom that cannot be shaken, let us be thankful, by which we may offer to God acceptable worship with reverence and awe; ²⁹ for our God is a consuming fire.

WHY & WHEREFORE

God's voice thundered at Sinai and the earth shook. Now in the Son who became *man*, God has spoken again. Another shaking remains—a final tremor that only what is eternal will survive. We already have begun to receive a kingdom that cannot be shaken. Our proper response is gratitude expressed in worship, from hearts filled with awe and reverence. The God who invites us to bring him our gifts of worship is also a consuming fire.

UNPACKING THE TEXT

12:25 Our author opened this epistle with the statement that God has spoken. Now he warns the reader not to refuse God who is speaking.

Again he contrasts Mount Sinai (from which God spoke to Israel) with the voice from heaven (which has been addressed to us). Israel's redeemed generation heard God's voice from the fearsome smoke and thunder and fire of Sinai. Sadly, they refused to heed his warnings and were destroyed (Hebrews 3:8-4:11). How much less will we escape if we reject God who has now spoken from heaven!

12:26 At Sinai, God spoke and his voice shook the earth (Exodus 19:18; Psalm 18:7; 68:8; 114:4). Now he promises to shake heaven and earth—the entire universe (Haggai 2:6). The language comes from Haggai's remarks to civil and religious leaders during the dedication of the postexilic Temple about 516 B.C. To our author, they describe the end of the world that now is.

12:27 Because God said he would shake all things "once more," our author reasons that this shaking will remove everything that is not ultimately permanent. In other words, the physical creation will finally come to an end (Hebrews 1:10-12). When that occurs, only the heavenly order of things, now invisible except to the eyes of faith, will remain.

12:28 We await a kingdom of the heavenly order, presently invisible and permanently unshakable. It is appropriate that we be thankful, as we offer God acceptable worship with reverence or pious respect and awe or godly fear.

12:29 Despite the assurances of God's gracious acceptance throughout this book, we must always live before him with reverence and awe. Divine grace which God pours out on us demands no less. For the irreverent and rebellious, our God is still a consuming fire (Deuteronomy 4:24). We love and trust God in response to his mercy. However, we also revere him and tremble in response to his holiness. Faith does not mean frivolity. Assurance does not permit audacity. (This verse and its counterpart in the Old Testament were the source for the title of my book, *The Fire That Consumes: A Biblical and Historical Study of the Doctrine of Final Punishment*, www.iUniverse.com, 2001, 500 pages, trade paper.)

HEBREWS 13:1-8

Practical Duties Set Out

¹ Let brotherly love continue. ² Do not neglect to show hospitality to strangers, for by doing this some have entertained angels without knowing it. ³ Remember those who are in prison, as though you were in prison with them, and those who are mistreated, since you yourselves are also in the body. ⁴ Let marriage be held in honor by all, and the marriage bed be kept undefiled; for God will judge fornicators and adulterers. ⁵ Keep your lives free from the love of money, and be content with what you have; for he himself has said, "I will never leave you or forsake you." ⁶ So we can confidently say:

"The Lord is my helper;
I will not be afraid;
what can man do to me?"

⁷ Remember your leaders, who spoke the word of God to you. Consider the outcome of their way of life and imitate their faith. ⁸ Jesus Christ is the same yesterday and today and forever.

WHY & WHEREFORE

For twelve chapters in our Bibles, the author of Hebrews has told the Story and has urged us to respond to it by faithful lives of reverent worship and persevering faith. It is the Story of the Son of God who became *man*, who lived and died as one of us, who now represents us in person as our man in heaven. When the Father is ready, Jesus will appear to us again, bringing the salvation he already has perfected, provided and procured for his patient and persevering people. From time to time, our author has interrupted the Story to encourage us and admonish us, to warn us and to inspire. Now, in this final chapter, our unknown author concludes his written sermon with a few closing admonitions, a beautiful benediction and a handful of personal remarks.

UNPACKING THE TEXT

'Loves' to Embrace and to Avoid

13:1 Our author's first exhortation here is to continue in "brotherly love." Outside Christian circles, "brotherly love" referred only to affection based on physical kinship, and unbelieving orators mocked Christ's followers because they regarded one another in this way. Our author asks his readers to "continue" in brotherly love because they already practiced it and had done so for some time (Hebrews 6:10; 10:32-34).

13:2 Love for God's children is manifested in many ways. Our author urges his readers not to neglect showing hospitality. The Greek word translated "hospitality" literally means a love of strangers. Some commercial lodging was available to first-century travelers in the form of private inns. Most often, however, these establishments ranged from ill-kept to dangerous. Besides being expensive, they often were bawdy as well. For these reasons, Jews and Christians regularly opened their homes to traveling fellow-believers in need of hospitality.

Jesus had taught that kindness shown to his people was kindness done to him (Matthew 25:35-40). Because hospitality involved both endorsement and support, John cautioned against withholding it from those who confessed the apostolic gospel (3 John 5-10), and he warned against extending it to teachers who did not (2 John 6-11). The *Didache*, a second-century Christian handbook, contains detailed instructions concerning traveling preachers and teachers. A later Roman writer named Lucian called Christians gullible, charging that every tramp could find food and housing by convincing them of his religion.

Hospitality can also bring unexpected rewards, our author notes, reminding us that some have entertained angels without knowing it. We immediately remember stories of Abraham (Genesis 18) and Lot (Genesis 19), of Gideon (Judges 6), of Samson's parents (Judges 13) and perhaps others. Whenever we extend hospitality to a stranger we potentially show kindness to an angel of God.

13:3 Brotherly love is also manifested by identifying sympathetically with believers in prison (Hebrews 10:34) or who are otherwise mistreated (literally "have it bad") for their faith in Jesus Christ.

13:4 Again (see Hebrews 12:16) our author urges sexual purity, this time within marriage itself. Marriage is honorable and is to be held in honor. The original text has no verb and either translation is appropriate. The person who honors marriage will maintain an undefiled bed, free from adultery (a violation against the marriage) and from impurity or fornication in general. The root of the words translated "fornication" and "prostitute," when spelled in English letters, is "porn." Even if these sins are hidden from other humans, God knows them and he will judge.

13:5 Having urged love of fellow-believers (v. 1) and love of strangers (v. 2), our author now warns against love of money, which is covetousness (literally "love of silver"). Instead of covetousness, which indicates that one is seeking security in money, our lives should reflect contentment that comes from trusting in God. This is not inconsistent with conscientious work.

Contentment is born from trust in God's promises never to desert or to abandon his own (Genesis 28:15; Deuteronomy 31:6, 8; Joshua 1:5; 1 Chronicles 28:20; Isaiah 41:17; Matthew 6:25-30). Our author emphasizes the divine promise by stacking negatives in the original Greek. It is as if God says: "No, I will not leave or forsake you—no, not ever!"

13:6 Trusting God's promise we can confidently respond, in words taken from Psalm 118:6,

> "The Lord is my helper;
> I will not be afraid;
> What can man do to me?"

As throughout this epistle, faith's essence is to so trust the invisible God that we obey him persistently despite all distractions and opposition.

13:7 The original recipients of Hebrews were at least second-generation believers (Hebrews 2:3-4). As examples of persevering faith, our author now urges them to remember those who formerly taught them and led them in the life of faith. Their lives were admirable in outcome and they merit consideration by these believers whom they once mentored. Whether this outcome was revealed in death by martyrdom or simply by a faith-filled finish, we do not know. Either outcome deserves contemplation and imitation. Some translations speak of "those who had the rule over" these readers, translating a participle from which comes our word "hegemony." However, the traditional majority phrase "your leaders" reflects more accurately both the verbal root involved and the true spirit of Christian leadership.

Jesus Is Always Constant

13:8 However valuable, committed or caring these leaders had been to those they led, they had now passed on. Such is the way of life, which makes the next statement all the more significant: "Jesus Christ is the same yesterday and today and forever!" Throughout this epistle, our author has emphasized the permanence of Jesus and the salvation he accomplished and now guarantees for his people.

The temporal referents "yesterday," "today" and "forever" are probably from the author's perspective. *Yesterday* is the author's recent past during which Jesus lived, died, rose to life again, ascended and received

---

Jesus Remains the Same

- Jesus is the same in his eternal being—yesterday and today and forever. Our parents, mentors and teachers will all pass away and we will have to carry on without them, but Jesus remains the same. We will die and those who depended on us can lean on us no more, but Jesus remains the same. All that is created deteriorates, grows old and finally passes away, but Jesus remains the same (Hebrews 1:10-12, quoting Psalm 102:25-27).

- Jesus is the same in his obedience and fidelity to the Father—yesterday and today and forever. Throughout his life on the earth, Jesus was faithful to the Father every "today" (Hebrews

3:1-2, 13). That is why he became a *man;* that is the reason God gave him a body. He came to do God's will and he did what he came to do (Hebrews 10:5-7). Like all of humankind, Jesus lived one life, died one death and was judged one time for the life he lived in the flesh (Hebrews 9:27-28). His life was perfect and it will never be anything less. God's verdict on that life is final and it will never change. It is not subject to rehearing, reversal or appeal. The bodily life-record of Jesus our representative is final, fixed and fantastic in the sight of God. The believer's standing with God is as stable and sure as its author, source and guarantor.

- Jesus is the same in his all-sufficient sacrifice for sin—yesterday and today and forever. When he had done God's will regarding all that God desires and all that God detests, Jesus offered his faithful life in his body on the cross—the same body in which he had done the Father's will—as a gift and sacrifice to the Father. That gift perfectly pleased the Father and satisfied his deepest desire. It can never be supplemented and it will never need repeating. By this one offering Jesus has perfected forever those who come to God through him (Hebrews 10:12-14).

- Jesus is the same in his intercessory priesthood for his people— yesterday and today and forever. Because the Father was eternally pleased with the gift of Jesus' faithful life, he raised him from among the dead and, fulfilling David's prophetic declaration (Psalm 110:1), positioned him in highest honor at his own right hand. There Jesus sits as high priest for his people, by his very human presence in heaven providing them admission and access to the Father. Because Jesus' priesthood rests on his life that will never break down, he always lives to make intercession for those who come to God through him (Hebrews 7:16-17, 23-25). Salvation is secured in the person of the Son—the Son at God's right hand—our man in heaven.

glory; *today* is his present, as he writes this epistle to encourage and to cheer those for whom he cares the most; *tomorrow* is his future during which he, his first readers and indeed us as well, all complete our respective individual journeys. Whatever any believer encounters, regardless of the temptation he faces or the persecution she endures, despite boredom or weariness, each must always remember and each can always say: "Jesus Christ is the same yesterday and today and forever."

HEBREWS 13:9-16

Believers' Altar and Sacrifices

[9] Do not be carried away by various and strange teachings; for it is good for the heart to be strengthened by grace, not by foods, which have not benefited those who have been occupied with them. [10] We have an altar from which those who serve the Tabernacle have no right to eat. [11] For the bodies of those animals whose blood is brought into the sanctuary by the high priest as a sacrifice for sin, are burned outside the camp. [12] Therefore Jesus also suffered outside the gate in order to sanctify the people through his own blood. [13] Let us then go to him outside the camp, bearing his reproach. [14] For here we have no lasting city, but we seek the city that is to come. [15] Through him then let us continually offer a sacrifice of praise to God, that is, the fruit of lips that confess his name. [16] Do not neglect to do good and to share, for with such sacrifices God is pleased.

WHY & WHEREFORE

Although Jesus remains the same, distractions constantly take new forms. Now our author warns against novel teachings about foods, calling his readers back to the great sin offering that truly strengthens the hearts of those nourished by it—a sin offering which Old Testament priests could not eat. This sacrifice is Jesus himself, who was made an outcast, cut off from the fellowship of Israel. Those who follow him risk similar expulsion, but the city from which they are expelled is itself destined to be destroyed. Meanwhile, Jesus' people offer spiritual sacrifices of praise and worship and by sharing with their fellow-man.

243

UNPACKING THE TEXT

Don't be Carried Away

13:9 Our author warns his readers not to be borne away as if by a stream from the unchanging Jesus Christ, allured by new teachings that float past from time to time and entice with their foreign novelty ("strange") or pretty colors ("various"). More specifically, he cautions about teachings involving foods, teachings that distract from grace and that have proven to be of no benefit to those who have become occupied with them.

We are left wishing for more details about these teachings. Are the teachings Jewish in origin? If so, do they involve disputes over kosher food such as clean and unclean meats? Are they concerned with sacrificial meats of the Levitical system, some of which were eaten by the priests and/or by the people? Might this refer to some kind of Jewish fellowship meal as mentioned by Josephus?

Or is our author concerned with Gentile teachings ("strange"=foreign)? Some first-century believers faced such issues as eating meat associated with pagan idols (1 Corinthians 8) or ascetic food-rules growing out of gentile philosophy (Colossians). The Mediterranean world of the first-century was saturated with Hellenistic or Greek ideas. The first readers of Hebrews might have encountered some variety of Platonic thought that had floated down from the past. They might as easily have come upon Gnostic or proto-gnostic notions which would blossom later into full flower.

Some commentators see ghosts of Platonism in our author's remarks about the original, true, heavenly tabernacle and the earthly tabernacle which was its later, temporary copy. Our author's emphasis on the humanity of Jesus and his mortal body, like the First Epistle of John, strikes against Gnostic doctrine which equated materiality with evil and which denied that Jesus was true God and true man. All these things might be included in the "strange teachings" against which our author warns. We simply cannot say for sure.

Whatever the precise details involved, the point here is plain. For believers in Jesus, the sacrifice of first importance results in a distribution of grace that strengthens the heart, not in a sharing of meat that strengthens the body.

Outside the Camp with Jesus

13:10 To the unbelieving Jews, those who followed Jesus seemed to be the poorer for it. According to the Jesus-followers, their high priest was in heaven—invisible to earthly worshipers. Their sacrifices were spiritualized—praise to God and sharing with the neighbor (see v. 15-16). Nor did they have a visible altar as the Jews did. Never mind that our altar is invisible; it is real none the less, and it provides benefits the Levitical priests had no right to enjoy.

13:11 The Law of Moses required animal sacrifices for a variety of circumstances. The people brought the animal to the priests to be slaughtered and offered to God. In most cases, the priests were entitled to eat some or all of the meat of the sacrificial animal (Leviticus 6-7). The notable exception was the sin offering. The ritual for that sacrifice required the priest to take some of the animal's blood into the sanctuary, and to burn the animal's body outside the camp (Leviticus 6:30). On the Day of Atonement, the high priest sprinkled blood of the sin offerings inside the Most Holy Place, and the carcasses of the sacrificial animals were burned outside the camp (Leviticus 16:11, 15, 27).

Jesus' offering of himself was the Sin Offering *par excellence,* and by that event Jesus fulfilled the symbolic meaning of the Day of Atonement. On the cross, Jesus made his sacrifice once for all time, and God indicated his approval of that sacrifice by raising Jesus from the dead. As our high priest, Jesus then ascended to heaven where he sprinkled and purified the heavenly sanctuary with his own blood. Under the sacrificial rules of the Mosaic Law, the Levitical priests were forbidden to "eat" (and thus to benefit from) this sacrifice.

13:12 The parallels continue. In the case of a sin offering, the body of the sacrificial animal was burned outside the camp. Corresponding to the figure, Jesus also suffered outside the gate of Jerusalem and outside the camp of Israel, in order to sanctify the people through his own blood.

Throughout the Old Testament Scriptures, to be put "outside the camp" is to be expelled from the fellowship of God's covenant people and, in a sense, from the presence of God himself. Carcasses of animals offered for sin are burned outside the camp (Leviticus 4:21). It is the place of unclean things and of people who have been defiled by unclean things (Numbers 5:1-3). Those who have infectious diseases reside there (Leviticus 13:46). This is the site of executions (Numbers 15:35-36) and the location of latrines (Deuteronomy 23:12). It is a shameful site, where refuse is burned, a disgusting place crawling with maggots whose hunger is never satisfied (Isaiah 66:24).

13:13 Because they had followed Jesus, the first readers of Hebrews were feeling shunned and shut out by their former friends and associates (whether their former society was Jewish, Gentile or mixed). Such excommunication certainly carries a reproach—but the reproach in this case is *Jesus'* reproach (Hebrews 11:26). Nothing is more important than being with Jesus, even when that requires isolation and exclusion from the community. However, this reproach is far outweighed by the fact that Jesus' death is the only sacrifice for sin God will accept. One prominent Hebrews scholar argues that the phrase "outside the camp" refers to the heavenly sanctuary where Jesus now intercedes for his people (Thompson, "Outside the Camp ...," 59-61).

13:14 As we saw earlier, God's faithful people in all ages are faith-pilgrims in search of a city that is better and more permanent than any city found on earth (Hebrews 12:22-24). They cannot see that city now. Yet they confidently believe God's promise that it will come. For, truth be told, even the earthly Jerusalem was no "lasting" city. Indeed, Roman armies either had destroyed it already, or would shortly do so, when our author wrote this epistle. (For lists of scholars holding each view, see Walker, "Jerusalem in Hebrews 13:9-14 and the Dating of the Epistle.") Our author makes a pun of sorts; the word translated "lasting" and the word translated "that is to come" sound very much alike.

13:15 Although Jesus has made the perfect sin-offering once for all time, his people make other sacrifices to God continually through him (see Hebrews 7:25). Ours are sacrifices of praise, the same term used in the Greek Old Testament for the peace-offering of thanksgiving (Leviticus 7:12-15). We also offer the "fruit of lips" by confessing our faith in Jesus Christ, an idea rooted in Old Testament worship of God (Psalm 50:12-15, 23; 141:2; Hosea 14:2).

13:16 If believers offer some "vertical" sacrifices (praise and confession directed to God), they also offer sacrifices on the "horizontal" plane. This they do whenever they do good to others or share with those in need (Amos 5 21-24; Micah 6:6-12). The verb translated "to share" can also be translated as "to have fellowship."

Personal Closing Words

¹⁷ Obey your leaders and submit to them, for they keep watch over your souls and will give an account. Let them do this with joy and not with grief, for that would be unprofitable for you. ¹⁸ Pray for us, for we are sure that we have a clear conscience, desiring to live honorably in all things. ¹⁹ I particularly urge you to do this so that I may be restored to you the sooner.

WHY & WHEREFORE

Again our author urges his first readers to follow their godly leaders who watch out for their spiritual welfare, and who will answer to God one day for that oversight. He then affirms his own integrity and clear conscience, expresses a desire to rejoin his readers where they are, and requests their prayers to that end.

UNPACKING THE TEXT

13:17 Our author returns to practical instructions concerning relationships with Christian leaders (see 13: 7). "Leaders" here translates a participle meaning those who persuade through proper use of words. The faith community is to submit to their guidance because they are persuaded to do so. There is no hint of autocratic "bosses" who demand obedience based on naked authority. Those who are led submit willingly.

On the other hand, these leaders have been charged with a divine assignment to watch for the spiritual wellbeing of those who compose the community of faith. This is a serious obligation—the word translated "watch" literally means staying awake at night—and leaders will give account to God for their work. If believers do submit to such leading, the leaders will report to God with joy. If believers do not follow their guidance, the leaders will still report. However, they will do so with grief, an outcome that will not benefit either the leaders or those for whose welfare they watch.

Old Testament spiritual leaders were also charged to be watchmen (Ezekiel 3:17-21; Ezekiel 33:1-9). The duty described is that of a shepherd ("pastor"). In several ways this passage resembles Peter's similar charge to those whom he calls "elders" (1 Peter 5:1-5). However, function is more important than form and the work matters more than any particular title or office.

13:18 Pray for us, the author urges, for we are sure (having been persuaded) that we have a clear conscience, and even now desire to live honestly in every respect. Had someone accused the author of evil or suspected him of any wrongdoing? Is he responding to criticism? As with so many other details in the background of this ancient writing, we are left in the dark. The author simply makes his request and affirms his integrity. He does not even identify those who with himself constitute the "we."

13:19 Whatever the situation, it seemingly hindered or delayed the author's speedy reunion with his readers. Now he intensifies his request for their prayers, which he hopes will result in his restoration to them. He speaks of being restored to them, not simply of joining them as if for the first time. This word-choice might imply an involuntary separation resulting from his imprisonment, or even his required presence elsewhere on gospel mission. All we know for sure is that he is not with his original readers. He hopes to be with them soon, and to that end he now requests their prayers.

HEBREWS 13:20-21

Benediction

[20] Now may the God of peace, who brought up from the dead our Lord Jesus, the great Shepherd of the sheep, through the blood of the everlasting covenant, [21] equip you with everything good to do his will, working in us that which is pleasing in his sight, through Jesus Christ, to whom be glory forever and ever. Amen.

WHY & WHEREFORE

Our author closes with a prayer that God will fully equip his readers to do all that God wishes and empower them to do what pleases him. He asks this with confidence in God's *power* (he brought Jesus back from death), his *persistence* (Jesus is the great Shepherd of his people) and his *purpose* (through the blood of the everlasting covenant).

UNPACKING THE TEXT

13:20 Warnings are good, encouragement is appropriate and exhortations are necessary. Yet they all appeal to the human will and emotions. None of them is effective unless God equips and empowers the recipient to respond by doing what pleases God. Aware of this, our author now concludes his sermon with a simple but magnificent benediction.

For his readers' present needs and their unknown future, he entreats "the God of peace." For a troubled people this is a comforting designation of God—whether that trouble comes from external opposition or from internal discouragement and fatigue. People experiencing trouble need *peace*—a place of respite, a period of repose. From time immemorial, God himself has been a refuge for his people to which they can always come (Psalm 71:3). David celebrates God's rescue from his enemies in soaring poetry, repeatedly declaring that God is his refuge (2 Samuel 22:3, 32, 33). Jesus' people also have fled for refuge. They have found it in Jesus, the source of strong hope—our *man* in heaven (Hebrews 6:18).

However, God performed his greatest act of deliverance when he rescued our Lord Jesus himself. He delivered Jesus, not from impersonal death in general, but specifically from among *the dead*—that great company of all who have died since Cain first killed his brother Abel. God raised the holy and obedient Jesus from among those who, because of sin, had come under the power of the devil. This is our author's only direct reference to Jesus' resurrection, although he has alluded to it since his first mention of Jesus at God's right hand in heaven.

Jesus Christ is not only the sacrificial lamb, he is also "the great Shepherd of the sheep" who laid down his life for the sheep (John 10:11, 15, 17, 18). God once brought Israel out from the sea as his flock with Moses and Aaron as their shepherds (Psalm 77:20; Isaiah 63:11). Now he has brought Jesus the great Shepherd up from among the dead. God raised Jesus "by the blood of the everlasting covenant"—a reference to Jesus' own blood that represented his life and evidenced his death. Jesus' life and death, his *representative* life and death, were planned before the world began by agreement between Father and Son.

Faithfully fulfilling the agreement made between Father and Son before the world began, Jesus lived and died as representative for his people. On the cross he offered his body and shed his blood. Then, fulfilling the eternal covenant between himself and the Son, God raised Jesus up from death and promoted him to a place of glory at his own right hand in heaven.

13:21 Our author prays that the very God who raised Jesus from the dead will also provide his people with all good things. The purpose for this provision is to equip (the same word sometimes means "to repair") them to do God's will. The prayer continues with a request that God himself will work (literally "do" or "make") in his people to produce everything that gives him pleasure.

As is common in Christian prayers, whether in the first century or the twenty-first, this benediction ends by ascribing majesty—either to God the Father or to Lord Jesus. From a grammatical standpoint, the phrase best refers to God the Father. However, it is not inconsistent with biblical teaching to apply the phrase to both.

Final Remarks

²² I appeal to you, brothers, bear with my word of exhortation, for I have written to you briefly. ²³ I want you to know that our brother Timothy has been released, with whom, if he comes soon, I will see you. ²⁴ Greet all your leaders and all the saints. Those from Italy greet you. ²⁵ Grace be with you all.

WHY & WHEREFORE

Our author closes what he here calls a "word of exhortation" and which he regards as "brief." He informs the first readers of Timothy's "release," which he believes might enable him to visit them in the near future. He extends general greetings, forwards greetings from certain unidentified Italians, and closes with the supreme Christian wish that his readers enjoy God's grace.

UNPACKING THE TEXT

13:22 Our author calls his writing a "word of exhortation," a term used elsewhere in the New Testament for a discourse or informal sermon (Acts 13:15). This is a written sermon, and it does not follow the usual form of an epistle. Our author has written "briefly," as he sees it, for he had much more he might have said (Hebrews 5:11; 11:32). Indeed, one can read this entire "word of exhortation" in about an hour.

13:23 Timothy (presumably Paul's protégé whose name two New Testament books bear) has been "released" or "set at liberty"—either from some incarceration or by having completed some mission or assignment. Now that Timothy is free to travel, our author hopes the two of them might soon visit the readers. Neither Scripture nor history reports Timothy being in prison.

13:24 The writer sends his own greetings to the entire community of faith for whose exhortation he has written. This strongly suggests that someone will read the document in an assembly that includes the believers in general ("the saints") as well as their leaders (Colossians 4:16; 1 Thessalonians 5:27).

He also forwards greetings from "those from Italy." This tells us that the author writes while with some believers from Italy. He does not say if they are in Rome or somewhere else. We also do not know whether his readers are in Rome or elsewhere.

13:25 Our tour of Hebrews is now over. As he leads us up the path to the gate where we first entered, our author bestows a traditional Christian benediction: "Grace be with you all." This is no mere formality. Our author sincerely entrusts us to God's divine favor. As we continue our own pilgrimage of faith, recharged and renewed by the message of Hebrews, surely we can wish for nothing more (Hebrews 2:9; 4:16; 10:29; 12:15, 28; 13:9).

BIBLIOGRAPHY

Books Specifically Concerning Hebrews

Anderson, David R. *The King-Priest of Ps 110 in Hebrews* (Studies in Biblical Literature, Vol. 21). New York: Peter Lang, 2001.

Archer, Gleason L., Jr. *The Epistle to the Hebrews: A Study Manual.* Grand Rapids: Baker Book House, 1957.

Attridge, Harold W. *The Epistle to the Hebrews* (Hermeneia—A Critical and Historical Commentary on the Bible). Philadelphia: Fortress Press, 1989.

Barrett, C. K. "The Eschatology of the Epistle to the Hebrews," *The Background of the New Testament and Its Eschatology* (Hon. C. H. Dodd), edited by W. D. Davies and D. Daube. Cambridge: The University Press, 1956.

Bruce, F. F. *The Epistle to the Hebrews* (The New International Commentary). Grand Rapids: William B. Eerdmans Publishing Company, 1964.

Calvin, John. *Commentary on Hebrews* (Calvin's Commentaries). Volume 22. Grand Rapids: Baker, 2005.

Clarke, Adam. *Commentary and Notes.* Volume 6. Nashville: Abingdon Press, 1977.

Craddock, Fred B. *The Letter to the Hebrews* (The New Interpreter's Bible). Vol. 12. Nashville: Abingdon Press, 1998.

Croy, N. Clayton, *Endurance in Suffering: Hebrews 12:1-13 in its rhetorical, religious, and philosophical context.* Cambridge: Cambridge University Press, 1998.

deSilva, David A. *Perseverance in Gratitude: A Socio-Rhetorical Commentary on the Epistle "to the Hebrews."* Grand Rapids: William B. Eerdmans Publishing Company, 2000.

Delitzsch, Franz. *Commentary on the Epistle to the Hebrews* (Clark's Foreign Theological Library). Two volumes. Edinburgh: T. & T. Clark, 1887.

Dods, Marcus. *The Epistle to the Hebrews* (The Expositor's Greek Testament). Volume 4. Grand Rapids: William B Eerdmans Publishing Company, 1961.

Ellingworth, Paul. *The Epistle to the Hebrews: A Commentary on the Greek Text* (The New International Greek Testament Commentary). Grand Rapids: Wm. B. Eerdmans Publishing Co., 1993.

Filson, Floyd V. *"Yesterday": A Study of Hebrews in the Light of Chapter 13* (Studies in Biblical Theology, Second series, 4). Naperville, Illinois: Alec R. Allenson, Inc., 1967.

Fudge, Edward W. *Our Man In Heaven: An Exposition of the Epistle to the Hebrews.* Grand Rapids: Baker Book House, 1973.

Gench, Frances Taylor. *Hebrews and James* (Westminster Bible Companion). Louisville: Westminster John Knox Press, 1996.

Gelardini, Gabriella (Editor). *Hebrews: Contemporary Methods—New Insights* (Biblical Interpretation Series, Vol. 75). Leiden & Boston: Brill, 2005.

Girdwood, Jim & Verkruyse. *Hebrews* (The College Press NIV Commentary). Joplin, Missouri: College Press, 1997.

Goodspeed, Edgar J. *The Epistle to the Hebrews* (The Bible for Home and School). New York: The Macmillan Company, 1908.

Greenlee, J. Harold. *An Exegetical Summary of Hebrews.* Dallas: The Summer Institute of Linguistics, 1998.

Guthrie, Donald. *Hebrews* (The Tyndale New Testament Commentaries). Downer's Grove, Ill.: IVP, 1983.

Guthrie, George H. *Hebrews* (The NIV Application Commentary). Grand Rapids: Zondervan, 1998.

Hagner, Donald A. *Hebrews* (New International Biblical Commentary). Peabody, Mass.: Hendrickson Publishers, 1990.

Holladay, Carl R. "The Riddle of Hebrews," *A Critical Introduction to the New Testament: Interpreting the Message and Meaning of Jesus Christ.* Nashville: Abingdon Press, 2005.

Hughes, Philip Edgcumbe. *A Commentary on the Epistle to the Hebrews.* Grand Rapids: Wm. B. Eerdmans Publishing Co., 1977.

Johnson, B. W. *The People's New Testament With Notes.* Nashville: Gospel Advocate Company, 1889-1891.

Johnson, Luke Timothy. *Hebrews: A Commentary* (The New Testament Library). Louisville: Westminster John Knox Press, 2006.

Kistemaker, Simon. *The Psalm Citations in the Epistle to the Hebrews.* Amsterdam: Wed. G. Van Soest N.V., 1961.

Koester, Craig R. *Hebrews* (The Anchor Bible). New York: Doubleday, 2001.

Kurianal, James. *Jesus Our High Priest: Ps 110:4 as the substructure of Heb 5:1-7, 28* (European University Studies, Vol. 693). New York: Peter Lang, 2000.

Lane, William L. *Hebrews* (Word Biblical Commentary). 2 volumes. Dallas: Word Books, 1991.

Lenski, R. C. H. *The Interpretation of the Epistle to the Hebrews.* Columbus, Ohio: The Wartburg Press, 1946.

Leschert, Dale F. *Hermeneutical Foundations of Hebrews: A Study in the Validity of the Epistle's Interpretation of Some Core Citations From the Psalms* (NABPR Dissertation Series, No. 10). Lewiston, NY: The Edward Mellan Press, 1995.

Lightfoot, Neal R. *Jesus Christ Today: A Commentary on The Book of Hebrews.* Grand Rapids: Baker Book House, 1976.

Lindars, Barnabas, SSF. *The Theology of the Letter to the Hebrews* (New Testament Theology). Cambridge: Cambridge University Press, 1991.

Long, Thomas G. *Hebrews* (Interpretation: A Bible Commentary for Teaching and Preaching). Louisville: John Knox Press, 1997.

Marohl, Matthew J. *Faithfulness and the Purpose of Hebrews: A Social Identity Approach.* (Princeton Theological Monograph Series, 82). Eugene, Ore.: Pickwick Publications, 2008.

Milligan, Robert. *Epistle to the Hebrews* (The New Testament Commentary). Nashville: Gospel Advocate Company, 1963.

Mitchell, Alan C. *Hebrews* (Sacra Pagina Series, Vol. 13). Collegeville, Minn.: Liturgical Press, 2007.

Moffatt, James. *A Critical and Exegetical Commentary on the Epistle to the Hebrews*. Edinburgh: T. & T. Clark, Ltd., 1924.

Morris, Leon. *Hebrews* (The Expositor's Bible Commentary). Vol. 12. Grand Rapids: Zondervan Publishing House, 1981.

Nairne, Alexander. *The Epistle to the Hebrews*. Cambridge: The University Press, 1921.

Pink, Arthur W. *An Exposition of Hebrews*. 2 volumes. Grand Rapids: Baker Book House, 1967.

Pfitzner, Victor C. *Hebrews* (Abingdon New Testament Commentaries). Nashville: Abingdon Press, 1997.

Rhee, Victor (Sung-Yul). *Faith in Hebrews: Analysis within the context of Christology, Eschatology, and Ethics* (Studies in Biblical Literature, Vol. 19). New York: Peter Lang, 2001.

Robinson, Theodore H. *The Epistle to the Hebrews* (The Moffatt New Testament Commentary). New York: Harper and Brothers Publishers, no date.

Rotherham, Joseph B. *Studies in the Epistle to the Hebrews*. Joplin, Missouri: College Press, Reprint edition, no date.

Thompson, James. *Hebrews* (Paideia Commentaries on the New Testament). Grand Rapids: Baker Academic, 2008.

Thompson, James. *The Letter to the Hebrews* (The Living Word Commentary). Austin, Texas: R. B. Sweet Co., Inc., 1971.

Woods, Clyde. "Eschatological Motifs in the Epistle to the Hebrews," *The Last Things* (Hon. W. B. West, Jr., edited by Jack P. Lewis). Austin: Sweet Publishing Company, 1972.

Wright, Tom. *Hebrews for Everyone* (The New Testament Guides for Everyone). Louisville, Ky.: Westminster John Knox Press, 2004.

Periodicals

Adams, J. Clifford, "Exegesis of Heb VI. 1f," *New Testament Studies*, 13 (March 1967), 378-385.

Attridge, Harold W. "Heard Because of His Reverence (Heb 5:7)," *Journal of Biblical Literature*, 98/1 (March 1979), 90-93.

Attridge, Harold W. "The Uses of Antithesis in Hebrews 8-10," *Harvard Theological Review*, 79/1-3 (January-July 1986), 1-9.

Baab, Otto J. "The God of Redeeming Grace: Atonement in the Old Testament," *Interpretation*, 10/2 (April 1956), 131-143.

Baugh, Steven M. "The Cloud of Witnesses in Hebrews 11," *Westminster Theological Journal*, 68/1 (Spring 2006), 113-132.

Brooks, Walter Edward, "The Perpetuity of Christ's Sacrifice in the Epistle to the Hebrews," *Journal of Biblical Literature*, 89 (June 1970), 205-214.

Brown, Raymond Edward. "Does the New Testament Call Jesus God?" *Theological Studies*, 26/4 (December 1965), 545-573.

Bruce, F. F. "Recent Contributions to the Understanding of Hebrews," *The Expository Times*, 80 (September 1969), 260-264.

Bruce, F.F. "The Kerygma of Hebrews," *Interpretation*, 23/1 (January 1969), 3-19.

Clifford, Richard, S.J., and Khaled Anatolios, "Christian Salvation: Biblical and Theological Perspectives, *Theological Studies*, 66/4 (December 2005), 739-769.

Cortez, Felix H. "From the Holy to the Most Holy Place: The Period of Hebrews 9:6-10 and the Day of Atonement as a Metaphor of Transition," *Journal of Biblical Literature*, 125/3 (Autumn 2006), 527-547.

Cosby, Michael R. "The Rhetorical Composition of Hebrews 11," *Journal of Biblical Literature*, 107/2 (June 1988), 257-273.

Croy, N. Clayton. "A Note on Hebrews 12:2," *Journal of Biblical Literature*, 114/1 (Spring 1995), 117-119.

Dahms, John V. "First Readers of Hebrews," *Journal of the Evangelical Theological Society*, 20/4 (December 1977), 365-375.

DeYoung, Kevin. "Divine Impassibility and the Passion of Christ in the Book of Hebrews," *Westminster Theological Journal*, 68/1 (Spring 2006), 41-50.

Elllingworth, Paul. "The Unshakable Priesthood: Hebrews 7:24," *Journal for the Study of the New Testament*, 23 (February 1985), 125-126.

Elliott, Ralph H. "Atonement in the Old Testament," *Review & Expositor*, 59/1 (January 1962), 9-26.

Emmrich, Martin. "Hebrews 6:4-6—Again! (A Pneumatological Inquiry)," *Westminster Theological Journal*, 65/1 (Spring 2003), 83-95.

Enns, Peter. "Creation and Re-Creation: Psalm 95 and Its Interpretation in Hebrews 3:1-4:13," *Westminster Theological Journal*, 55/2 (Fall 1993), 255-280.

Gleason, Randall C. "The Eschatology of the Warning in Hebrews 10:26-31," *Tyndale Bulletin*, 53/1 (2002), 97-120.

Gleason, Randall C. "The Old Testament Background of the Warning in Hebrews 6:4-8," *Bibliotheca Sacra*, 155/617 (January-March 1998), 62-91.

Gudorf, Michael E. "Through a Classical Lens: Hebrews 2:16," *Journal of Biblical Literature* 119/1 (Spring 2000), 105-108.

Gurtner, Daniel M. "LXX Syntax and the Identity of the NT Veil," *Novum Testamentum* 47/4 (2005), 344-353.

Hahn, Scott W. "A Broken Covenant and the Curse of Death: A Study of Hebrews 9:15-22," *Catholic Biblical Quarterly*, 66/3 (July 2004), 416-436.

Harmon, Steven R. "Hebrews 2:10-18," *Interpretation*, 59/4 (October 2005), 404-406.

Higgins, A. J. B. "The Priestly Messiah," New *Testament Studies*, 13 (March 1967), 211-239.

Horbury, William, "The Aaronic Priesthood in the Epistle to the Hebrews," *Journal for the Study of the New Testament*, 19 (October 1983), 43-71.

Howard, George. "Hebrews and the Old Testament Quotations," *Novum Testamentum*, 10/2-3 (April-July 1968), 208-216.

Howard, Wilbert Francis. "Epistle to Hebrews," *Interpretation*, 5/1 (January 1951), 80-91.

Hughes, Philip Edgcumbe. "The Blood of Jesus and His Heavenly Priesthood in Hebrews. Part I: The Significance of the Blood of Jesus," *Bibliotheca Sacra*, 130/518 (April-June 1973), 99-109.

Hughes, Philip Edgcumbe. "The Blood of Jesus and His Heavenly Priesthood in Hebrews. Part II: The High-Priestly Sacrifice of Christ," *Bibliotheca Sacra*, 130/519 (July-September 1973), 195-212.

Hughes, Philip Edgcumbe. "The Blood of Jesus and His Heavenly Priesthood in Hebrews. Part III: The Meaning of 'The True Tent' and 'The Greater and More Perfect Tent," *Bibliotheca Sacra*, 130/520 (October-December 1973), 305-314.

Hughes, Philip Edgcumbe. "The Blood of Jesus and His Heavenly Priesthood in Hebrews. Part IV: The Present Work of Christ in Heaven," *Bibliotheca Sacra*, 131/521 (January-March 1974), 26-33.

Huxhold, Harry N. "Faith in the Epistle to the Hebrews," *Concordia Theological Monthly*, 38 (October 1967), 657- 661.

Kidner, Derek. "Sacrifice: Metaphors and Meaning," *Tyndale Bulletin*, 33 (1982), 119-136.

Koester, Helmut. "Outside the Camp': Hebrews 13:9-14," *Harvard Theological Review*, 55/4 (October 1962), 299-315.

Konkel, August H. "The Sacrifice of Obedience," *Didaskalia* (Otterburne, Man.) 2/2 (April 1991), 2-11.

Lee, John A.L. "Hebrews 5:14 and 'EXIS': A History of Misunderstanding," *Novum Testamentum*, 39/2 (April 1997), 151-176.

Lefler, Nathan. "The Melchizedek Traditions in the Letter to the Hebrews: Reading through the Eyes of an Inspired Jewish-Christian Author," *Pro Ecclesia*, 16/1 (Winter 2007), 73-89.

Leithart, Peter J. "Womb of the World: Baptism and the Priesthood of the New Covenant in Hebrews 10:19-22," *Journal for the Study of the New Testament*, 78 (June 2000), 49-65.

Lewis, Edwin. "Creator and Creature: Atonement, Its Means and Methods," *Interpretation*, 4/2 (April 1950), 143-155.

Lightfoot, Neil R. "The Saving of the Savior: Hebrews 5:7ff," *Restoration Quarterly*, 16/3-4 (1973), 166-173.

Little, Hervey G. "Christ for Us and in Us: An Essay on Incarnation and Atonement," *Interpretation*, 10/2 (April 1956), 144-156.

Long, Thomas G. "Bold in the Presence of God: Atonement in Hebrews," *Interpretation*, 52/1 (January 1998), 53-69.

MacLeod, David J. "Christ, the Believer's High Priest: An Exposition of Hebrews 7:26-28," *Bibliotheca Sacra*, 162/647 (July-September 2005), 331-343.

MacLeod, David J. "The Cleansing of the True Tabernacle," *Bibliotheca Sacra*, 152/605 (January-March 1995), 60-71.

McNair, Bruce G. "Luther, Calvin and the Exegetical Tradition of Melchisedec," *Review & Expositor,* 101/4 (Fall 2004), 747-761.

McRay, John. "Atonement and Apocalyptic in the Book of Hebrews," *Restoration Quarterly,* 23/1 (1980), 1-9.

Mathewson, Dave. "Reading Heb 6:4-6 in Light of the Old Testament," *Westminster Theological Journal,* 61/2 (Fall 1999), 209—225.

Mayhue, Richard L. "Heb 13:20: Covenant of Grace or New Covenant? An Exegetical Note," *Master's Seminary Journal,* 7/2 (Fall 1996) 251-257.

Most, William O. "A Biblical Theology of Redemption in a Covenant Framework," *Catholic Biblical Quarterly,* 29 (January 1967), 1-19.

Nelson, Richard D. "'He Offered Himself': Sacrifice in Hebrews," *Interpretation,* 57/3 (July 2003), 251-265.

Nongbri, Brent. "A Touch of Condemnation in a Word of Exhortation: Apocalyptic Language and Graeco-Roman Rhetoric in Hebrews 6:4-12," *Novum Testamentum,* 45/3 (2003), 265-279.

Omark, Reuben E. "Saving of the Savior: Exegesis and Christology in Hebrews 5:7-10," *Interpretation,* 12/1 (January 1958), 39-51.

Paul, M.J. "The Order of Melchizedek (Ps 110:4 and Heb 7:3)," *Westminster Theological Journal,* 49/1 (Spring 1987), 195-211.

Peterson, Robert A. "Apostasy in the Hebrews Warning Passages," *Presbyterion,* 34/1 (Spring 2008), 27-44.

Proctor, John. "Judgement or Vindication? Deuteronomy 32 in Hebrews 10:30," *Tyndale Bulletin,* 55/1 (2004), 65-80.

Rhee, Victor (Sung-Yul). "Christology and the Concept of Faith in Hebrews 5:11—6:20," *Journal of the Evangelical Theological Society,* 43/1 (March 2000), 83-96.

Saunders, Landon. "'Outside the Camp': Hebrews 13," *Restoration Quarterly,* 22/1-2 (1979), 19-24.

Schenck, Kenneth L. "A Celebration of the Enthroned Son: The Catena of Hebrews 1," *Journal of Biblical Literature,* 120/3 (Fall 2001), 469-485.

Scott, Julius J. *"Archegos:* the Salvation History of the Epistle to the Hebrews," *Journal of the Evangelical Theological Society,* 29/1 (March 1986), 47-54.

Selby, Gary S. "The Meaning and Function of *Syneidesis* in Hebrews 9 and 10," *Restoration Quarterly,* 28/3 (1985-1986), 145-154.

Smalley, Stephen S. "The Atonement in the Epistle to the Hebrews," *The Evangelical Quarterly, 33* (January-March 1961), 36-43.

Smillie, Gene R. "'*O Logos Tou Theou'* in Hebrews 4:12-13," *Novum Testamentum,* 46/4 (2004), 338-359.

Stewart, R. A. "The Sinless High-Priest," *New Testament Studies,* 14 (January 1967), 126-135.

Still, Todd D. "*Christos* as *Pistos:* The Faith(fullness) of Jesus in the Epistle to the Hebrews," *Catholic Biblical Quarterly,* 69/4 (October 2007), 746-755.

Stott, Wilfrid, "The Conception of 'Offering' in the Epistle to the Hebrews," *New Testament Studies,* 9 (January 1962), 62-67.

Swetnam, James. "A Suggested Interpretation of Hebrews 9:15-18," *Catholic Biblical Quarterly,* 27/4 (October 1965), 373-390.

Thompson, James W. "Hebrews 9 and Hellenistic Concepts of Sacrifice," *Journal of Biblical Literature*, 98/4 (December 1979), p 567-578.

Thompson, James W. "Outside the Camp: A Study of Heb 13: 9-14," *Catholic Biblical Quarterly*, 40/1 (January 1978), p 53-63.

Thompson, James W. "'That Which Cannot be Shaken': Some Metaphysical Assumptions in Heb 12:27," *Journal of Biblical Literature* 94/4 (December 1975), p 580-587.

Thompson, James W. "The Epistle to the Hebrews and the Pauline Legacy," *Restoration Quarterly*, 47/4 (2005), p 197-206.

Thompson, James W. "The Hermeneutics of the Epistle to the Hebrews," *Restoration Quarterly*, 38/4 (1996), p 229-237.

Thompson, James W. "The Structure and Purpose of the Catena in Heb 1:5-13," *Catholic Biblical Quarterly*, 38/3 (July 1976), p 352-363.

Thompson, James W. "The Underlying Unity of Hebrews," *Restoration Quarterly*, 18/3 (1975), p 129-136.

Tune, Mike. "Why Should You Quit?" *Restoration Quarterly*, 27/4 (1984), 221-226.

Vos, Geerhardus. "Hebrews, the Epistle of the Diatheke," *Princeton Theological Review*, 13 (1915), 587-632; 14 (1916), 1-61.

Walker, Peter W. L., "Jerusalem in Hebrews 13:9-14 and the Dating of the Epistle," *Tyndale Bulletin*, 45/1 (1994), 39-71.

Wallace, David. "The Use of Psalms in the Shaping of a Text: Psalm 2:7 and Psalm 110:1 in Hebrews 1," *Restoration Quarterly* 45/1-2 (2003), 41-50.

Weiss, Herold. *"Sabbatismos* in the Epistle to the Hebrews," *Catholic Biblical Quarterly*, 58/4 (Oct. 1996), 674-689.

Willis, Timothy. "'Obey Your Leaders': Hebrews 13 and Leadership in the Church," *Restoration Quarterly*, 36/4 (1994), 316-326.

Wolf, Herbert C. "Main Types of the Doctrine of the Atonement." *Lutheran Quarterly*, 15:3 (August 1963), 250-265.

Worley, David R. "Fleeing to Two Immutable Things, God's Oath-Taking and Oath-Witnessing: The Use of Litigant Oath in Hebrews 6:12-20," *Restoration Quarterly*, 36/4 (1994), 223-236.

Other Books

Aland, Aland, Karavidopoulos, Martini and Metzger, (editors 4th Revision), *The Greek New Testament*. New York: United Bible Societies, U.S.A., 1983.

Arndt, William F. and F. Wilbur Gingrich (editors). A *Greek-English Lexicon* of *the New Testament and Other Early Christian Literature*. Chicago: The University of Chicago Press, 1963.

Berkouwer, G. C. *The Person of Christ*. Translated from the Dutch by John Vriend. Grand Rapids: William B. Eerdmans Publishing Company, 1969.

Bernard, Thomas Dehany. *The Progress of Doctrine in the New Testament*. New York: American Tract Society, 1907.

Chandler, Vee. *Victorious Substitution: A Theory of the Atonement.* A dissertation submitted to Trinity College and Seminary. Undated. (Author's address is 2415 Saddle Club Road, Burlington, NC 27215).

Cullman, Oscar. *The Christology of the New Testament.* London: SCM Press, Ltd., 1963.

Dix, Gregory. *Jew and Greek.* London: Dacre Press, 1967.

Edersheim, A. *The Temple, Its Ministry and Services.* New York: Fleming H. Revell Company, no date.

Hatch, Edwin and Redpath, Henry A. *A Concordance to the Septuagint,* 2nd edition. Reprinted. Grand Rapids: Baker Book House, 1998.

Hillers, Delbert R. *Covenant: The History of a Biblical Idea.* Baltimore: The Johns Hopkins Press, 1969.

IDB = The Interpreter's Dictionary of the Bible. Edited by George Arthur Buttrick. Four volumes. New York & Nashville: Abingdon Press, 1962.

Jocz, Jakob. *The Covenant.* Grand Rapids William B Eerdmans Publishing Company, 1968.

Kittel, Rudolf (editor). *Biblia Hebraica* [The Hebrew Old Testament] Stuttgart: Wurttembergische Bibelanstalt, 1966.

McKnight, Scot. *A Community Called Atonement. (Living Theology,* Tony Jones, editor.) Nashville: Abingdon Press, 2007.

Moulton, James Hope and George Milligan. *The Vocabulary of the Greek Testament Illustrated from the Papyri and Other Non-Literary Sources.* London: Hodder and Stoughton, 1963.

Philips, A. Th. (translator). *Prayer Book for the Day of Atonement.* New York: Hebrew Publishing Company, 1931.

Polkinghorne, John R. *Traffic in Truth: Exchanges Between Science and Theology.* Minneapolis: Fortress Press, 2002.

Rahlfs, Alfred (editor). *Septuaginta.* Stuttgart Wurttembergische Bibelanstalt, 1962.

Schweizer, Eduard. *Church Order in the New Testament: Studies in Biblical Theology.* London: SCM Press, Ltd., 1961.

Smith, J. B. *Greek-English Concordance to the New Testament.* Scottdale, Pennsylvania: Herald Press, 1955.

Stalker, James. *The Atonement.* New York: A. C. Armstrong and Son. 1909.

Thayer, Joseph Henry (editor). *Greek-English Lexicon of the New Testament.* Grand Rapids: Zondervan Publishing House, 1963.

TDNT = Theological Dictionary of the New Testament. Edited by Gerhard Kittel, translated by G. W. Bromiley. Six volumes. Grand Rapids: William B. Eerdmans Publishing Company, 1964-1968.

Wright, G. Ernest. *God Who Acts: Studies in Biblical Theology.* London: SCM Press, Ltd., 1969.

Wright, N. T. *Surprised by Hope: Rethinking Heaven, the Resurrection, and the Mission of the Church.* New York: HarperOne, 2008.

Also by Edward Fudge

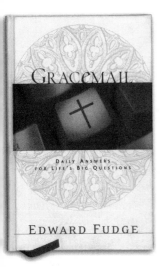

Gracemail
Daily Answers for Life's Big Questions

$12   451 pages, cloth   ISBN 0-89112-489-6

"My name is on the long list of those who've been touched by the pen of Edward Fudge. God has graced this friend with the knowledge of what matters—and what doesn't."

—MAX LUCADO

The Great Rescue
The Story of God's Amazing Grace

$9.95   150 pages, paper   ISBN 0-9714289-3-X

"*The Great Rescue* is at once a gripping novel and a compelling theology text. It unfolds the sweeping panorama of God's redemptive work, taking the reader from Genesis to Revelation. The resulting picture is truly a masterpiece of grace."

—JAMES SWEENEY, Western Seminary, Portland, Oregon

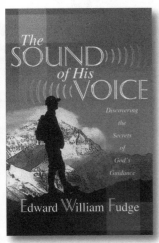

The Sound of His Voice
Discovering the Secrets of God's Guidance

$10.95   160 pages, paper   ISBN 0-9714289-4-8

The author tells the story of how he discovered some of the ways God guides our daily steps. It will encourage you to seek—and to discover—God's guidance for your own life.

LEAFWOOD
P U B L I S H E R S
www.leafwoodpublishers.com
Toll Free 1-877-816-4455

The Meditative Commentary Series

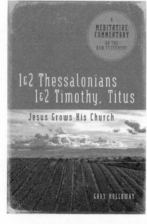

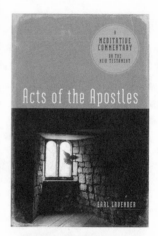

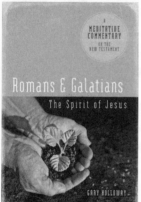

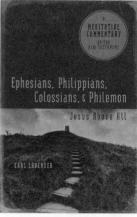

Matthew
Jesus Is King
by Gary Holloway
$13.99   ISBN 0-9767790-1-3

Thessalonians, Timothy, & Titus
Jesus Grows His Church
by Gary Holloway
$11.99   ISBN 0-89112-503-5

Acts of the Apostles
Jesus Alive in His Church
by Earl Lavender
$13.99   ISBN 0-89112-501-9

Romans & Galatians
The Spirit of Jesus
by Gary Holloway
$11.99   ISBN 0-89112-502-7

Luke
Jesus Is Savior
by Earl Lavender
$13.99   ISBN 0-89112-500-0

1 & 2 Corinthians
Jesus, Cross, Church
by Earl Lavender
$11.99   ISBN 978-0-89112-568-6

Ephesians, Philippians, Colossians, & Philemon
Jesus Above All
by Earl Lavender
$9.99   ISBN 978-0-89112-561-7

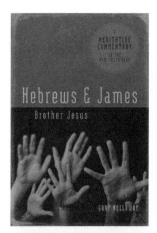

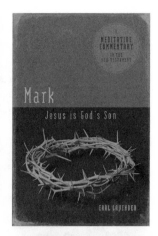
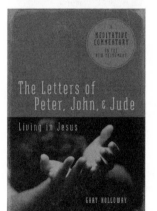

Also Available

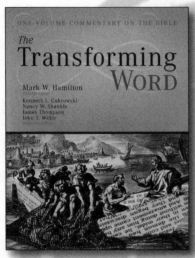

The Transforming Word
One Volume Commentary on the Bible

General Editor

MARK W. HAMILTON (Ph.D., Harvard University),
Associate Professor of Old Testament, Abilene
Christian University

Associate Editors

KENNETH L. CUKROWSKI (Ph.D., Yale University)
NANCY W. SHANKLE (Ph.D., Texas A & M University)
JAMES THOMPSON (Ph.D., Vanderbilt University)
JOHN T. WILLIS (Ph.D., Vanderbilt University)

1136 pages, $69.95 cloth
ISBN 978-0-112-521-1

   This volume contains a commentary on each book of the Bible. The reader should expect to gain an understanding of (1) the organization and arguments of each biblical book, (2) the main historical issues bearing on its interpretation, and (3) the theological meaning of each book. It also includes additional articles on the background of the Old and New Testaments.

"The editors and authors should be commended for their work on this milestone publishing event. . . . a valuable addition to anyone's library, particularly someone who does not have a commentary on every book of the Bible."

—TERRY BRILEY, Dean, College of Bible and Ministry, Lipscomb University, Nashville, Tennessee

"What a wonderful gift to churches and those who teach in them! Ministers and Sunday school teachers will benefit greatly from the good judgment and clear articulation of the Bible's message found in this commentary."

—JERRY L. SUMNEY, Lexington Theological Seminary

An ideal reference tool for small group Bible study leaders, adult Sunday School teachers, preaching ministers, elders, and all serious students of the Scriptures.

1-877-816-4455 toll free
www.abilenechristianuniversitypress.com

Abilene Christian University Press